Palgrave Macmillan Studies in Family and Intimate Life

Titles include:

Harriet Becher
FAMILY PRACTICES IN SOUTH ASIAN MUSLIM FAMILIES
Parenting in a Multi-Faith Britain

Jacqui Gabb
RESEARCHING INTIMACY AND SEXUALITY IN FAMILIES

David Morgan
RETHINKING FAMILY PRACTICES

Eriikka Oinonen
FAMILIES IN CONVERGING EUROPE
A Comparison of Forms, Structures and Ideas

Róisín Ryan-Flood
LESBIAN MOTHERHOOD
Gender, Families and Sexual Citizenship

Palgrave Macmillan Studies in Family and Intimate Life
Series Standing Order ISBN 978–0–230–51748–6 hardback
(*outside North America only*)

You can receive future titles in this series as they are published by placing a standing order.
Please contact your bookseller or, in case of difficulty, write to us at the address below with
your name and address, the title of the series and the ISBN quoted above.

Customer Services Department, Macmillan Distribution Ltd, Houndmills, Basingstoke,
Hampshire RG21 6XS, England

Photograph from the exhibition 'Ecce Homo' © Elisabeth Ohlsson-Wallin, reproduced with permission.

Lesbian Motherhood

Gender, Families and Sexual Citizenship

Róisín Ryan-Flood
University of Essex, UK

First published 2009 by
PALGRAVE MACMILLAN

Palgrave Macmillan in the UK is an imprint of Macmillan Publishers Limited, registered in England, company number 785998, of Houndmills, Basingstoke, Hampshire RG21 6XS.

Palgrave Macmillan in the US is a division of St Martin's Press LLC, 175 Fifth Avenue, New York, NY 10010.

Palgrave Macmillan is the global academic imprint of the above companies and has companies and representatives throughout the world.

Palgrave® and Macmillan® are registered trademarks in the United States, the United Kingdom, Europe and other countries.

ISBN-13: 978–0–230–54541–0   hardback
ISBN-10: 0–230–54541–6   hardback

This book is printed on paper suitable for recycling and made from fully managed and sustained forest sources. Logging, pulping and manufacturing processes are expected to conform to the environmental regulations of the country of origin.

A catalogue record for this book is available from the British Library.

A catalogue record for this book is available from the Library of Congress.

10   9   8   7   6   5   4   3   2   1
18   17   16   15   14   13   12   11   10   09

Transferred to Digital Printing 2010

Contents

List of Tables

Acknowledgements

I am grateful to many friends, family and colleagues during the birthing of this manuscript. Diane Perrons and Rosalind Gill provided invaluable support and intellectual input. They continue to inspire me as friends and colleagues. Barbara Hobson and Linda McDowell have also been inspiring role models and offered encouraging advice. Ken Plummer and Don Kulick were typically generous with their time and insight. I am grateful to Christina Bodin for her hospitality and wisdom. Julie Shanahan, Roona Simpson, Giovanni Porfido, Tamara Herath, Kellie Burns and Scheherezade Soodeen have always offered encouragement and a listening ear. Ulrika Nyh was my constant companion and advisor and remains a friend for life. Thanks also to Philippa Grand at Palgrave for all her help and support for this project. Rachel Jones provided invaluable assistance in preparing the manuscript. I thank my sisters Siobhán and Mary, and my brothers Seán, Cormac and Ryan for their enthusiasm and merriment throughout. Finally, I thank my parents, Ann and Seán, for all their wonderful support over the years. Their commitment, energy and generosity can never be repaid.

Permission has been obtained to reprint extracts from the following:

Ryan-Flood, R. (2005) 'Challenging Heteronormativity: Discourses of Fatherhood Among Lesbian Parents', *Sexualities: Studies in Culture and Society*, 8(2): 189–204.

Permission has also been given to reproduce an image from 'Ecce Homo' by the photographer Elisabeth Ohlsson-Wallin.

1
Introduction – Charting the Lesbian Baby Boom

On February 14th 1999, a national newspaper in the UK carried the headline 'LESBIANS CAN MAKE BETTER PARENTS'. This claim was extraordinary in a number of ways. Firstly, in a socio-political context that is frequently unsupportive of lesbian parents, the fact that a newspaper – the Sunday Express – would carry a leading story about lesbian mothers that was very positive, seemed entirely unexpected. Secondly, the nature of the story, which referred to research by the British sociologist Gillian Dunne, suggested that lesbians could perform better as parents than heterosexuals. This appears to be a radical claim given the fact that lesbian and gay parenting is more often seen as a problematic anomaly in popular culture, particularly British tabloid press. The article loosely referred to Dunne's conclusion that lesbians were more likely to engage in egalitarian divisions of labour in the home and to find creative ways of achieving this. She did not in fact at any time claim that lesbians could make 'better' parents, rather, that lesbian relationships potentially allowed for new ways of managing work and care that did not rest on a traditional sexual division of labour. The headline is also revealing for its comparison between lesbian and heterosexual parents, the latter being the norm to which other families are inherently always compared. In a sense then, the newspaper article echoes a number of questions that are also present in academic work on lesbian parenthood.

The fact that lesbian parents were the subject of the newspaper story is perhaps unsurprising, given that images of lesbian motherhood are increasingly widespread in popular culture. From television characters such as Carol and Susan in *Friends*, or Kerry Weaver and Sandy Lopez in *ER*, to celebrity mothers like comedienne Rosie O'Donnell and musician Melissa Etheridge, lesbian motherhood is a source of compelling storylines and public fascination. This proliferation of images reflects the fact that a growing number of lesbian women are choosing to embark on parenthood in the context of an openly lesbian lifestyle. Academic work on lesbian parenthood has largely focused on the children in these families and the implications of growing up with non-heterosexual parents. The research has overwhelmingly concluded that having lesbian parents does not affect children adversely and that their psychological development is similar to children with heterosexual parents. This work has played an important role in refuting myths about lesbian and gay parents in social life, and has been significant in the development of more equitable laws in some countries regarding custody, adoption and access to assisted conception. Nonetheless, like the newspaper headline cited above, academic research on lesbian and gay parent families has largely centred around questions of sameness and difference – to what extent these families are either 'ordinary' or 'unique'. This incorporates questions not only about the psychosocial development of children, but also what constitutes a 'real' – and legitimate – family, as well as the division of labour among parents. Queer theory has often attached a strong importance to those practices and identities that challenge hegemonic categories of sexuality and heteronormative lifestyles. This emphasis is reflected in some queer theoretical work that is critical of lesbian and gay lifestyles that potentially endorse the notion of the 'good' gay citizen. Lesbian mothers often occupy an uncomfortable place in academic work, torn between the pressure to be 'normal' in order to challenge homophobic critics, and the subversive imperative of queer theory.

What does the teleological nature of discourses of sameness/difference and assimilation/transgression to considerations of lesbian parenting reveal about the discursive landscape in which lesbian familial modes of relatedness are constructed? I would argue that it is indicative of the socio-political context in which lesbian parenting occurs. In a social context where lesbian and gay parenthood remains controversial, research emphasising a similar or even superior performance by lesbian parents in relation to an implicit heteronormative comparative standard refutes homophobic claims that heteronormative family forms are the best or only ideal context in which to raise children. Indeed, the research illustrating that a lesbian or gay identity is in no way incompatible with effective parenting played a significant role in the struggle for equitable citizenship. The challenges to an emphasis on normativity from queer theorists illustrate the central role that notions of subversion and transgression play in much queer theory. Ahmed (2004) has provided a very thoughtful contribution to these debates where she warns against either idealising or dismissing lesbian parent families and suggests that a more productive approach is to view them as inhabiting norms differently, thereby avoiding a reductionist assimilation/transgression analysis.

Rather than assess their relative success in challenging heteronormativity or their assimilative dimensions, my wider analysis is concerned with locating lesbian parents as social actors and citizens within two specific national contexts. The debates about potential assimilation or subversion among lesbian parent families often overlook the importance of context to understandings of lesbian parents' experiences. In this way, what lesbian parents' choices reveal about wider understandings of gender and kinship are left unexamined. This book attempts to uncover the ways in which lesbian parents' choices and experiences are illustrative of broader understandings of kinship in relation to family formation, everyday interactions and social policy. The approach taken in this book is therefore critical of the emphasis on transgression that has dominated recent queer theoretical work and instead explores the meanings of kinship apparent in lesbian women's narratives of parenthood. In this way, their negotiation of broader discourses of kinship are unravelled. Lesbian parents' choices and experiences may be characterised by both assimilative and subversive elements. The point of this analysis is not to assess the extent to which they either conform to or destabilise heteronormativity, rather it is to explore how lesbian parenthood gives rise to new understandings of contemporary kinship in two European states. In this book, the experiences of lesbian parents' are explored in relation to sexual citizenship in two distinct welfare states, and the everyday spaces of parenthood – reproductive healthcare, child-centred spaces of daycare and schools, and local neighbourhoods.

Lesbian motherhood

Although 'lesbian' and 'mother' are often considered to be oppositional categories, in fact many lesbians are mothers. Some lesbians become mothers in a heterosexual relationship prior to coming out. A rather more recent phenomenon is that of lesbians who choose to become parents in the context of an openly lesbian lifestyle. The women's movement, the Lesbian, Gay, Bisexual and Transsexual (LGBT) rights movement, and developments in reproductive rights and technologies have enabled all women – heterosexual and lesbian – to explore a wider range of possibilities than was perhaps previously imaginable. In a discussion of lesbian families in the United States, Slater (1995) suggests that lesbians who came out during the 1970s were unlikely to have children, in contrast to earlier, more closeted generations of lesbians who often had children within heterosexual relationships. She also attributes this generational difference to critiques of motherhood within the burgeoning women's movement, which coincided with the development of a more accessible lesbian community. Thus, many lesbians opted for a childless lifestyle. In Slater's view, the equation of coming out with a political choice not to become a parent politically marginalised lesbian mothers. She suggests that young, politically active lesbians thus 'unwittingly' reinforced the social dichotomy between lesbianism and motherhood. In perceiving the choice to opt out of motherhood as a necessary part of emancipation, these younger lesbians 'left unchallenged the accompanying social oppression of women who were both lesbians and mothers' (Slater, 1995: 90). While her analysis focuses on politically active lesbians, it nonetheless reveals the changing discourses of motherhood within lesbian communities over time.

Slater (1995) highlights a new generation of lesbian women. These younger lesbians are distinct from the previous two groups – lesbians who became mothers within the context of a heterosexual marriage and lesbians who made a political choice to reject motherhood – that preceded them. Lesbians are now having children after coming out. This situation has also been enabled by changes in reproductive technologies and adoption services. For example, since the early 1980s some sperm banks have established insemination programs that are open to women irrespective of marital status or sexual orientation. Adoption has also become a possibility for some lesbians, although it is typically restricted to single women and women who present themselves as heterosexual. In any event, many lesbians choose the 'low tech' option of a known sperm donor. Slater (1995) suggests that lesbian mothers may also have become politically organised as a result of custody battles with ex-husbands. Thus, lesbian parents have become politically mobilised at the same time that new reproductive technologies and established lesbian communities has made motherhood a more visible option for lesbian women. The culmination of these changes has been a shift in perception among lesbians regarding motherhood, which is an increasingly viable possibility. Lesbians are now becoming parents individually or in couples outside of heterosexual marriages, a markedly new demographic development. The themes explored within the literature on lesbian parents and their children reflect the relatively recent development of this family form, as it largely addresses issues of children's well-being and family formation.

Previous research on lesbian parenting

According to Morningstar (1999), the literature on lesbian parent families falls into two main categories: psychological outcome studies of children of lesbians – most of which concern children who were conceived in a previous heterosexual relationship – and psychological and socio-cultural accounts of the experiences of lesbian mothers and their families. I would add a third category, that of more recent theoretically-oriented work examining lesbian parenting in terms of practices and symbolic meanings. Nonetheless, as Morningstar (1999) notes, the first category is by far the largest. Thus, the body of research on lesbian parents with children has focused primarily on the children of gay and lesbian parents, rather than the parents themselves. In addition, most research has been carried out in British or North American contexts, which arguably have more established histories of lesbian parenting, due to the location of metropolitan centres associated with LGBT commercial and political spaces.

The majority of previous research has examined the developmental pathways and general well-being of these children in comparison to children raised by heterosexual parents. The emphasis in research on children reflects pervasive myths about the incompatibility of a lesbian or gay identity with effective parenting. Opponents of lesbian and gay parenting rights (such as adoption or access to new reproductive technologies) frequently posit such claims as children growing up with lesbian or gay parents will become gay themselves or that 'homosexual' parents (particularly gay male) will abuse their children (Hicks, 2005). In fact, no study has produced evidence to lend credence to these myths.

Numerous authors have highlighted the similarities between children of lesbian parents and children who grow up with heterosexual parents (e.g. Tasker & Golombok, 1998; Johnson & O'Connor, 2002). Patterson (1992) provides a comprehensive overview of 'outcome studies' since the 1970s on children with lesbian parents. She notes that the children are consistently rated similarly to the children of heterosexual mothers in all areas of psychological development, including separation-individuation, emotional stability, moral judgement, object relations, gender identity and sexual identity. However, the studies she refers to focus almost exclusively on children born within a heterosexual arrangement. Patterson (1994) carried out a study of children born to or adopted by openly lesbian parents. She investigated the self-concept, behavioural adjustment and sex role behaviour of 37 children, who were found to follow a standard trajectory of psychological development. Her findings support her earlier conclusion in the 1992 review that children are not adversely affected psychologically as a result of having lesbian parents, although children in the 1994 study were found to feel more stressed than children in other families. Patterson suggests that this may be due to the fact that their lives are actually more stressful than the lives of children in more traditional families. On the other hand, she also found that children with lesbian parents were more articulate about their emotions than other children in the study, which could account for their greater propensity to articulate stress. Concern for children's well-being in lesbian households may also stem from an awareness of homophobia in society and the potential difficulties of growing up in a marginalised and stigmatised family – rather than simply homophobic attitudes – and it is notable that children with lesbian parents do not appear to be adversely affected.

Some studies identify positive traits associated with growing up with lesbian parents. For example, children of lesbian and gay parents often see themselves as more open-minded and aware of diversity than their peers with heterosexual parents (see Stacey & Biblarz, 2001). Lott-Whitehead & Tully (1999), based on their study of 45 lesbian mothers, suggest that there are many positive aspects of lesbian parent families, including openness about difference in general. A number of families in their study experienced a high level of stress, but the parents consciously attempted to protect their children's well-being in the face of potential homophobia. In the context of political debates about lesbian and gay parenting rights, several European governments have commissioned reports investigating the well-being of children raised by lesbian and gay parents, which have also concluded that a lesbian or gay identity is not incompatible with effective parenting. For example, the Swedish government released a report based on the findings of a special commission, in which it was clearly stated that lesbian and gay parents can provide loving supportive environments for their children (SOU, 2001).

Stacey & Biblarz (2001) are critical of what they view as the tendency in research to downplay potential differences between the children of lesbian and heterosexual parents. They provide a thorough overview of previous research and argue that the children of lesbian parents may in fact be different, but that this difference is manifested in *positive* ways. For example, they suggest that children may develop in less gender-stereotypical ways, a finding which previous authors fail to acknowledge. Stacey and Biblarz suggest that this is due to a conflation of a 'no difference' outcome with a position that indicates there is no need for social concern regarding lesbian and gay parenting. While they acknowledge the necessity for combating homophobic stereotypes of lesbian and gay families, Stacey and Biblarz suggest that this should not be done in ways that presume any potential difference will be negative. Irrespective of whether children of lesbian parents are either no different from other children, or are positively affected by their upbringing, the considerable body of research indicating that having a lesbian mother or parents is not detrimental to children has played a significant role in the evolution of legal rights for lesbian parents, including the regulation of adoption and access to new reproductive technologies. In addition, custody battles formerly automatically awarded custody to a heterosexual spouse, a situation which has since changed dramatically largely due to the research refuting arguments about the negative impact of lesbian parents on their children. This research has clearly been necessary in the context of a homophobic society in which lesbian parents face legal discrimination and social stigma. Nonetheless, Patterson (1992) suggests that researchers turn their attention to more productive aspects of research, given the growing level of awareness and acceptance that the children of lesbian and gay parents are not adversely affected as a result of their parents' sexual orientation.

Socio-cultural accounts of lesbian parenting

The second main category of work on lesbian parenting consists of largely socio-cultural accounts of the experiences of lesbian parents (Hanscombe & Forster, 1982; Pollack & Vaughn, 1987; Benkov, 1994; Nelson, 1996; Moraga, 1997; Hicks & McDermott, 1999; Wells, 2000; Saffron, 2001) and the legal implications of lesbian parenting for the relationship between gender, sexuality and the state (Beresford, 1998; Lehr, 1999; O'Donnell, 1999; Bernstein & Reimann, 2001). A number of themes emerge from this literature. These include: the difficulties of communicating plans to parent to family of origin; considerations influencing the preference for a known or unknown donor; and the effects of 'biologically asymmetrical' (Pies, 1988) relationships to children within a lesbian couple, such as the legal vulnerability of the co-parent. Lesbians choosing parenthood face a variety of complex decisions that involve counteracting deeply embedded social norms. This process can be challenging but also liberating. The creation of lesbian and gay parent families requires rethinking hegemonic assumptions about the nature of kinship. This facilitates a reflexive engagement that can produce new insights about all family relationships.

Lesbian co-parents

The literature on lesbian motherhood from the 1970s frequently addressed custody concerns with respect to children from prior heterosexual relationships. As more lesbian couples are openly planning to have children together, many highlight the precarious legal status of co-parents with regard to their children as a major concern. In many countries, same-sex couples do not have access to the benefits accrued to married heterosexual couples and in those nation-states where they can register in same sex partnerships, they are often not extended rights of adoption. While the lack of legal and social definitions concerning the role of co-parents can be stressful, writings by lesbians concerning their decision to have children together reiterate their view of the decision as a joint one with equal responsibility expected from both partners. Some express confidence in their role as a co-parent, which they derive from the experience of raising a child. Various anthologies contain stories of women's commitment to raising a child together after a relationship ends (e.g. Pollack & Vaughn, 1987; Saffron, 2001).

Muzio (1999: 209) in her psychoanalytic account of lesbian motherhood argues that a co-parent is at risk of becoming reduced to 'mimicry', which Irigaray (1985) describes as the role historically relegated to the feminine. However this can be overcome by mimesis – the self-conscious adoption and subversion of the feminine role. 'To play with mimisis is thus, for a woman, to try to recover the place of her exploitation by discourse, without allowing herself to be simply reduced to it...to make "visible," by an effect of playful repetition, what was supposed to remain invisible' (Irigaray, 1985: 76). Women may therefore employ mimesis as a strategy to transform subordination into affirmation and to subvert any notion of a coherent identity. Muzio (1999: 209) suggests that lesbians raising children have the possibility to explore as mothers and co-mothers 'the feminine' in a context 'unbounded by overt masculine ownership'. Lesbian parenting couples may therefore mimic each other's interpretations of their roles in a way that transforms them. This could result in new ways of thinking about gender and parenting.

Reconsidering masculinities, parenthood and relatedness

Lesbians who achieve parenthood by using the services of a sperm bank are perhaps among the most controversial of lesbian parent families. The existing literature suggests that the decision about whether to use a known or an unknown donor is a complex one. Morningstar (1999) in her account of the developmental pathways of lesbian families, suggests that the possible legal threat posed by a known donor to the couple and especially to the co-parent, causes many lesbian couples to favour insemination with an anonymous donor. In my view this is a large generalisation and cannot be assumed for lesbians within all nation-state contexts. The findings regarding discourses of fatherhood explored in Chapter 3 for example challenge Morningstar's claim. However, the distinction Morningstar makes between the legal claim of a known donor and an anonymous donor is an important one as it suggests that donor anonymity among lesbian couples is therefore not motivated simply by the issue of involvement, but of legal security. These considerations have become complicated by the option of donor identity disclosure that is offered by some clinics, including the Sperm Bank of California, which offers a lesbian-friendly service. Donor identity disclosure enables any subsequent child to contact the donor upon reaching the age of 18.

The issue of lesbians using sperm banks to become pregnant is particularly controversial, partly because any information regarding paternity is usually unavailable to children. This is a situation that some argue is an infringement of children's rights (e.g. Freeman, 1996). Vanfraussen *et al.* (2001) examined 41 children's attitudes towards donor identity disclosure in lesbian parent families in Belgium. Although 54 per cent of children were content with donor anonymity, the remaining 46 per cent desired more information. The researchers found no clear indicators regarding which children express a preference for more information, as this was not determined by their parents' stance on the issue, although boys appeared to have a slightly greater wish for more information. They therefore recommend a flexible system offering anonymous and open-identity donors in order to meet the potential needs of each individual family. Scheib et al. (2000) interviewed heterosexual and lesbian parents who chose donor insemination (DI) in the US and found a marked preference for donor identity disclosure among all participants in their study, regardless of sexuality. Interestingly, both lesbians and heterosexual women expressed a strong preference that donors be physically similar ('matching') to their partner. The authors argue that this suggests that matching serves functions beyond concealing the non-biological relationship of the social father to the child. I would argue however, that it could serve a similar purpose in lesbian families, where partners may also wish biological markers to be less evident, as will be discussed further in Chapter 3.

Donovan (2000) argues that lesbian parents challenge hegemonic discourses about fatherhood in constructing their family forms. This perspective is supported by Brewaeys et al.'s (1993) work. In a study of lesbian and heterosexual couples' motivations for using DI in Belgium, they found that heterosexual participants perceived themselves as becoming 'more normal', in contrast to lesbian parents, whose choice of DI in the context of a lesbian relationship represented an exacerbation of their difference in society. In addition, while heterosexual couples emphasised secrecy regarding DI, lesbian parents intended to disclose information about the circumstances of their children's conception. It must be noted however, that lesbian parents had less choice in this issue, as social fathers in heterosexual couples could pass as the biological father. In a follow up study of identity-release sperm donor recipients in the US, Scheib *et al.* (2003) found almost no parents regretted using an identifiable donor. Disclosure did not impact negatively on families, irrespective of sexual orientation or relationship status, although heterosexual couples were less likely to be open about the means of conception with children, family and friends. Father absence is hardly exclusive to lesbian families, nor characteristic of all lesbian parenting arrangements. Concerns about the single mothers and lesbians who parent independently of men, while ostensibly 'in the best interests of the child', may constitute part of a conservative discourse that idealises a heteronormative nuclear family form (Thompson, 2002).

Inventive Mothers – equality and kinship among lesbian parents

A small body of more recent research examining the practices and meanings of lesbian parenting represents a move towards new ways of thinking about lesbian parent families, including work that addresses lesbian parenting from psychological and psychoanalytical perspectives (Schwartz, 1998; Laird, 1999; Malone & Cleary, 2002; Sullivan, 2004). These theoretical analyses have been centrally concerned with the creative potential for reformulating notions of kinship and new ways of achieving egalitarian relationships. Research on lesbian motherhood has suggested that lesbian couples demonstrate more egalitarian living arrangements than heterosexual couples. Dunne (1998) argues that while motherhood provides lesbians and heterosexuals common ground on which to interact, the sexuality and gender dynamics of the relationship between lesbian parents parenting as two women together 'necessitates the transformation of the boundaries, meaning and content of parenthood and facilitates the construction of more self-reflexive, egalitarian approaches to financing and caring for children'.[1] In this way, she argues, lesbian motherhood represents a fundamental challenge to existing gender structures. Even when parenting was not a shared project, lesbian mothers experienced enormous support from partners and domestic work was shared equally. Unlike in many, particularly middle-class, heterosexual relationships where women anticipate financial dependence on their male partner while the child is young, the mothers she studied waited until they had achieved work goals which promised long-term financial security before having children. This work is particularly interesting because it examines lesbian parenting from a feminist perspective, addressing the division of domestic labour.

This concern with the egalitarian potential of lesbian parenting carries with it the underlying question of how similar or different lesbian parents are from heterosexual parents. Not all authors share the view that they are particularly different. Lewin (1993) in research carried out in the late 1970s and early 1980s, found that the lifestyles of lesbians with and without children were dissimilar enough so that lesbian mothers felt they had more in common with other mothers than with childless women. In a later article, she suggests that analyses which portray lesbian mothers as either 'resisters or accommodators' in relation to gender norms, are too simplistic. She argues that lesbian mothers may be both or neither. In her view, a more accurate interpretation of lesbian parenting narratives is that they are 'strategists, using the cultural resources offered by motherhood to achieve a particular set of goals' (1993: 350). These goals and resources are shaped by the heterosexist and gender differentiated social context. In Lewin's view, although many lesbian parents are 'conscious resisters', others may willingly adjust to traditional values where possible. Their behaviour may be viewed as transgressive (in which case they are seen as resisters or subversives), or (along with lesbian/gay marriage) as assimilation into heterosexual norms and values, an abandonment of the subversive potential of queer sexualities. Lewin notes that the search for 'cultures of resistance' vital to feminist theory and analysis should not limit accounts of women's lives to narratives of victimisation. On the other hand, she warns against complacency when evidence of resistance is uncovered, as both interpretations may 'fail to reveal the complex ways in which resistance and accommodation, subversion and compliance, are interwoven and interdependent, mutually reinforcing aspects of a single strategy' (p. 350). The theoretical literature on lesbian parenting has also examined the possibilities for new formulations of kinship. Weston's (1992) classic work suggests that the importance of biology to kinship is displaced among lesbian and gay communities, where rejection from families or origin often leads to the formation of new 'families we choose', based on friendship, love and choice. Hayden (1995) challenges the dichotomy of resistance/accommodation and suggests that debates about the normative or creative values attached to kinship formation among lesbian and gay people in Lewin and Weston's work highlight the centrality of biology to conceptualisations of kinship in American society. She further argues that the symbolic role of biology may be reconfigured in lesbian parent family forms, where biology may become a more flexible concept. These explorations of the potential for lesbian parent families to develop new practices and deconstruct the meanings attributed to categorisations such as 'kinship' and 'motherhood' represent new ways of examining lesbian motherhood experience.

In a provocative article, Butler (2002) asks 'is kinship always already heterosexual?' She questions the legitimation of sexuality and queer relationships through the lens of marriage. Noting the vulnerability of queer subjects who are denied formal recognition in terms of exclusion from the associated rights and benefits typical of marriage – including health care benefits and custody of children – she nonetheless underlines the importance of retaining a sense of queer kinship that exists outside the confines of marriage or civil partnership. She argues that to construe marriage as the only terrain within which to consider queer kinship would potentially pathologise other forms of queer relatedness and render them unthinkable and perhaps even unimaginable, ultimately containing lesbian and gay life within a normative framework: 'The life of sexuality, kinship and community that becomes unthinkable within the terms of these norms constitutes the lost horizon of radical sexual politics, and we find our way 'politically' in the wake of the ungrievable' (Butler, 2002: 40). This questioning of the possibilities that may be excluded from the terrain of kinship is also applicable to a consideration of lesbian parenting. What are the assumptions informing the regulation of lesbian parent families in the recent turn to legal frameworks? The legislative response has largely constructed lesbian parent families in accordance with a nuclear family model of two 'married' residential parents. This overlooks other potential ways of conceptualising kinship within lesbian parent families – such as the existence of more than two parent figures, either through the involvement of co-parents and donors or through polyamorous relationships. The wider context of sexual citizenship for understanding lesbian parents' experiences, choices and possibilities is important in exploring the plurality of lesbian parent family forms in place.

The research study

This book draws on a comparative study of lesbian motherhood in Sweden and Ireland. The impetus for the Swedish/Irish context comparison is rooted in my own biography as a researcher. I am from

Ireland and previously lived in Sweden for just over a year in 1996–1997, when I carried out research on rape crisis services while based at Stockholm University. During my sojourn in Sweden, I became aware of two distinct differences between Sweden and Ireland in relation to sexual politics, parenting and gender equality. The first was the prominent place of lesbian and gay equality issues in the media and political debate in Sweden, compared to Ireland. Registered partnerships (same sex 'marriage') had been introduced in Sweden the previous year and there was a sense of momentum regarding sexual equality as a result. Swedish media – including television, radio and newspapers – frequently examined lesbian and gay rights issues.

The second major difference concerned the construction of parenting norms in policy and society. I was frequently struck by the number of Swedish men with prams I noticed in shops, neighbourhoods and on public transport. The dual breadwinner model of parenting and emphasis on participatory fatherhood contrasted with the male breadwinner and female caregiver model traditionally more characteristic of Ireland. When later contemplating a new study on lesbian motherhood, these images returned to my mind and I became curious about the possible impact of different socio-cultural contexts on lesbian women's perspectives on kinship and equality. In addition, I discovered that although lesbians had a more visible public presence in Sweden, parenting was more explicitly restricted to heterosexuals, as the registered partnership laws clearly stated that all parenting rights – including adoption and access to new reproductive technologies (NRTs) – were prohibited for lesbian and gay people. Ireland in contrast lacked a comprehensive legal framework that expressly excluded lesbians from access to NRTs and at that time there was one clinic that openly provided its services – including anonymous donor insemination – to lesbian women. I decided to do comparative research between Sweden and Ireland in order to explore how lesbians were embedded in local contexts where social policy and hegemonic discourses endorsed particular family forms. I became interested in lesbian parents' conceptualisations of notions such as motherhood, gender and kinship and how they negotiated these understandings within particular cultural and policy frameworks.

The research study consisted of interviews with 68 lesbian parents (n = 40 in Sweden, n = 28 in Ireland), representing 42 family units (n = 24 in Sweden and n = 18 in Ireland). The majority of the fieldwork took place in 2000–2001, although I have kept in touch with most participants and some follow up contact has included further interviews, phone calls and email correspondence post-fieldwork. The majority of the sample were white, with one mixed-race participant. Most participants conceived children while in their thirties. Although there were a range of class identifications and incomes in the study, the majority of participants worked in a 'professional' category (n = 28 in Sweden and n = 16 in Ireland). However, the remainder of the sample – approximately one third – worked as technicians, in trades and the service industry. Swedish participants were more likely to have higher education, with 90 per cent of Swedish women interviewed having a university degree (n = 36), compared to 71 per cent of Irish participants (n = 20). The majority of the families consisted of one child at the time of interview and most children were under twelve, with approximately two thirds of all children in the study under the age of five years.

Openness and visibility

The process of recruitment for the study faced rather more challenges in Ireland than in Sweden. While lesbian parenthood was a hotly debated topic in the media in Swedish society during fieldwork, lesbian parents had a much lower profile in Ireland. This difference in visibility had in some ways accrued Irish lesbians certain advantages. They were not specifically prohibited by law from accessing assisted reproduction services, unlike their Swedish counterparts. This reflected the general lack of awareness of lesbian parenthood in Ireland at the time. The lack of visibility was reflected in participants' discourses and strategies. Lesbian and gay activism in Ireland has been influenced by anti-imperialist politics. The concept of an indigenous lesbian and gay politics carries particular significance among Irish activists (Rose, 1994; Bowyer, 2001). Thus, confrontational models of queer activism are often viewed as a cultural import and therefore problematic. Nonetheless, increased lesbian and gay visibility and established events such as the annual Pride parade in Irish cities have been utilised by Irish LGBT communities in the struggle for equality. Although considerable advances have been made in recent years and research indicates growing levels of acceptance, especially among young people (Inglis, 1998), homophobia remains widespread.

Upon embarking on fieldwork in Ireland, I soon observed the contrast with Sweden in terms of the very different levels of media and political debate about queer parenting. I became aware of what seemed to me a deafening silence regarding lesbian parenting, arriving as I was from a context where it was a source of intense discussion. This is not to undermine the greater prominence given to lesbian and gay issues in contemporary Irish media, where they have a much higher profile than in previous decades. However, it was illustrative of the different political moments in both countries and the politicised meanings of visibility for participants. In contrast to Swedish participants, for whom 'speaking out' about their families constituted an important political gesture, Irish participants tended to live out their lesbian identities in a more segregated way.

The dynamics of openness and (in)visibility were also evident when recruiting participants for the study. While Swedish women were generally eager to be interviewed and it was easy to find a generous number of participants for the study, recruitment in Ireland was much more difficult. Irish lesbians seemed far more wary of participating in a research study that would potentially expose their families to greater visibility in Irish society. This therefore raised an ethical quandary: would it be preferable to avoid doing such research at this time, rather than expose participants to the disciplinary power of public discourse, in Foucauldian terms? Was the fact that it was more difficult to recruit in Ireland a sign that some lesbian parents were resisting my efforts to document aspects of their lives that they might prefer to remain hidden? Ultimately I concluded that even if this was the case, the fact that a substantial number of women did agree to participate suggests that this was not the only resistance discourse available. In the interim the social climate in Ireland has changed considerably, with media such as television and radio programmes including positive representations of lesbian parents and their families.[2]

Context, kinship and normativity

This book explores lesbian parents' experiences along three axes of analysis: context, kinship and normativity. The most obvious element of this study that pertains to context is the cross-national comparison. There is a dearth of research on lesbian parent families in diverse national contexts, which restricts understandings of the ways in which their narratives are shaped by specific socio-political concerns. In addition, it overlooks the role of social policy in contributing to women's ability to form autonomous households. Much social policy relating to families is informed by heteronormative assumptions. The differing nature of these assumptions in these two countries highlights wider understandings of 'the family'. A cross-national exploration of lesbian parent experience highlights the role of the state in mediating women's economic status and ability to access medical services – such as assisted conception – and kinship possibilities including second parent adoption, or the formal legal recognition of co-parents. Chapter 2 explores cross-national differences in gender, families and citizenship. However, context refers not only to the cross-cultural dimension of the study in terms of country of residence, but incorporates broader concerns about the significance of place and space. Thus, the exclusion of lesbian parents from specific service providers and their experiences of particular spaces – such as hospitals and schools – are a recurring analytic theme and interrogated further in Chapter 4. A contextualised approach to lesbian parenting enables a fuller and more nuanced interpretation of their narratives and experiences.

The second analytical theme explored in the book is that of kinship, or the relational choices and possibilities of lesbian parents. Contemporary research on families often examines the ways in which individuals are continually constructing and reconstructing their intimate relationships. More recently, the role of state legislation in regulating intimate relationships has also been an area of interest. New reproductive technologies and the separation of sexuality and child-bearing facilitated by increased reproductive control potentially render a tectonic shift in our understandings of the role of motherhood in women's lives. Participants in this study are clearly involved in the creation of new family forms, raising interesting questions about the changing nature of familial relatedness and broader interpretations of categories such as 'mother/ parent' in contemporary society. This research addresses the kinship discourses and relational matrices of lesbian parents. Chapter 3 examines reproductive decision-making and constructions of fatherhood among lesbian parents. In Chapter 5, the ways in which biology is imagined and constructed in these family forms is explored, with particular reference to the role of co-parents.

A concern with Otherness and normativity constitutes the third axis of analysis throughout this text. As already noted, much theoretical and empirical work on lesbian parents explores the extent to which they are either similar to, or different from, heterosexual parents, particularly in research concerned with the impact of their sexuality on their children. Research emphasising the similarity or normative behaviour of the children of lesbian parents compared to those raised by heterosexual parents has played an important role in improving the situation for lesbian parents in custody disputes with ex-husbands for example and has paved the way for legislative provisions supportive of lesbian and gay parenting. More recent work examines the possibility of lesbian parent families manifesting positive differences, compared to their hetero-sexual counterparts. Chapter 6 examines debates about sameness and difference in lesbian parents families and considers the ways in which gender is (re)produced in the interview narratives about their family prac-tices. The final chapter considers the implications of the research findings for theoretical debates about families, subjectivity and citizenship.

Relatively little is known about the lives of the new generation of les-bians choosing motherhood in local contexts, despite the significance of their existence to social and theoretical debates about diverse topics including gender, kinship and equality. The overwhelming emphasis in much previous research on the well-being of their children has played an important political role in refuting offensive homophobic myths. Indeed the well-being of children should always be a necessary com-ponent of considerations of new intergenerational family forms. It must be noted however that this argument may often be used not in chil-dren's best interests, but rather to further the political agenda of the interlocutor, as has been the case in homophobic rhetoric invoking lesbian parents as an example of the breakdown of 'family values'. Nonetheless, it is increasingly acknowledged that lesbian and gay parents do not compromise their children's well-being by virtue of their sexuality. As a result, researchers are turning their attention to more productive aspects of lesbian parent families.

An intersectional analysis that addresses dynamics of gender, sexuality and citizenship enables an interpretation of lesbian mothers' narratives in which they are acknowledged as gendered sexual subjects. This facil-itates an exploration of discourses of biology, kinship and gender among lesbian parents whereby their experiences and perspectives are con-textualised within frameworks of domination and hegemonic ideals. This book therefore attempts to address the experiences of lesbian parents in diverse local contexts in an effort to reconsider notions of resistance and subjugation within previous theoretical work and critically analyse the efforts of lesbian parents to create and establish meaningful con-ceptualisations of their families in often unsupportive contexts.

2
Gender, Families and Social Change

Bell & Binnie (2000) argue that all citizenship is sexual citizenship. In other words, citizenship is mediated by sexual identity. The ability to have your partnership legally recognised, to seek redress for sexual orientation discrimination in the workplace, to become an adoptive parent, to feel safe in expressing your sexual identity in public spaces – through words, physical affection with a partner, or appearance: all of these are mediated by the nation-state context in which you live. Narratives of citizenship often assume a heterosexual citizen (Valentine, 2001). Thus, welfare states traditionally developed policies that catered largely to a heterosexual nuclear family. Discussions of family, particularly references to 'the family' often assume that the two parent model of kinship is an inevitable expression of biological reproduction. Yet, as Schneider (1984: 75) pointed out, kinship is an 'empirical question', not a 'universal fact'. Stacey (1990: 2) similarly described family as 'a locus not of residence, but of meaning and relationships'. Cross-cultural studies have illustrated the variety of understandings of kinship in place (Herdt, 1984; Bauer & Thompson, 2006). The heterosexual nuclear family model is one type of family form but many others have and do exist across time and place. Welfare states and public policy are increasingly forced to respond to the plurality and individuality of kinship forms in contemporary society. The variety of families – including lone parents, divorced parents, blended families, intergenerational extended families, friends as family and so on – present particular challenges and pleasures. This diversity in families is often attributed to the breakdown of the nuclear family, which is held up as a nostalgic signifier of a bygone era. However, as Davidoff (2006) points out, the assumption that families have moved from simple to complex forms in recent years is highly problematic. The rise of the two parent nuclear family model is associated with the development of industrial capitalism,[1] but 'family' has always been and remains, a complex ever evolving narrative. Morgan (1996) suggests that it is perhaps more helpful to speak of 'family practices' rather than 'family', as the latter term too often invokes a monolithic notion of kinship. The term 'family practices' allows for a fluidity of interpretation, definition and identity. An approach that addresses family practices implies that families are what families do, rather than view kinship in the traditional structural sense.

The extensive literature on gender and citizenship (Lewis, 1993; Lister, 1997; Sainsbury, 1994, 1996, 1999) offers invaluable insights into the ways in which women's rights are constructed, overlooked or eroded by state policy. Yet this literature has rarely incorporated a critical concern with sexuality. Women's relationship to the state has always been mediated by their status in relation to fertility and partnership – as mothers, childless women, and wives or spinsters. Lesbian women occupy a complicated relationship to the state and citizenship practices in terms of their gender and sexuality. This chapter will address the intersection of gender, sexuality and citizenship. The ways in which families are constructed by social policy and legislation in Sweden and Ireland will be explored. The dominant cultural and policy discourses of 'the family' will be outlined. It will also examine the particular constraints and challenges faced by lesbians as citizens, particularly in relation to reproduction and the construction of new family forms. Hobson (2003) has characterised these two approaches in terms of citizenship frames as 'gender-distinctive' (Ireland) and 'universalist' (Sweden). Thus, Ireland like many post-colonial societies, has a history and culture reflecting the dominant nationalist emphasis on traditional family forms and a strong male breadwinner role (Nandy, 1983; Meaney, 1991). In contrast, Sweden has a longer tradition of women's participation in the paid labour force and clearly encourages men to participate more in caring for children (Björnberg, 1998; Bergqvist *et al.*, 1999). An examination of the social welfare and legislative context for lesbian parents in Sweden and Ireland highlights constraints and possibilities within two distinct welfare states. This is illustrated in the gendered nature of social policy, in addition to the differential treatment of lesbian subjects. In this chapter, family law and social security systems in Sweden and Ireland will be addressed in terms of gender and sexuality politics in order to situate lesbian parents within local social systems.

Gender, sexuality and citizenship in Ireland

The particular configurations of marriage and motherhood in Ireland are often attributed to the influence of a nationalist political heritage in the context of postcolonialism. Numerous writers have highlighted the gendered imagery of women in Irish symbolic figurations of 'the nation' (Nash, 1993; Smyth, 1997), particularly in Irish literature. These range from representations in which 'Mother Ireland' mourns the loss of her sons[2] to a beautiful young woman making sacrifices for her beloved.[3] Gray & Ryan (1997) suggest that these two examples, which are most often referred to in analyses of nationalist imagery in Ireland, tell us little about women's actual lives and that even within nationalist discourse gender is invoked in multiple and complex ways. Anthias & Yuval-Davis (1993) explore the utilisation of gender as a symbolic resource in nationalist and postcolonial discourse. They suggest that women 'both signify and reproduce the symbolic and legal boundaries of the collectivity' (p. 28) through their actions, including motherhood in the context of heterosexual marriage. Thus, women are prohibited from specific behaviours – such as particular forms of dress, or pre/extra-marital sexual relationships – that are seen to compromise collective national/ethnic honour. Smyth (1991: 11) suggests that women are symbolically invoked in Irish nationalist rhetoric 'in a discourse from which women, imaginatively, economically, politically disempowered, are in effect and effectively excluded'. This serves to construct women as an integral part of nationalist symbolism while simultaneously denying women's own agency and subjectivity.

Nandy (1983), with reference to colonialism in India, has argued that the colonised man has been constructed as feminine by colonial powers. Nationalist responses have often taken the form of a polarisation of gender roles, where notions of womanhood are used to assert the masculinity of the colonised man. This results in highly differentiated gender norms persisting long after colonialism has officially ceased, as these new norms continue to act as a symbol of the power of male subjects. Thus, women are not simply a symbolic resource for 'the nation', women's bodies also become the terrain in which power is exercised.

Meaney (1991) applies principles of Nandy's work to a consideration of gender relations in Ireland. She highlights similar anxieties to those outlined by Nandy as the origin of the distinctive regulation of relationships and reproductive rights in Ireland, as illustrated through concerted debates about marriage, contraception and abortion. In her view, prohibitive abortion laws in Ireland are indicative of 'the extent to which women only exist as a function of their maternity in southern Ireland' (p. 188). She argues that 'a deep distrust and fear of women' is paradoxically grounded in the idealisation of the mother in Irish culture as an omnipotent and 'dehumanised' figure. While this may be historically accurate, it seems a slightly overly pessimistic analysis now, given the important reforms to marriage and reproductive rights that have taken place in the interim.[4] A more contemporary analysis is offered by Gray & Ryan (1997: 529–30), who explore some of the changes in the relationships between 'woman', women and Irish national identity. They argue that representations of women in the 1990s are more 'diffuse' than in the 1920s (the period when the Irish Free State emerged) and that symbols of 'women and Irishness need to be understood within changing economic, social and political contexts'. Nonetheless, they acknowledge that some continuities remain in the ways that symbols and representations of women are deployed.

Motherhood and the Irish constitution

The original 1922 constitution of the Free State, which was agreed in negotiations with the UK government, contained no overtly religious or moral overtones. The 1937 constitution, however created new provisions based on middle-class nationalist ideals and was formulated in explicitly nationalist and religious language. The 'special position' of the Catholic Church was asserted in Article 44 (removed in 1972), in which it was recognised as 'the guardian of the faith of the great majority of the citizens'. Another article affirmed the centrality of the nuclear family: 'the family as the natural primary and fundamental unit group of society, as a moral institution possessing inalienable and imprescribable rights antecedent to and superior to all law' (Article 41.1). In the same article, women's participation in and contribution to society was relegated to motherhood within marriage and the private sphere: 'the state shall, therefore, endeavour to ensure that mothers shall not be obliged by economic necessity to engage in labour to the neglect of their duties in the home' (Article 41.2.2); and to 'guard with special care the institution of marriage' (41.3.1). The ban on divorce was formalised in another article: 'No law shall be enacted providing for the dissolution of marriage' (41.3.2). This unique combination of religious doctrine and oppressive gender relations reflected the close relationship between the Catholic Church and state policy in subsequent decades until the 1970s (Lentin, 1998).

Thus the Republic of Ireland has a constitution which explicitly addresses issues pertaining to traditional gender roles. The special status given to the family in the constitution has formed the background for debates about women's rights. Family law reform has largely focused on women's rights and divorce. There have been enormous constitutional and legal changes concerning these issues in the past 30 years. Many of these changes have emerged as the result of campaigns by feminist activists.

Fathers and the Irish Constitution

Freeman & Richards (2006) note that in a socio-legal framework, motherhood is traditionally established through birth, whereas paternity is affirmed through marriage. This is certainly the case historically in Irish law. The emphasis on marriage in the Irish constitution has had consequences for unmarried fathers. In the mid-1960s, a case arose of an unmarried father whose biological child was to be given up for adoption by the mother without his consent or consultation. He attempted to obtain legal support for his parental claim on the child (The State (Nicolaou) v. An Bord Uchtála, Supreme Court, 1966). However, the court ruled that the mother had sole authority in any decision regarding adoption. In distinguishing between the biological father and those whose consent for the adoption was required by legislation, it was stated:

'When it is considered that an illegitimate child may be begotten by an act of rape, by a callous seduction or by an act of casual commerce by a man with a woman as well as by the association of a man with a woman in making a common home without marriage in circumstances approximating to those of married life, and that, except in the latter instance, it is rare for a natural father to take any interest in his offspring, it is not difficult to appreciate the difference in moral capacity and social function between the natural father and [those whose consent was required under the statute]'.[5]

Connolly (1995) points out that Nicolaou, a man who was committed to taking responsibility for his child, was not differentiated by the Court from men who take no interest in their children. The Court therefore permitted all unmarried fathers to be treated differently by the law to mothers because some unmarried fathers would be unwilling to meet the responsibilities of parenthood. In this case the Court also upheld that an unmarried mother has, by virtue of Article 40.3.1 of the Constitution, 'a personal right to the care and custody of her child, but that an unmarried father possesses no constitutional right to either custody of or contact with his child' (Connolly, 1995:15). The Status of Children Act, 1987, established that an unmarried father could apply to the courts to be appointed guardian of his child. Connolly (1995) notes that it seems unlikely that this would have benefited Nicolaou, as an unmarried mother may still give her child up for adoption without the consent of the child's father. This development interestingly distinguished between prospective adoptive married parents and unmarried fathers, implicitly supporting the former as the more appropriate family context in which to raise a child. In this case, the Court affirmed that an unmarried father has no constitutional right to the guardianship of his child, and stressed that the legislative right was one to apply to court to be appointed guardian, not a right to be appointed guardian.

The treatment of widowers differs slightly to that of unmarried men. In 1984, the Irish High Court overturned a legislative provision whereby a widow could adopt regardless of whether she was already a parent but a widower could only adopt if he already had custody of another child (O'G v. Attorney General).[6] The Court ruled that this was in violation of the widower's constitutional right to equality before the law. The original provision was clearly based on the notion of sexual difference enshrined in the Irish constitution, in which women are essentially predisposed to nurturing motherhood, while men's contribution to family life is that of a breadwinner. This construction of womanhood has been highly influential in legislative provision. The emphasis on women's role as caregiver rather than paid worker, is also evident in the history of women's employment in Ireland.

Employment

It was not until the 1970s that the Oireachtas[7] began to address gender equality in relation to employment. Ireland's accession to the European Community played a significant role in the development of Irish social policy, as restrictions regarding women's employment had to be removed as a condition of Ireland's entry to the EEC in 1973. A commitment to equality of pay between men and women is clearly stated in the Treaty of Rome of 1957. The European Council subsequently passed two Directives (1975, 1976) advising every Member State to introduce laws regarding gender equality in relation to pay and terms and conditions of employment (Cook & McCashin, 1997).

Many of the barriers to women's labour force participation that were in place prior to Ireland's membership in the EEC seem archaic today. In 1973, the ban on married women participating in public sector employment in Ireland was finally removed with the introduction of the Civil Service (Employment of Married Women) Act. Similar prohibitions were overturned in other semi-state and private sectors within the same timeframe. For example, an Aer Lingus ban on married air hostesses was lifted in 1973 following union negotiations. The 1973 Act removing the marriage ban was the first step in a series of important legislative acts in Ireland during the 1970s. The three main anti-discrimination Acts were the Anti-Discrimination (Pay) Act 1974, the Employment Equality Act 1977 and the Maternity (Protection of Employees) Act 1981. The Unfair Dismissals Act in 1993 amended Employment Law to include sexual orientation as a category covered by the law. Several authors note that although being forced to resign or retire on marriage may seem incredible to many younger Irish women, only one generation of Irish women have come of working age in a climate which is free from the ban itself, as well as from the family ideology of female caregiver/male breadwinner that it reinforced and that remains enshrined in the Constitution (Smyth, 1988; Smyth, 1997; Mahon, 1998). Nonetheless, the effects of the marriage ban are still experienced by many women of the previous generation.

The gendered ideology of the family embedded in the Irish Constitution has been highly influential in shaping Irish laws. As a result, many women have been forced to choose between a career and motherhood. This is reflected in the fact that Irish women have had the lowest labour market participation rate in the EU. While it has increased considerably it continues to rank low by EU standards. The most significant change in the Irish female labour force has been the increased participation rates of married women. Most of this increase has taken place since 1971 with the rate more than trebling from 7.5 per cent in that year to 29 per cent in 1992. By 2002, the percentage of married women in paid employment had risen dramatically to 46 per cent.[8] Young married women in particular are remaining in the labour market and combining earning and caring responsibilities.[9]

Clearly, there is much room for improvement regarding the facilitation of women's participation in the paid labour force. Childcare provision remains weak and the introduction of publicly subsidised universal childcare would make an enormous difference to Irish women's lives. However, the ideology of motherhood whereby mothers are the most appropriate carers of young children has been traditionally entrenched. In any event the rising cost of living in Ireland may necessitate dual breadwinner roles. Extensive parental leave reform would also impact positively on women's choices regarding labour market participation. Despite the anti-discrimination laws that are now in place, Irish women still face significant gender inequalities – including the gender wage gap (Smyth, 1997).

Families and the social security system

The Irish constitution provides a gendered construction of citizenship, whereby women's primary role pertains to motherhood and the domestic sphere, while men correspondingly are viewed as breadwinners and participate in the public sphere. This gendered ideology has informed subsequent Irish social and welfare policies. Women were assumed to be economically dependent on men until the mid-1980s. Married women were not entitled to the same amount or duration of unemployment benefit as single women and all men. In contrast, a married man was automatically entitled to claim his wife as a dependent irrespective of whether she was in fact earning, while a married women had to show actual dependency before she could claim her husband as a dependent. Women, as single parents, could claim an allowance, but this was denied to men in the same situation. Interestingly, although lesbian and gay relationships are generally disadvantaged under familial regimes such as Ireland's, lesbian and gay couples on social welfare may not be subject to the limitation rules which apply to heterosexual couples. As their relationship is not recognised, they may be considered individual claimants, rather than face restrictions on the benefits they receive as a recognised family unit – a restriction that further impoverishes the most vulnerable families (McLaughlin & Yeates, 1999).

Childcare provision in Ireland is among the most expensive in Europe and the lack of good quality affordable childcare has been identified as a barrier to women's participation and retention in the workforce (O'Connor, 1998; Galligan, 1998). A report published in 2000 found that the average cost of childcare in Ireland is 20 per cent of average earnings. For women with low earning potential it may therefore be financially detrimental to participate in paid employment (P2000 Expert Working Group).[10] Parents who cannot afford the prohibitive costs of private childcare are forced to rely on relatives (often grandmothers). Waiting lists for preschools and montessoris tend to be extensive. Although a system of health board pre-schools does exist, again the waiting list is lengthy and priority is given to children who are at risk in the home. Some organisations, including large companies and semi-state organisations sometimes provide workplace crèches, but these are seen as a bonus rather than an obligation (Prendiville, 1995; O'Connor, 1999). In short, Irish social policy is traditionally characterised by a male breadwinner model and heteronormative assumptions, including an emphasis on marriage. These policy frameworks have important implications for lesbian women in Ireland.

Lesbians in Ireland

Lesbian lives in Ireland are 'marked by prejudice and discrimination on the one hand, and by celebration and pride on the other' (Moane, 1997: 439). Coinciding with the development of second wave feminism in Ireland in the early 1970s, lesbian groups began to form and act both as support groups and to engage in political struggle. Irish lesbians have been involved in both the women's movement and the lesbian and gay movement. In 1978, lesbians instigated new initiatives around exclusively lesbian issues. The same year, the first lesbian conference was held in Trinity college Dublin, and the Dublin Lesbian Line Collective was formed. Various lesbian-oriented events began to take place on an annual basis and soon there was a proliferation of lesbian groups throughout the country, although largely concentrated in urban areas. In 1991, Dublin Lesbian Line, the Dublin Lesbian Discussion Group (later known as First Out), and Cork Lesbian Line presented written submissions to the Second Commission on the Status of Women (1993), in addition to an oral presentation to the Commission by Dublin Lesbian Line. The document submitted by the Dublin Lesbian Line emphasised lesbians' rights as participatory citizens (Moane, 1997). The final report of the Commission made a number of recommendations pertaining to lesbians, including legislative change safeguarding workers from unfair dismissal on the grounds of sexual orientation and the integration of lesbian and gay sexuality awareness in the sex education curriculum in Irish schools. Later the same year a co-ordinating group called Lesbians Organising Together (LOT) was formed. This group aimed to act as a support and resource for lesbians in Dublin and became the first lesbian group to receive NOW (New Opportunities for Women) funding for an outreach and education programme (Lesbian Education and Awareness – LEA). LEA ran a high-profile campaign urging greater acceptance of lesbians during 1999.[11]

Lesbians have also been active in campaigns for legislative change. Homosexual activity remained technically a criminal offence in Ireland until 1993, even though prevailing codes of practice for government agencies condemned discrimination on the basis of sexual orientation and the Prohibition of Incitement to Hatred Act (1989) ostensibly included sexual orientation. The Gay and Lesbian Equality Network

(GLEN) ran a very public campaign and lobby to repeal the legislation on male homosexuality (successfully attained in 1993). However, as lesbians were not included in that legislation they remained largely absent in the accompanying public debate (Prendiville, 1997). In 1993 homosexuality was finally decriminalised, and the new law also introduced an equal age of consent. Sexual orientation has been included in the Unfair Dismissals Act (1993), the Employment Equality Act (1996) and the Equal Status Act (2000). However, the latter two incorporate exemptions on the grounds of religion, therefore rendering lesbians and gay men particularly vulnerable. Nonetheless, these changes indicate that significant progress has been made in advancing lesbian (and gay) rights in Ireland in the last two decades. Despite this, lesbian parents have largely retained a low profile and lesbian parenting issues have not been highlighted in the LGBT movement's political agenda until very recently. The growing awareness of lesbian parenthood is often linked to campaigns around same sex partnerships and marriage reform, which highlight lesbian and gay family units.

Parenting rights

The constitutional emphasis on marriage is reflected in family law and has interesting implications for lesbian parents. In the case of married parents, both names are recorded on a child's birth certificate and joint guardianship is automatic. An unmarried biological mother is automatically considered the sole guardian and her name is included on the birth certificate. An unmarried father must prove paternity and then apply separately to the Registrar of Births, Marriages and Deaths if he wishes to have his name documented on a child's birth certificate. However, a successful outcome primarily acts to ensure the child's inheritance from the father's estate. The father must apply to the courts in order to obtain guardianship rights, access and custody. Although the status of illegitimacy was abolished by the Status of Children Act (1987), a birth mother cannot record the father's name without his consent (Prendiville, 1997). During the past decade, there has been considerable media debate about the 'rights of fathers' in Ireland. This period has also witnessed the formation of several fatherhood rights groups.

The custody of the children of separated or divorced lesbian mothers is left to the discretion of the courts. The judiciary is supposed to allocate custody according to the best interests of the child/ren and the sexual orientation of parents is ostensibly irrelevant. However, 'hearsay' evidence is admissible and lesbian mothers are often afraid to reveal their involvement with another woman in court, in case it influences the court's decision regarding custody arrangements. Nevertheless there have been a number of reported cases where the lesbian mother was open about her sexual orientation with a favourable outcome (Prendeville, 1997). There is no legal recognition of lesbian and gay partnerships in the Republic of Ireland, although Northern Ireland, as part of the UK, has implemented civil unions for same sex couples. There is an increasing level of political debate about same sex partnership and it is now the primary site of LGBT activism in Ireland. Lesbian co-parents have no formal legal rights as parents.

Insemination, fostering and adoption

Donor insemination (DI) was first introduced into Ireland in 1982 and is predominantly obtained privately. Only one clinic has publicly provided DI for all women, regardless of sexuality. It is possible for Irish lesbians to obtain DI in Ireland, but can be difficult in practice, as not all clinics are supportive of lesbian clients. The fact that a relatively conservative society such as Ireland does at least in theory allow lesbians to access donor insemination, a possibility that was denied to Swedish lesbians through legislation at the time of fieldwork, may seem surprising. According to McDonnell (1999: 70), the preferred institutionalised response in Ireland to new reproductive technologies (NRTs) has been 'to defer public debate and to leave policy frameworks to the self-regulatory activity of the medical profession.' This contrasts with the response of Nordic countries, where national ethics committees and widespread public debate have informed the regulation of NRTs. In Ireland, the potential legal and ethical implications of NRTs were ignored in normative discourses that depicted them as a resource for heterosexual married couples with fertility difficulties. Thus, the introduction of NRTs in Ireland did not precipitate a public crisis. McDonnell (1999) notes that the pronounced absence of public debate about NRTs has meant that public discourse has not been influential in their regulation. In the UK, the possibility of single and lesbian women accessing NRTs was publicly debated. But this concern was not raised in Irish media or political debate, rather NRTs were normalised by the profile given to childless married couples who were the presumed consumers of this medical assistance. While the availability of the service to non-married couples, lesbian and single women was not prohibited, 'they did not emerge as a legitimate subject or public with distinct needs and claims' (McDonnell, 1999: 76). She further argues that the invisibility of lesbians and single women who may avail of the service is not only taken for granted, 'but it is adopted as a strategy of inverted logic to avoid open contestation over competing claims' (1999: 76). Thus, the claims of non-married and lesbian couples are removed from the terms of any potential debate. The absence of political or legislative disputes on NRTs has meant that public contestation and, hence, public debate have been absent in the Irish context. O'Donnell does note however, that international public discursive events have become an important reference for mobilising public concern in Ireland. It may also be the case that the liberal market policies of Ireland and Britain facilitate access to private services, unlike in a social democratic society such as Sweden. This appears to have been the case in Finland, where a more liberal market regime has meant that private clinics have provided their services to single and lesbian women.

In Ireland, adoption is restricted to heterosexual couples, with clear guidelines that couples must satisfy to be eligible. The adoption organisations are predominantly private voluntary bodies, although there are also some denominational groups. However, many lesbians continue to bypass these formal channels by becoming pregnant through informal arrangements with known donors. The adoption laws are therefore most restrictive to lesbian co-parents and infertile lesbian women. Fostering is arranged by Regional Health Boards, which are state agencies. Interestingly, the severe shortage of foster carers in Ireland has led some health boards to advertise for foster parents in Irish lesbian and gay press since the 1990s, although this does not appear to have been noticed by the mainstream Irish media.

Gender, sexuality and citizenship in Sweden

The struggle to attain equal rights for women in relation to paid employment developed quite differently in Sweden compared to Ireland. In 1939 Sweden passed an Act outlawing the dismissal of women on the grounds of marriage, pregnancy or childbirth, legislation that was exceptional in an international context at the time (Gustafsson, 1994). It arose as a result of feminist campaigns responding to a government commission, which in 1935 recommended that married women be dismissed from employment in order to help combat the economic depression that the country was experiencing. Feminists argued that if married women left the paid workforce, working-class women would be unable to afford to marry and have children. As Sweden was at the time facing a population crisis, these arguments appealed to the pronatalist concerns of the government (Hobson, 1993; Gustafsson, 1994).

Swedish economic policies in the 1960s aimed to increase the labour supply of married women. Sweden was facing a labour shortage during this time period and married women were identified as a labour resource to solve this problem. Gustafsson (1994) suggests that one reason for increased support of married women in the labour force was that Sweden (as opposed to for example Germany) did not view immigrants as guest workers, instead extending full citizenship rights to them. Thus the economic costs of immigrant workers (who were entitled to bring their families and to Swedish language instruction) were far greater than simply bringing married women into the workforce.

Gender equality and 'the family'

A new discourse emerged on inequality between women and men (jämställdhet) in Sweden during the late 1960s. Gender inequality was attributed to both women's lack of participation in paid work and the gendered division of labour in the home. The message in the major social policy investigation of sex roles at that time, Women's Life and Work (Dahlström, 1962), was that in addition to encouraging women to participate in the paid labour force, men's attitudes towards carework needed to change. This would alter existing gender relations by depriviliging the male breadwinner model and would also be positive for men, who would benefit from greater involvement in family life and carework. The report undermined those rare instances where women were privileged as individuals through the construction of gender roles, for example in custody cases where the mother was automatically assumed to be the most appropriate primary caregiver. In addition, this new approach called for the abolition of widows' pensions, the last bastion of women's economic protection under a male breadwinner system. However, this challenge to existing gender ideologies was not framed within the language of power, but rather as an issue of education and socialisation (Bergman & Hobson, 2002).

Policy discourse assumed that women and men's working lives would become more and more similar over time, as men would also shoulder responsibility for carework. According to this perspective, women's liberation would be achieved through equal participation in paid employment, thus reflecting the roots of the social democratic welfare state in class-based emancipatory politics. Many of the policy ideas of the time are often attributed to a progressive group of social scientists and political activists, Group 222. This group was composed of men and women across several political parties.[12] Interestingly, Swedish men have played an active role in feminist debates about gender equality. This is perhaps a reflection of the construction of gender equality ideology in Sweden, where 'equality meant equality between the sexes, emancipation meant emancipation of women *and* men' [italics as they appear in the original text] (Bergman & Hobson, 2002: 105).[13]

Sainsbury (1996: 163) highlights the impact of direct payment of children's allowance to mothers as a contributing factor to the undermining of the father-breadwinner model in the 1940s. However, Bergman & Hobson (2002: 105) suggest that 'the real turning point' occurred in the 1970s with policy interventions that further undermined the male breadwinner system. Thus, tax reforms founded on the premise that all workers be treated as individuals removed the marriage subsidy that was paid to men married to housewives. In addition, the tax rate of married women's salaries was formerly calculated by adding the wife's wages to her husband's and then taxing them at the highest rate. This practice was also abolished. Bergman & Hobson (2002) note that widows' pensions represented 'the last residue' of the male breadwinner model and were finally phased out in the late 1980s.

Swedish equality discourse emphasises the benefits of shared parenthood for women and men, in addition to the advantages for children in attending the public childcare system. Nonetheless, this rhetoric co-exists with prevalent ideas about the importance of mothers' accessibility to their children. Swedish research clearly shows that women's work orientation correlates to their occupation and social position. As a result, highly educated women who have professional, independent jobs are strongly committed to both work and the family. In contrast, research on women with less advantaged socio-economic status are primarily oriented toward family life and as a result their working lives are organised around a caregiving role (Elvin-Nowak, 1999).

Several researchers have pointed out that modern femininity in Sweden is based on participation in fields that in previous decades were considered the domain of men, such as paid employment. Lifestyles based on more traditional gender roles (such as becoming a full-time housewife) are no longer regarded as a positive expression of femininity (Haavind, 1998). Elvin-Nowak (1999) found this line of reasoning consistent with the findings of her research on motherhood in contemporary Sweden. She uncovered a discourse of motherhood in which the child's needs are central, but where the mother, in accordance with the equality discourse, is also expected to find her well-being external to the child and family. She concludes that in Sweden women acting as a sole caregiver after their child/ren's infancy, face criticism because their situation is considered to represent 'blatant subordination and excessively traditional femininity' (p. 61). Swedish discourses of gender equality in which women's and men's life paths are expected to approximate one another produce a normative understanding of femininity and masculinity in which both women and men are expected to want and enjoy a life independent of their partner and child: 'The mother who questions this by giving up a job outside the home thus also questions the ideology of equality, and becomes a representative for an ideal considered to be antiquated' (Elvin-Nowak, 1999: 63).

However, women are nonetheless in a double bind, as mothers who prioritise a job or career over the family risk even greater disapproval. Since motherhood is constructed around accessibility, women in paid employment are constantly judged as to the performance and integration of their roles as worker and mother. According to Elvin-Nowak (1999: 72), the mother who does not prioritise her child breaks an invisible taboo: 'This mother actualises the gender neutrality norm from the ideology of equality, which is seldom desirable in reality'. Thus, women face a complex balancing act of roles, expectations and subjectivity.

Fatherhood in Sweden

Bergman & Hobson (2002) provide an illuminating overview of the historical context for the changing relationship between gender, fatherhood and social policy in Sweden. They argue that the Swedish welfare state has played a unique and active role in the normative regulation of fatherhood. This is illustrated through the introduction of policies reserving part of the parental leave allowance for fathers and laws that enforce the obligations of biological fathers to their children after divorce through a system of shared custody.

Sweden began to regulate the formal acknowledgement of paternity for children born outside marriage in the first decades of the twentieth century. Unlike many countries (including Ireland) where paternity is related to marriage, a law passed in Sweden as early as 1917 required that the paternity of all children be established. The impetus behind this legislation was concern for the material well-being of unmarried mothers and their children, as Sweden had one of the highest illegitimacy rates in Europe at that time. In addition, infant mortality was higher among children born outside of marriage and they were more likely to be in fostercare and orphanages. The 1917 act also obliged men to make an economic contribution to their children's upkeep, regardless of marital status (Bergman & Hobson, 2002). A further legal change in the postwar era ensured the inheritance rights of children with unmarried parents (Björnberg, 1998). More recently, Swedish legislation has moved from a protection of the rights of children born outside marriage, to an emphasis on the right of a child to know the identity of her or his biological parents. However, the increasing emphasis on biological paternity from the early twentieth century also reflects efforts to ensure that men were not held responsible for the maintenance of someone else's biological child. Furthermore, it has been suggested that the emphasis on biological fatherhood was contiguous with eugenicist discourses of the 1930 and 1940s. In 1933 a law was passed allowing for blood tests establishing the identity of biological parents (Bergman & Hobson, 2002).

Legal practice also began to emphasise the role of biology in the regulation of fatherhood. Bergman & Hobson (2002) note that despite the plurality of family forms and constellations, biological fatherhood remains crucial to the coding of men as fathers in the Swedish welfare state. Following the publication and subsequent discussion of a government commission on Family and Marriage, a dramatic change in the construction of fatherhood took place during the 1970s. The role of fathers as financial providers was replaced with an emphasis on men as participatory fathers. The rights of the child were considered paramount and the relationship between individual parents was not to interfere with their responsibilities and rights with regard to parenting. As a result, men were now conferred with official decision-making rights, irrespective of whether they were residential parents or not. Joint custody is strongly supported in the event of relationship breakdown between parents and is considered to be in the best interests of children. Changes to the Parental Code in 1998 now allow courts to rule in favour of joint custody even when one parent is opposed to it. Even in situations where a biological father has lost contact with a child or children and their mother's new partner has been involved in raising them, the biological father is entitled to demand visitation rights or custody (Hobson & Bergman, 2002). Perhaps the most dramatic indication of the social policy efforts to ensure that men participate in family life, is the *'pappa månad'* or father's month, introduced in 1994 as part of the parental leave provisions. According to this law, one of the 12 months of parental leave available to parents is reserved for fathers (and one month for mothers) and is not exchangeable. This provision for fathers was extended to two months in 2003.

However, an examination of the impact of social policy on men's behaviour reveals disappointing results. While studies indicate that children are the primary motivation for Swedish men to adjust their professional activity to their family lives (Björnberg, 1998) and more Swedish men than men in other countries base their identity on their family life, men's involvement in household work and in childcare remains lower than that of women. Men do one third of what their partners do, even when both have full-time jobs. Thus, Björnberg (1998) argues that men tend to be child-oriented but less motivated to do housework. In Sweden, about 30 per cent of fathers take up some part of parental leave. Although Swedish feminists have expressed disappointment with this low percentage, given the incentives to fathers, it is still reflective of the more active fathering role in Sweden, relative to many other countries. The recent extension of the period of parental leave reserved for fathers from one month to two months reflects an effort to encourage men to play a more active role. Despite the problematic implications of certain aspects of the active fathering discourse in Sweden, in many ways it represents a move away from gendered essentialist notions of biological motherhood and often constitutes an effort to ensure that men share caring responsibilities. However, in the view of Bergman & Hobson (2002: 124), the emphasis on biological fatherhood in Sweden has meant 'celebrating participatory fathering, while at the same time not disturbing the division of labour within the family or the gendered inequalities in the labour market'. Irrespective of whether the emphasis on participatory fatherhood has been emancipatory or not, it has become central to Swedish men's identities (Plantin, 2001) and to Swedish family discourses.

Employment

The Swedish welfare state has supported women's participation in the workforce with subsidised public childcare and generous parental leave. This is reflected in Swedish women's employment rates, which are comparable to men's. Perhaps more surprisingly, Sweden has one of the highest fertility rates in Europe, although it has dropped substantially in recent years from 2+ in 1989 to 1.5 in 2002.[14] Hoem (1990) attributed the high fertility rate in Sweden to progressive social policy that enabled women to combine work and care responsibilities. Chesnais (1996) compared Sweden with Italy and also concluded that policies designed to facilitate the integration of work and care responsibilities in fact contribute to higher fertility rates. The recent decline in Swedish fertility has been attributed to increasing unemployment and reduced levels of financial support for families. Although the level of support remains higher in Sweden than in most other European countries, Hoem & Hoem (1996) suggest that Swedes have experienced considerable 'relative deprivation' in recent years and this has influenced their fertility.[15]

The high labour market participation rate of Swedish women is one indication of the level of support for female employment.[16] Support for the dual earner family is reflected in generous parental leave allowances (including leave days to care for sick children), in addition to job security ensuring that posts remain open while parents are on leave. All workers are entitled to five weeks of vacation annually, a further incentive to women's participation in the labour force (Hobson, 1993). The conditions of solo mothers provide another example of the extent to which the male breadwinner model has been undermined in Sweden. As Hobson & Takahashi (1997) note, solo mothers in Sweden experience much lower levels of poverty compared to their counterparts in many other Western countries. Nyberg (2002) suggests that although the capacity of Swedish solo mothers to support themselves through paid employment has been affected by the economic decline of the 1990s, it has improved significantly since the 1970s. However, women's capacity to form autonomous households has improved through higher transfers, rather than higher labour market earnings.

Analyses of the historical trajectory of Swedish family policies concur that important initiatives took place in the 1930s and 1940s (Hirdman, 1989, 1998; Bergman & Hobson, 2002).[17] From the late 1960s, expert discourses connected gender equality to men's roles in the family and the dual parenting model. Swedish media debated sex roles and equality in the family throughout the late 1960s and early 1970s (Hirdman, 1998). This had different implications for women and men. While women were encouraged to participate in the paid labour force, men were expected to play a more active caring role in family life. Although these discussions challenged hegemonic motions of masculinity and the construction of men as breadwinners, they were not radical in the sense that they were centred around the traditional nuclear family (Leira, 1993; Sainsbury, 1996). To some extent, the sex role debate addressed the consequences for family life of women's widespread entry into the labour market. Bergman & Hobson (2002: 106–7) suggest that 'in a society with a history of social engineering it is not surprising that the dual earner family model would authorize experts to define new parenting styles and with the loss of the full time housewife, the construction of explicit norms for fathering'. Swedish women's mass entry into the labour market has not been accompanied by men participating equally in domestic work. Recent decades have however witnessed men becoming more active in family life (Björnberg, 1998).

Families and the Social Security System

The public provision of childcare was a fundamental demand of the Swedish women's movement in the 1960s and 1970s and 'day-care for all' was a popular feminist slogan (Bergqvist, 1999). Eighty-seven per cent of children up to six years of age in Sweden are registered in some form of childcare (Statistics Sweden, 2002). Parents are entitled to 12 months of paid parental leave (usually at 80 per cent of their salary, although there are ceiling levels). This can be extended over a longer period of time if parents choose to take a smaller payment each month.[18]

Sweden became the first country to introduce a reform of parental leave that included fathers in 1974. This policy innovation was explicitly meant to contribute to equality between women and men. It was based on the assumption of the dual breadwinner family. Parents were seen as economically independent individuals, both with obligations and rights in respect of their children as well as the labour market (Bergqvist, 1999). Parental leave allowance has been set at relatively high levels of compensation, which has minimised loss of income. In Sweden, the scheme includes a 'father's month' and a 'mother's month', the entitlements to which are not transferable between parents (unless there is an unknown father, as in the case of children conceived through DI, but this can cause complications with local social security offices).

Marriage and cohabitation

Sweden has a long tradition of low marriage rates in addition to high rates of cohabitation and births outside marriage (Bergman & Hobson, 2002). Many couples do not marry until after the birth of a child or children, if at all.[19] Although it has been argued that the Swedish preference for cohabitation is indicative of a decline in the institutionalisation of the family (Popenoe, 1988), nuclear family ideology nonetheless remains strong in Sweden. The lesser importance attached to marriage in Scandinavian countries, including Sweden, has implications for understanding the development of registered partnerships for same sex couples there.

Søland (1998) examines the discursive landscape accompanying the introduction of registered partnerships in Denmark. She argues that marriage has lost symbolic value in Denmark and has therefore been extended to same sex couples because it no longer represents the locus of normative family ideologies. In her view, lesbian and gay actors and organisations have been too conformist in their pursuit of this possibility and have unquestioningly accepted middle-class ideals of 'decent lifestyles'. As a result registered partnerships may create a new normative framework of gay life that excludes 'less respectable' modes of homosexual lifestyles. She is strongly critical of a politics of assimilation and suggests that the queer movement should retain a commitment to diverse lifestyles and visions of kinship. Halvorsen (1998) in her discussion of the Registered Partnership Act that was passed in Norway in 1993, also illustrates that the passage of this legislation is indicative of the extent to which cohabitation has become an acceptable norm among heterosexuals. She notes that relatively few couples registered their partnership and suggests that the Act has symbolic rather than practical value. In Halvorsen's view, lesbian and gay people are obtaining formal rights in areas that are of declining social and symbolic value, as the demarcation of new boundaries for the legitimising of relationships and lifestyles are occurring elsewhere. This analysis also appears to be applicable to the Swedish context. Thus, while legislation extends the rights of marriage to lesbian and gay couples in the Nordic countries, parenting remains far more controversial, as illustrated by the legislative restrictions for lesbians and gay men concerning adoption and assisted conception.

Lesbians in Sweden

A survey of attitudes towards homosexuals in Sweden was widely reported in Swedish media during fieldwork.[20] The changes in attitudes over the previous 20 years were hailed as an indication of major progress. In 1980, only 30 per cent of Swedish people felt comfortable about having a homosexual as a friend. By 2000, as many as 70 per cent indicated that they did not object to having homosexual friends. Whether this news is worth celebrating is debatable, but the study did indicate some striking findings concerning the last bastion of heterosexuality in Sweden – the family. Over 60 per cent of respondents did not support lesbian and gay adoption. Interestingly, only 51 per cent of the 668 adult Swedish residents surveyed supported same sex marriage, despite the introduction of registered partnerships in 1995 (Landén & Innala, 2002). Nonetheless, Sweden is often considered to be one of the most progressive countries in the world concerning lesbian and gay rights.

Homosexuality was decriminalised in Sweden as early as 1944 and RFSL[21] (The Swedish Federation for Gays and Lesbians) was established in 1950. The first openly gay Swedish public figure came out in 1951 and lesbian and gay social life has been increasingly visible in Sweden since the late 1950s. Interestingly, it has been a principle of Swedish law since 1955 that the sexual orientation of parents should not influence custody disputes (SOU, 1984: 63, 274). In 1973 the Swedish parliament declared after a vote that Sweden should view homosexuality as equal to heterosexuality. In 1978 the age of consent was made the same for heterosexuals and homosexuals. Section 9 of the Penal Code, the Prohibition Against Unlawful Discrimination (1976) was extended in 1987 to include sexual orientation (Widegren & Ytterberg, 1995). In 1999 this was further amended to include more extensive obligations in relation to employment. Lesbian couples are afforded a measure of legal protection through the recognition of cohabiting relationships (the sambo law) and the law on registered partnerships. The sambo law does not give rights of inheritance and also excludes certain social benefits.[22] Registered partnerships (gay marriage) came into effect in 1995. The partnerships were almost identical to heterosexual marriage, except for the crucial distinction of parenting rights. Registered partners are expressly prohibited by law from adoption, fostering, assisted insemination, fertility treatment and parental leave. Finally in 1999, an Ombudsman against Discrimination because of Sexual orientation,[23] was appointed by the government.

A Swedish lesbian lone mother has the right to the same benefits as any other Swedish lone mother. However, there are complications in the case of lesbians (and single heterosexual women) who become pregnant through insemination at a sperm bank abroad, as the name of the father has to be declared on the birth certificate (and in order to qualify for lone parent benefit). This situation with the birth certificate does not apply to heterosexual couples who conceive by insemination.

Biological parents are automatically awarded custody upon the birth of a child. However, legislative changes that came into effect in January 2003 allow lesbian and gay people to adopt. This includes the possibility of second parent adoption for lesbian co-parents, although it is dependent upon the biological father rescinding all formal rights. Given that many Swedish lesbians parent with involved donors (see next chapter), this situation does not allow for all possible configurations of lesbian parent families, where there may be more than two active parents.

Insemination, adoption and fostering

A paternity case in Sweden in 1981 involving a child who was conceived by insemination served as the impetus behind a nationwide controversy over donor insemination. The Swedish lower court pronounced the child in question 'fatherless', when the social father challenged paternity on the basis that insemination had taken place without his consent. The 'Haparanda case' sparked a debate which resulted in the introduction of legislation regulating donor insemination in 1984. Three mandatory conditions concerning DI were introduced: psychosocial screening of prospective parents; the registration of DI births in the National Population Register; and the anonymity of donors was outlawed, introducing a system of open donor identity. This latter innovation was framed in terms of the 'child's right to know' (Liljestrand, 1995). According to Liljestrand (1995: 271) the debate over DI that raged in Sweden in the early 1980s was 'a smokescreen for issues other than the child's best interests'. She further contends that DI was constructed as a social problem within the terms of the debate because it represented a challenge to normative frameworks and ideologies. In addition, she argues that the possibility of single or lesbian women conceiving children through DI constituted a central dimension of this threat. In Liljestrand's view, this is because they would enable the conception of children who would grow up without a father and knowledge of their paternity.

Donor insemination was only available to married heterosexual couples in Sweden at the time of fieldwork. Unmarried heterosexual women and all lesbians were prohibited by law from being inseminated within the health care system or private clinics. Swedish lesbians could travel to neighbouring Denmark, where a single clinic in Copenhagen offers DI services to single heterosexual women and lesbians. Interestingly, Sweden is the first country in the world that has a system of compulsory donor identity disclosure for DI services. Thus, heterosexual couples who utilise this service in Sweden cannot choose an anonymous donor, as all donors must agree to make their identity known to any future child when she or he turns eighteen. This stipulation provides a particularly clear illustration of the emphasis on biological fatherhood and knowledge of bio-paternity in a Swedish context. There have been difficulties in achieving a sufficient supply of donations for Swedish sperm banks however, resulting in lengthy waiting lists for heterosexual couples who wish to use this service. A consequence of this which has been completely absent from discussions in Sweden is that heterosexual Swedish couples are also travelling to Denmark for the purpose of donor insemination.[24]

Despite the introduction of registered partnerships in 1995, adoption was restricted to heterosexual couples and single people in Sweden until new legislation in 2003 enabled same sex couples to adopt. Although single lesbians were not formerly excluded in the previous adoption prohibitions, it seemed unlikely that a lesbian who was open about her sexuality would be approved for adoption. A Supreme Court verdict from 1993 denied a man living with another man the right to adopt a child on his own (Berggren, 1995). The new legislation includes second parent adoption, where a lesbian or gay man can become a legally recognised parent of their partner's biological child. This is a tremendous advance from the previous restrictions on lesbian and gay parenting rights in Sweden and represents the culmination of years of activist lobbying and governmental investigation. The primary legal vulnerability has been the lack of formal recognition of co-parents. However, adoption by a co-parent can only take place if she and her partner are in a registered partnership. It cannot be awarded retrospectively in cases where a couple had split up by the time the legislation came into effect, but had continued to parent together. The legal situation with regard to fostering is less clear. A lesbian couple, cohabiting or registered partners, might be allowed to become foster parents as there is no law against it. Berggren (1995) refers to a single case of a gay male couple becoming foster parents for a gay teenage boy but notes that while fostering gay and lesbian teenagers is therefore possible, it remained exceptional.[25]

Several Members of Parliament have proposed motions to change the law on adoption and insemination since 1995, culminating in recent legislative changes. From 1st July 2005 lesbian couples have had access to insemination at a hospital clinic under the same rules as for heterosexual couples. This right is for both couples that live together (sambos) and registered partners. All couples accessing this service are tested and evaluated (medical, psychological and social circumstances) and insemination will happen if it can be assumed that the child will grow up under 'good circumstances' ('goda förhållanden'). The co-parent becomes the second parent by law through the same process as a social father to a child conceived via donor insemination in a heterosexual marriage. She has to sign a paper before witnesses either prior to the birth or after, confirming her role as parent.[26] Although the discourse around lesbian and gay parenting in Sweden has ostensibly been centrally concerned with the welfare of the child, it should be noted that such debates concerning 'the best interests of the child' often take a homophobic form. Interestingly, with the publication of the Swedish government report (SOU, 2001: 10) indicating that children of lesbian and gay parents are not harmed by their parents' sexuality, the discussion became more focused on adoption. The Ombudsman against Discrimination on the grounds of Sexual Orientation (HomO), has suggested that the debates within the commission were overshadowed by the issue of adoption.[27] There was considerable popular concern that extending adoption rights to lesbians and gay men would have a negative impact on heterosexual prospective adoptive parents, as most adoptions involve children born abroad and their countries of origin might object to sending children to Sweden to be raised by same sex couples.[28]

However, it is clear from my research that although second parent adoption is a crucial issue for lesbian parents, international adoption is not the means by which many would choose to become parents. In fact, assisted reproduction is a very important issue for lesbians wishing to embark on parenthood. The laws on adoption were revised in June 2002 to include lesbian and gay parents. Assisted reproduction therefore remained the last barrier to full legal equality between heterosexual and homosexual parents in Sweden. After intensive campaigning, legislative changes came into effect in 2005 that offered assisted conception services to single women and lesbians in registered partnerships. In contrast, Irish lesbians have accessed these services due to their relative invisibility whereby they are not formally recognised through the act of prohibiting them from using assisted reproduction services. It must be noted however that this research took place prior to the innovative legislative changes regarding adoption and assisted conception that have recently been introduced in Sweden.

A comparative study of lesbian parenting in Sweden and Ireland

Comparative analysis of lesbian parents in these two social contexts facilitates an exploration of the ways participants negotiate hegemonic discourses of kinship while situated differently from the norm. An examination of the experiences of lesbian parents highlights how individual societies facilitate or restrict women's autonomy according to their sexuality. According to Reinharz (1992), there is a paucity of feminist cross-cultural research. Oyen (1990: 1) argues that there is an increasing demand for comparative studies due to the 'growing internationalisation and the concomitant export and import of social, cultural and economic manifestations across national borders'. She further argues that this globalising trend may require that researchers doing comparative studies shift their emphasis from 'seeking uniformity among variety to studying the preservation of enclaves of uniqueness among growing homogeneity and uniformity'. Further, overarching comparative analyses can obscure significant aspects of local social policy formulations. Clearly, Ireland and Sweden have distinctive approaches to gender, parenting and citizenship, which are coded in their legislation and social security systems. The contrast between the two in

terms of social policy frameworks regarding gender and familial relationships is significant. There is considerably more support for women's
autonomous households in Sweden, as illustrated by women's greater
participation in the labour market and the availability of parental leave
and subsidised childcare, all of which affect women's choices regarding
the financial and employment implications of motherhood. Queer activism has become increasingly networked on an international scale over
the past twenty years and this is reflected in the growing emphasis on
transnationalism in queer research (Corber & Valocchi, 2003). Yet the
Nordic countries, including Sweden, have more formal rights and a high
level of media visibility for lesbians, gays and bisexuals than many other
countries. This contrasts with the Republic of Ireland, where lesbians and
gay men have fewer legal rights, less recognition and are more marginalised from mainstream discourses than in Sweden (McDonnell, 1999).
Any advantages they may have compared to Sweden (in Ireland, access to
fertility treatment and DI, both in the private sector) appear to have been
accrued by their very invisibility. As policy-makers were not aware that
lesbians and gay men seek these services, they are not explicitly prohibited from using them. It may also be the case that the tendency toward a
liberal market policy in Ireland facilitates access to private services, unlike
in a social democratic society such as Sweden. These social policy differences shape the context for lesbian women's choices and experiences
in local contexts and are therefore pertinent to any analysis of lesbian
parenting.

Unlike comparative studies of welfare states that examine macro structural processes, the research for this book takes a qualitative approach,
exploring how lesbian women negotiate possibilities and limitations
within two welfare state contexts. Policy discourse and formulations
regarding gender, sexuality and 'the family' set the context for normative
understandings of kinship and equality politics. A comparative analysis of
lesbian parenting places the perspectives of lesbian parents at the centre
of analysis. Rather than simply compare their narratives to an implicit
(and unidimensional) heterosexual model, Irish and Swedish lesbian
parents' discourses are examined relationally to each other.

3
In Search of Doctors, Donors and Daddies: Lesbian Reproductive Decision-Making

Lesbian parents disrupt normative assumptions about the linear connection between heterosexuality and parenting. The most common representations of motherhood in Western society take place within a heterosexual matrix. Lesbians are actively discouraged from parenting by legislative prohibitions that restrict them from access to adoption, fostering and assisted reproduction. This is reflected in popular assumptions that a lesbian identity is incompatible with parenthood. During fieldwork in Sweden, I was introduced to a middle-aged Swedish man who enquired about my research topic. When I explained that I was interviewing lesbian mothers, he replied in a puzzled voice: *'Isn't that a bit of a contradiction?'* Although new reproductive technologies have developed at a rapid pace and despite the advances of the lesbian, gay and bisexual movement, including at that time almost daily articles in Swedish newspapers about homosexual parenting, procreation/reproduction often remains linked to heterosexual sexual activity in the popular imagination, as this example illustrates. In fact, alternative insemination is a straightforward process and requires little or no medical assistance. It is also the case that some lesbians become parents through fostering or adoption. Nonetheless, the fact remains (but perhaps not for much longer, given recent developments in gynogenesis[1]) that in order for a woman to become pregnant, a donor is required. Although not all participants in this study were biological mothers, a factor common to all parents was that she or her partner had conceived a child and experienced pregnancy.[2] The decision about whether to have a known or unknown donor, an involved or uninvolved donor and the practicalities of meeting donors or accessing clinics required considerable effort and discussion. In this chapter, the discourses of lesbian parents in Sweden and Ireland concerning finding and choosing a donor and issues of access with regard to sperm banks, will be explored. The ways in which social and institutional contexts influence reproductive decision-making among lesbian women in two distinctive welfare regimes illustrates their limitations and possibilities. Wider cultural discourses regarding 'the family' also featured in participants' accounts, where these norms and values were re-imagined.

Contrasting discourses of fatherhood among Swedish and Irish participants

For lesbians choosing biological parenthood, one of the first practical decisions concerns finding a donor and deciding whether or not they want this person to play an active role in a future child's life. The vast majority of participants chose to have a known donor. Sperm banks are difficult for Swedish and Irish lesbians to access. Nonetheless, most interviewees expressed a clear preference for a donor whose identity was known to them. Perhaps the most dramatic difference between Irish and Swedish participants was that Swedish lesbians were far more likely to choose an involved donor. In contrast, the most common situation among Irish participants was to choose a donor, whose identity remained secret. Such donors agreed that if the child became curious about the donor, he could be contacted by the child at some point in the future. This type of arrangement, where the donor's identity remained known only to the lesbian parents, was completely absent from Swedish participants' discussions and choices. Despite this difference regarding donor involvement, both samples generally shared a preference for their child to have access to knowledge of their paternal biological origins. These family constellations are summarised in the following table, where donor status is delineated in terms of donor anonymity or knowledge of his identity, and degree of donor involvement. The numbers refer to the arrangements chosen by individual families:

Table 3.1 Donor status among Swedish and Irish families at time of interview

	Known, involved donor	Known, uninvolved donor	Anonymous donor
Swedish	17	4	3
Irish	5	9	5
Total	22	12	9

Three of the Swedish families classified in the table above as having a known but uninvolved donor, originated as an arrangement with some donor involvement. After some time, the donors themselves chose not to maintain contact with the children, contrary to the initial agreement. The fourth Swedish family in the middle category involves a couple who conceived via insemination at a clinic, but imported semen from the Sperm Bank of California with the donor identity disclosure option (the child can access the donor's identity upon reaching the age of 18). This couple had an initial preference for a known and involved donor, but were unable to achieve this. In contrast, the Irish families with a known but uninvolved donor had all specifically chosen that arrangement from the beginning. It is worth noting that the degree of contact on the part of involved donors in Ireland, was very slight. There was a far greater amount of contact and degree of shared parenting on the part of donors in Sweden. Thus, there is a dramatic contrast between the two samples in terms of understandings of fatherhood.

Although five of the Irish families have been classified as 'anonymous donor' types, only three of these refer to usage of sperm bank services. One child was conceived through a one night stand with an untraceable man, another was a result of rape. All of the Swedish participant families classified in this category had undergone insemination with an anonymous donor at a clinic.

Choosing known donors

The reasons given for choosing a known donor were always explained in terms of the best interests of the child. The importance of having a known donor was far more entrenched among Swedish participants, with Irish parents more likely to view it as a preferable option rather than a necessity. Swedish participants referred to a child's right to know the identity of their father, adopted children's need to know their biological parents and a sense of guilt at having to face their future child's questions about a donor if his identity was unknown. In addition, the donors were most often very involved in the children's lives. Irish parents liked to leave the option open for their children in case they were curious in the future, but preferred to have little or no involvement on the part of donors:

We wanted to have a known donor, but we didn't want that the identity, we didn't want a father, we didn't want to share parenting with somebody else, but we wanted to know who the donor was ourselves and we wanted that information to be confidential.

– Eimear, Irish participant

The majority of Swedish participants expressed a strong belief that children have a 'right' to know their biological father and that to deny a child this right was either unconscionable or contrary to the welfare of the child. The importance of knowledge about one's biological origins was repeatedly articulated by most Swedish participants. An important difference between Irish and Swedish lesbian parents is that while a preference for a known donor was shared, the Swedish women also had donors who were involved in the children's lives. There were a number of reasons given for this. Swedish women expressed the importance of having a male role model (*'förebild'*) in a child's life. While they acknowledged that any man – not just the biological father – could fulfil this role, it was considered easier to have a father who was regularly involved in the child's life to provide this. It was also assumed that donors would want to be involved and that to choose a known donor required their involvement. The kind of steps taken by Irish women to ensure that a known donor was found who would also be uninvolved simply did not appear to have occurred to any of the Swedish participants:

We think because maybe for our sake it would be very easy to have an unknown father to do an insemination in Denmark for example, because we wouldn't have any compromises or negotiations you know. And there would be just one home and one base for the children, so there would be positive things for that too but we think that it's very important for a child to be able to know their roots at least being able to find out sometimes but if you go to Denmark you will never know so em we thought it was for the children's best that we would like to have a father.

– Magdalena, Swedish participant

Yeah and I suppose I was really quite strong on this one, I couldn't resolve it all for myself, I wasn't happy with the idea of a completely anonymous donor, it would have been very secure for us because there would never be any risk of someone trying to take the child off us or anything like that, so personally I wanted, my strong desire was to have a donor who would not have any involvement in raising the child and would not feel themselves as a parent but who would consider the possibility if at some point this person, if the child wanted to meet them, then that would be something they would consider. That they wouldn't rule it out so we had to talk about that quite a lot.

– Karen, Irish participant

Although the amount of contact that donors had with children in Sweden was often described as limited by participants, in fact it ranged from every day, to four or five times a year. The most common arrangement was for donors to see their children once or twice a week, usually involving an overnight stay. In cases where donors saw their children less often, participants usually expressed dissatisfaction with this and a desire for greater involvement on the part of the donor.

In Sweden, women who have a child are required by law to notify the authorities of the father's name. If the parents are not in a relationship, the father must make monthly payments for the maintenance of the child. He faces legal penalties if he fails to do so. The child maintenance is deducted by the state from his salary every month and given directly to the mother. If, through no fault of the mother, the father cannot be found, she will be given the maintenance from the state. However, if the woman refuses to disclose the father's identity, it is possible she may not receive the allowance. Biological fathers are strongly supported by law through the mechanism of automatic shared custody at the birth of a child and increasing legal promotion of joint custody in divorce cases. Hobson & Bergman (2002) argue that the Swedish welfare state represents a strongly institutionalised expression of biological fatherhood. It was the first country in the world to introduce a system whereby donor insemination at a clinic is accompanied by compulsory donor identity disclosure. This legislation was introduced in 1985 and remains unusual in an international context. There are significant benefits designed to induce men's greater participation in parenting, including the reservation of two months of the duration of parental leave for fathers. Irish family law retains a strong influence from the 1937 constitution, which defines the family within the context of marriage and a male breadwinner model. As a result, unmarried fathers are not automatically recognised by law and have to apply to the courts for joint guardianship. An unmarried mother has a personal right to the care and custody of her child, but an unmarried father possesses no constitutional right to either custody or contact with his child (Connolly, 1995). Although individual women may be able to use this situation to their advantage, guardianship in an Irish legal context is based on an ideology of motherhood that is clearly sexist, through the explicit construction of women's contribution to society within the confines of domestic motherhood.

Swedish participants seemed remarkably confident about their legal status as parents with regard to donors, despite the lack of legal recognition for non-biological parents. Not one expressed the fear that was so frequently articulated by Irish interviewees, that known donors might fight for custody or increased contact. The prospect of losing custody of children was a major concern for Irish participants. In marked contrast, Swedish women either welcomed men's involvement or accepted it as inevitable and went to immense lengths to secure amicable and equitable arrangements. In fact, one reason often articulated by Swedish women when explaining a preference for gay male donors, was that they would be more reliable in their commitment to a child, whereas heterosexual men might later start a family with a partner and lose interest in a child or children they had with lesbians:

> Maybe they [heterosexual men] find later on a woman that they want to create a family with and where comes Anton [son] in then? You know when he has new kids with his new home and a new family and maybe he forgets about Anton and a gay man would never do that, there's never a risk or a chance that he would meet a woman and create, start having a family.
>
> – Eva, Swedish participant

Four couples in the Swedish sample chose heterosexual men as donors who would be involved in the children's upbringing. One of these donors was already a close friend of the couple. The other three donors were in relationships with heterosexual female friends, who themselves suggested their partner as a donor. Only one of these arrangements worked out successfully. In two other cases, the donor lost interest after several years and chose not to remain in contact with the children. The fourth donor later married a woman who was uncomfortable with the situation and he now has less contact than was originally anticipated. Clearly, no generalisations can be made and one of these arrangements proceeded amicably. However, the other three cases may suggest that concerns expressed by participants about involving a heterosexual male donor are not unwarranted.

In contrast, among Irish participants with known and involved fathers, a gay man was seen as less threatening than a heterosexual man, because he would be equally as disadvantaged as the lesbian parents in a potential custody battle, on the basis of also being gay. Rather than expressing concern that a heterosexual father would lose interest, they worried that he might become *too* interested and have a legal advantage in a custody case because of his sexuality. Irish interviewees felt vulnerable to fathers who might develop an attachment to a child, particularly once the child was past infancy and required less work. Heterosexual men were seen to be more powerful in a legal context on the basis of their sexuality:

M: It felt less risky than involving a straight man.

G: In case anything went wrong, in terms of them changing their minds, that really they didn't want to go down the route of just having a donor relationship.

M: Yeah you know, custody issues or whatever, it just it might be riskier with a straight man.

– Maeve and Gráinne, Irish participants

As involved donors, gay men were also seen as a more practical option by both Irish and Swedish interviewees, because they understood the difficulties of coming out and the hardship of facing homophobia in society. In addition, gay men were seen to embody a more appealing form of masculinity than many heterosexual men. Gay men were perceived as challenging hegemonic masculinity in ways that were advantageous to parenting:

I don't want my kids to have a stereotyped male role, I don't like that, or a stereotypical female role model, as it's seen in this society. I really love and like it that our kids are in a gay community as well and I think it's necessary for all kids to see all diversity and for example I really love to see my kids, that they see both their fathers or other gay men who are not these stereotype, not this macho.

– Hanna, Swedish participant

In Sweden, having a known donor meant having an involved father. It was insufficient for a child to have knowledge of their paternity, a relationship with that person was also required. This was not just based on the potential difficulties of finding a donor who would agree to have no role in the child's life, but because among Swedish participants the importance of children having a relationship with their fathers was frequently reiterated. The emphasis on participatory fatherhood among participants can be seen as a reflection of broader discourses about the significance of fatherhood and biological relatedness in Swedish society. These normative discourses were acknowledged by one co-parent who had an initial preference for an anonymous donor at a sperm bank:

> There seems to be this incredibly strong need in Sweden for a child to know that they have a father somewhere so I figured oh well you know okay I accepted that after a while.
>
> – Anne, co-parent whose partner is Swedish

Among Irish interviewees, the preference for a known father was generally shared, although less prioritised than among Swedish participants. A known donor did not necessarily imply a relationship between children and the donor however. Given the dominant social norms regarding the nature of kinship and importance of biology, it is unsurprising that a known donor was preferable. Even if interviewees themselves considered biology to be unimportant in parenting, they recognised that broader social norms continually reinforce the significance of biological origins. It was therefore usually viewed as best for the child if this option existed. The distinction between a 'Dad' or 'Pappa' and a 'donor' or 'biological father' was occasionally referred to in interviews. The former was a social parent, whereas a donor is someone who is the biological male parent:

> They [children] explain that they have no Dad, a Dad is a relationship that you have with a person, but they have a father who is the person that made them.
>
> – Catherine, Irish participant

Some Swedish participants said that they might have gone to Denmark for anonymous donor insemination at a clinic if they had not found a known donor, but this was seen as a last resort, a desperate measure. Many however were clear that this was not something they could ever have considered because of the anonymity of the donor. For Swedish women, there were other advantages associated with having known fathers. Another parent was someone who also shouldered responsibility for childcare. When children spent time with their fathers, the lesbian parent or parents were free to spend time alone with their partner or devote their energies to other areas of life:

> We thought it was easier to find two men, one or two men here in Sweden and then we were talking also about this thing that it was good for our kids to have their fathers and it should be good for us

because then our kids could be with their fathers and we have some time for ourselves and all these things to do and going on vacations and all these things.

– Gunilla, Swedish participant

Men's participation in parenting was not seen as beneficial solely to children, it could also be advantageous to lesbian parents, who were able to share the practical aspects of childcare with involved donors. This enabled them to concentrate their energies in other areas of their lives as well. This can be seen as a reflection of a Swedish public discourse of participatory fatherhood dating from the 1970s, when women's entry to the paid labour market was encouraged and facilitated, along with men's greater involvement in family life. Both men and women were perceived to benefit from men's greater involvement in parenting.

Custody considerations among Irish lesbian parents

Three women in the Irish sample had children from a heterosexual marriage. Each had experienced prolonged custody battles and homophobia within the legal system. When they embarked on parenthood with their female partners, one chose to have a donor whose identity remained known only to them and the other two couples chose to inseminate at a sperm bank. Despite the fact that in Sweden fathers have the same rights as mothers and in Ireland fathers are only recognised if they are married to the mother of the child, this legal situation provided Irish participants with little or no sense of security. The legal system and instruments of the law were perceived as threatening and inherently unsympathetic to lesbians. Although the marriage bias in Irish law prevents recognition of unmarried fathers (and has traditionally exempted them from responsibilities), this was not considered to provide sufficient security. This was true for most participants, not only those couples where one partner had been through a custody battle with an ex-husband:

I don't think you can ever as a lesbian in this country depend on any legal system to support you, you know. That's how I feel about it anyhow [...] So I wouldn't have any faith in the Irish legal system whether or not there's legislation there to support us in any legal battle over a child.

– Síle, Irish participant

Once a case has come to court, families are very much at the mercy of judges. If a woman's ex-husband agrees to share custody with her, even partially, she runs the risk of being denied even this limited visitation should she challenge the case in court. While there have been enormous improvements in how lesbians are treated in Irish courts in recent years, Irish participants remained worried that homophobia would act against them in custody cases. It seems that the broader social context shapes women's perceptions of the range of choices available to them, regardless of legal protection or vulnerability. Although Sweden has a highly regulated code of fatherhood that confers men equal rights and responsibilities at the birth of a child, this was not perceived as threatening to lesbian parents. On the other hand, despite the lack of social rights (and responsibilities) afforded fathers in Ireland, Irish interviewees articulated concern that they would be losers in custody battles, on the basis of their sexuality. Choosing an uninvolved donor was therefore seen to provide them with a greater measure of security.

Finding a donor

The task of finding a donor was often a lengthy and intensive process. One participant estimated that over the past 15 years while searching for donors for her partner, herself and friends in their lesbian network, she had approached more than 500 men, of whom only 3 agreed. Although for a small minority of participants the donor was an immediately obvious candidate such as a close friend of many years standing, for most participants it took immense time and effort before finding a suitable person to agree to act as a donor.

There were numerous ways of meeting donors. The most common method of finding a donor was to enquire among friends and acquaintances. For lesbian women choosing parenthood, the donor is a person whom most often they become acquainted with in the context of embarking on parenthood. Unlike in heterosexual relationships, there is seldom a prior shared history of friendship or sexual intimacy. The relationship usually resulted from women's search for a donor. Some Swedish participants (n = 12) placed or answered advertisements in lesbian and gay publications or internet sites. Several other Swedish interviewees mentioned that they had considered it. Only one Irish couple in this study attempted to find a donor using this particular method. Although they received several replies, they did not respond to any of them. Despite the fact that this method of meeting donors was more common among Swedish participants, at least twelve advertisements appeared in the 'contacts' column of the Irish *Gay Community*

News from women looking for donors or from men wishing to act as donors, between 1997–2000 (Spillane, 2001). It may have been easier for Irish participants to find someone suitable within their acquaintance network, due to the lesser degree of involvement required. For Swedish women it was perhaps harder to find someone compatible, because of the degree of commitment that was necessitated in parenting as a shared project. Attempts to meet donors through ads on the part of Swedish participants were sometimes successful although in many cases, women encountered men whom they found distinctly unappealing options before finding someone who became the eventual donor.

This process was often described as demoralising and discouraging. One couple met with a man who answered their advertisement and during the course of the meeting they realised that he was a paedophile. They immediately left and called the police. The same couple also met a man whom they recognised as the donor for friends of theirs. He denied that he had any other children. Others described some of the men they encountered as disturbed and perverted, particularly the heterosexual men who responded to ads. Considerable caution was taken in meeting men contacted this way and participants were careful to check them out thoroughly:

> Yes, it was, kind of terrible, we put this ad in and that should have been an interesting study, to meet all those men! [Laughter] They were from like age 25 to 80 years old.
>
> – Viveka, Swedish participant

R: And how did you meet Mattias [biological father]?

Rg: Over the internet, an advertisement on the internet. I was giving up lots of times and Eva said no one more, we will try one more. No I don't want to, I'd given up, yeah several times and Eva said no one more time, one more time. And the more nutcases we met, oh I thought god it's no idea.

E: God some were nuts, straight guys, gay guys, you know.

Rg: After a while, all the straight guys was no way, no straight guys, because they were really nuts.

> – Regina and Eva, Swedish participants

Some participants who placed advertisements later went on to meet donors through friends or acquaintances. One Swedish couple, whose children were among the oldest in the sample, had attended a support group for lesbians contemplating parenthood. They also referred to the experiences of women in that group who had attempted to meet donors via advertisements. Some of these men wanted to watch the lesbian couple having sex in exchange for sperm, or for children to be conceived via intercourse.

Nonetheless, some participants had extremely positive experiences with their donors, whom they met through advertisements. These arrangements had worked out very successfully and now years later the donor had become an important part of their own life as well as their child's and was an established figure in their kinship network:

> And all by an accident, I don't know why, I was reading in this ad, there was a man who was looking for a lesbian woman or a lesbian couple and he wanted to have a child and I answered his ad and he called me two days later and he came to my apartment and it was like a big love [laughs], it was a strange feeling, he had been looking for a woman for a long time and he was living alone at the time too and I had been you know trying to find a possible or a man to have a child with and we met five weeks talking about everything and nothing.
>
> – Stina, Swedish participant

The difference between this search for a donor and traditional heterosexual scripts concerning a search for a partner is that the relationship between the lesbian woman or couple and the donor centres around conception. Often this is the only reason they meet in the first place. Just as some heterosexuals, lesbians and gay men advertise in personal columns for a sexual partner, so do some prospective parents seek to find a suitable donor/mother in the same way in queer publications or internet sites. The developing relationship between an involved donor and lesbian woman or couple is based on parenting and is a platonic relationship not a romantic one. Locating potential donors through advertisements provided women with a practical strategy for finding compatible fathers when they had exhausted their own networks of friends and acquaintances. It was a joint effort between partners and immense efforts were taken to ensure the trustworthiness and suitability of men who responded to advertisements.

UK Networks

One couple in the Irish sample conceived their second child while living in Britain. They belonged to a network of lesbian women interested in becoming parents. Another lesbian couple in this network contacted men through an advertisement in a gay publication and then vetted them for the rest of the group. They received 40 replies to their ad and accepted five of these men. The men who agreed to act as donors would arrive at the organising couple's home at short notice and obligingly provide the sperm, which this couple would take to a woman in another room to be used for insemination. The men would not know who was being inseminated and agreed to donate but have no parental responsibilities. Women usually chose to inseminate with several donors in the same month, in order to maximise the secrecy of the donor identity. The men however agreed that the children could contact them in the future if they were curious about them (assuming that it could be surmised who the father was). The men had no way of reaching the mothers however. In fact, all the children ended up bearing a strong resemblance to a particular donor, so there was no doubt about their paternity:

J: They'd come into the bathroom, jerk off into a beer mug, somebody would take it and use a syringe and do it

R: But they wouldn't know who was using it

J: No they'd be somebody else doing the, in somebody else's house as well [laughs], it wasn't even in our own house that we did it.

R: So I guess it was helpful that your friends knew these men

J: Yeah they had done a bit of vetting, we didn't do any vetting really...

B: I was going to throw out the man with the shoestring tie.

J: Oh you didn't like him

B: He looked like a country and western, he had this shoestring tie [J laughs] you know the kind of thing where you're like [J & B in unison] OH GOD! [laughter] But I don't know whether I threw that out or not anyway it wasn't him, so.

J:[...] We had all sorts of donors turning up who used to do it for nothing, it was really nice.
– Joan and Barbara, Irish participants

Their experience is typical of certain lesbian groups in the UK and US during the late 1980s, where networks of lesbians, often influenced by radical feminism, made similar arrangements with donors. The ethos of these groups was that women were parenting independently of men. Considerable lengths were taken to ensure the anonymity of the women. This was to prevent later intervention on the part of donors should they become curious about the children. Given the climate of hostility towards lesbian mothers at the time and the entrenched custody battles taking place between lesbian who became parents in heterosexual relationships and their former male partners, it is unsurprising that women would have been extremely concerned about their legal security as parents (Green, 1997). Some groups took the extra precaution of mixing the sperm of multiple donors together and use the resulting mixture for insemination. This US and UK phenomenon appears to be entirely absent from the discourses of lesbian parents interviewed for this study, apart from one couple who were living in Britain at the time they conceived their second child within one of these networks. There is a long history of emigration from Ireland to the US and UK, particularly during the 1980s, a time of high unemployment in Ireland. Many Irish lesbians and gay men emigrated during this period because of the unsupportive social climate in Ireland at that time. Given that their destination was often the US and the UK, it is probable that like this couple, some went on to become parents abroad. The recent economic boom in Ireland coinciding with increased social tolerance has encouraged the return of many emigrants. Two Irish couples in the study conceived at least one of their children while living abroad.

Most Irish participants found donors within their immediate network of friends and acquaintances. Occasionally a friend suggested or introduced a couple to a potential donor. Some of these men were heterosexual with left-wing politics and were willing to do the couple a favour by acting as a donor, provided there was a clear understanding that the arrangement required no parenting responsibilities. It was also the case that gay men often wanted more involvement than Irish participants were willing to consider. Unlike Swedish participants, who were concerned about a lack of commitment on the part of heterosexual men and welcomed greater involvement on the part of donors, Irish lesbian parents were unanimous in their desire to be the sole or primary parenting figures. Uninvolved donors in Ireland agreed that their identity should remain known only to the lesbian parents and be revealed at a later stage to the child, if she or he was interested. This suited everyone, as the lesbian parents wanted sole responsibility for the child while leaving the possibility of future contact between the child and the donor open, should the child express an interest in meeting him. These men were asked about their medical history and usually requested to undergo testing for HIV and other sexually transmitted diseases. The main concern, besides their medical health, was if they seemed likely to be trustworthy and responsible about upholding the condition of non-involvement:

> And so we asked him and he thought about it and he said yes and [...] we were saying that's fine but what about you know in five years time, when she's five [...] or she's twenty-two and decides I want to find out who this person is you know. He said well I'm okay about that [...] I think he was a pretty amazing person to be able to do that.
> — Aoife, Irish participant

Changing donors

Not all donors initially accepted went on to become the biological father. Sometimes arrangements were terminated by either party, due to unforeseen circumstances arising. One participant backed out of using a particular donor at the last minute when disconcerted by his behaviour and disclosure that there was mental illness in his family:

> J: And he was too embarrassed so he did it before I got there, then he realised he had to keep it warm so he put it in a yoghurt pot and into a pot of boiling water [D laughs] so that's what I was faced with when I got there
>
> D: This boiling, this yoghurt boiling! [laughs]
>
> J: And then he told me that his mother was mad and I thought, because [...] I knew there was a little bit of genetics in schizophrenia and I thought oh I don't know whether, I mean [laughs] he doesn't seem entirely biologically sound anyway! As soon as this knowledge was there I thought gee I think I might just leave it now.
> — Julie and Deirdre (partners), Irish participants

In some cases, women inseminated with several donors before becoming pregnant. Sometimes a donor declined to continue inseminating after a period of time, due to personal factors in the circumstances of his own life, such as a decision to move to a different country for example. Occasionally, the women became concerned that lifestyle factors were lowering a donor's sperm count and after a period of repeated disappointment, decided to find another donor. Sometimes the women themselves moved to a different geographical location and it became impractical to continue with the same donor. The search for donors was a difficult and demanding process and women were usually reluctant to begin their search anew. Some of these women went on to become pregnant via sperm banks.

Sperm banks – the clinic route and donor anonymity

Rates of conception via frozen sperm are substantially lower than for fresh sperm. According to the Sperm Bank of California, the possibility of a fertile heterosexual couple in their 20s conceiving from well-timed intercourse is about 20–25 per cent per cycle attempt. The chance of a fertile woman conceiving using frozen sperm is about 5–10 per cent per cycle attempt with a vaginal insemination and 10–15 per cent per cycle attempt with an intrauterine insemination. Freezing seems to cut down by about one-third the effectiveness of sperm. That is, it is likely to take approximately 30 per cent more inseminations to become pregnant with frozen sperm than with fresh sperm. A further deterrent to using a clinic's services is that it is a very expensive process and given the longer period of time it can take to become pregnant, the financial strain can become prohibitive. However, clinics offer the advantage of thoroughly screening donors for possible health problems to a degree unlikely to be achieved outside of a medical setting.

Swedish participants

Those participants who chose to use a clinic gave the issue of donor anonymity much consideration. It was not the ideal prospect for all the women who eventually opted for this possibility. Of the five Swedish couples who inseminated at a clinic, three had initially searched for a known donor. One couple, Sara and Åsa, had found a gay man who agreed to act as a donor and Sara inseminated with him for some time. They then discovered that he had fertility problems and Sara underwent a course of IVF privately abroad, as IVF was not available to lesbians in Sweden. This led to a pregnancy, which unfortunately resulted in a miscarriage. They considered inseminating with this man again but for various reasons he lost interest and as they were unable to find another donor, they finally decided to go to a clinic instead, where Åsa conceived.

They described themselves as extremely happy with this decision and during the interview, commented that they enjoyed being the only parents and not having to negotiate with a father or fathers. On the subject of donor anonymity, they felt that it was something they had to be open and honest about with their child from the beginning and were aware that she might experience this as a sense of loss. However, in their view it was better not to have the option of donor identity dis-closure at the age of eighteen, because a meeting with the donor as an adult could be potentially painful and a sense of finality was therefore preferable. Thus, having a sense of closure from the beginning might make this reconciliation to donor anonymity easier. They recognised that children may respond differently to this knowledge and that there was no way to predict how their daughter would react to having an anonymous donor. Despite this, they felt that if they were open about it and sensitive to how their daughter's feelings about this might change over time, it would be something that she could cope with:

> We are very much aware of it and have been all the time since we decided to do it this way and it's something that we have to sort of help her with and of course we don't know how she's going to react, because we think it's very individual, maybe she's going to be sad, maybe she's going to be totally fine, because she hasn't had anything else, so it's very difficult to say [...] and it can come into periods during her upbringing where she sort of has these questions and as long as we can give her the right answers and be honest about all the things, maybe she's going to be fine and okay you know the most important is that you love me and you did this because you really wanted to have me and hopefully that's the way it's going to be.
>
> – Åsa, Swedish participant

Another Swedish couple, Elin and Ylva, were unable to find a known donor, so they chose an anonymous donor insemination at a clinic. However, they inseminated only once there, which did not result in a pregnancy. They then met a man who agreed to act as a donor and play an active parenting role and they eventually had children with him. A third Swedish couple, Sylvia and Mia, who went on to insem-inate in Denmark had initially felt it was important to have a known father. So they placed an advertisement in a queer publication. However, after receiving some answers and meeting one man they changed their minds and decided to go to Denmark instead:

> It seemed too complicated when I faced the facts, no this would be too complicated and two parents would be enough for our kids.
>
> – Sylvia, Swedish participant

Interestingly, they were ambivalent about the possibility of donor iden-tity disclosure. Like Åsa and Sara, they perceived some disadvantages to this. The meeting between the donor and the child might not prove to be a positive experience. In addition, they recognised that not all children may be curious about donors:

> It's not like when she turns eighteen and she can knock on a door and hey that's Daddy. So I don't know, I mean for some people they want to find their genetic roots and you can never know that and hopefully it won't matter because we shall be two parents [...] I don't know if she would care or not, I mean I know adopted children who don't really care about their roots, so you can't really know.
>
> – Mia, Swedish participant

Only one Swedish couple had decided from the beginning to go to Denmark for insemination by an anonymous donor. They also realised that they did not want to negotiate parenting with a third parental figure:

> We want to decide everything. We don't want, even if it's a friend we don't want him to interfere in our lives.
>
> – Linnea, Swedish participant

Among Swedish participants, insemination at a clinic was usually a last resort. However, interviewees who had children in this way expressed great satisfaction with the arrangement. Although they recognised that there could be disadvantages for the child in terms of the donor's identity remaining secret, the possibility that children might not suffer because of this was also raised. This potential problem was seen to be outweighed by the benefits of raising children by themselves. It is certainly the case that Swedish participants who had known fathers went to great lengths to negotiate visitation and responsibilities. This necessitated ongoing discussion with fathers, requiring considerable effort, communication and commitment from all parties. Although this was not without its advantages, it was a demanding process. Lesbians who inseminated at a sperm bank, were able to raise their children as the primary parental figures, without negotiating the presence of a third parent. In addition, it was seen to benefit the child who did not have to go back and forth between two homes.

Irish participants

Like most participants, Irish parents Mary and Eileen initially attempted to conceive with a known donor. However, the (heterosexual) donor's girlfriend became pregnant unexpectedly and he decided not to continue with the inseminations. Mary and Eileen were devastated and Mary was particularly upset by the sense of a lack of control. They had been concerned in any case about custody issues and when this donor backed out, they decided to try a clinic:

> I just felt that like it was taken out of my hands, that like, because of other circumstances in his life like that he felt that he couldn't donate [...] also I was worried about custody and access [...] and I want to be able to take Fiona [child] out of the country, you know if we want to go away for holidays or live abroad [...] I decided that I didn't want to have to be counting on someone else's permission, someone who wasn't an active parent.
>
> – Mary, Irish participant

Again, the issue of potential custody battles was a major concern for Irish women who decided to inseminate at a clinic. Although emigration and travel was a feature of life for participants in both countries, the issue of mobility and fathers was seen as more complicated among Irish participants. Another Irish couple who had their child via donor insemination at a clinic, initially considered using a donor from another country. However, they were concerned that as he lived abroad, there would be continual pressure regarding travel arrangements. In addition, they were worried that in the future he might wish to obtain official visitation rights, in which case the child would possibly spend part of the year living in another country. The advantage of having a donor who lived abroad however, was that it facilitated less involvement. This is a difference between participants in the two countries. In cases where fathers lived some distance away or abroad, Swedish interviewees generally expressed a desire for greater involvement on the part of donors in the form of more contact with children.

The notion of donor anonymity was also accompanied by a critique of fatherhood and the view that biological fathers are not necessarily good fathers. While it was considered important to have men involved in a child's life, that role could be filled by any suitable man, either a friend or relative. It was not restricted to a biological father. On the issue of knowledge available to children about their biological origins, participants felt that not all children are curious about this and were optimistic that a child would feel satisfied with the parents and upbringing they received. Overall, Irish women were more likely to emphasise the increased sense of control and choice associated with a clinic and safety in terms of custody issues. Although autonomy was a feature of Swedish participants' accounts, they framed their discussions in terms of a preference for raising a child together without interference from or negotiation with a donor or donors. A child's knowledge about their biological origins was not considered to be more important than having a secure and loving home. Not all children were presumed to be curious about their paternity. The importance of being aware of and sensitive to a child's changing needs with regard to donor anonymity were articulated, as was the hope that being raised in a secure and loving environment, would be sufficient for any child.

Transnational journeys

Another Swedish couple who chose to use a clinic, Katarina and Elisabeth, were unsuccessful in their search for a donor. Eventually they decided to go to a clinic, but chose to use sperm imported from the Sperm Bank of California (SBC). The SBC offers the option of donor identity disclosure once a child reaches eighteen. Donors are asked whether they will agree to this information being disclosed and when a woman or couple are looking at the clinic's catalogue, they can choose a donor with this option. So they ordered sperm from the SBC, which was then sent to Denmark, where they travelled every month for the insemination. Katarina did eventually become pregnant, but sadly miscarried. Eventually they met a man who agreed to be a donor and take part in any future child's upbringing. Unfortunately, this man was planning to emigrate in the near future. So he obligingly travelled to Denmark and deposited some sperm at the clinic there. However, his semen reacted badly to the freezing process, lowering the possibility of a successful outcome. Their monthly trips to the clinic continued. After two years of inseminating in Denmark, they decided to undergo IVF in Finland. However, the clinic they attended there had a policy of using unknown donors at that time.[3] So Katarina and Elisabeth once again imported sperm from the SBC. It was sent to Finland to be used in the IVF attempt there. During a consultation with the specialist at the Finnish clinic prior to treatment however, they were told that there was the possibility of a change in the law in the near future, which would prohibit lesbians from accessing this service in Finland. If this occurred, the specialist suggested that the sperm vials be sent to St. Petersburg, where alternatively the IVF treatment could take place. Fortunately Elisabeth is proficient in Russian, otherwise their experience there could be complicated by a language barrier. Katarina later e-mailed me with her opinion about these events:

> Isn't this totally stupid. These little sperms have to travel around the whole world and me too before they will get into me...

This is an interesting illustration of the potentially international context for lesbians accessing assisted reproduction. Given that many countries restrict certain categories of women – particularly lesbians – from accessing sperm banks and fertility treatment, it is inevitable that women will travel abroad to avail themselves of these services. In this case, conception involved five countries: the US where the sperm originated; Sweden where the lesbian couple wishing to have a child are from; Denmark where alternative insemination took place; Finland where they attended an IVF consultation; and possibly Russia, if they were unable to carry out the IVF in Finland. In such cases, even if the donor identity disclosure option is available, the child and donor may not speak the same language. Katarina's comment ironically highlights absurdities encountered by lesbians seeking to become pregnant in this way. Due to legal prohibitions, if they wish to follow the Swedish ideal of having a known donor, they are literally forced to chase services with the donor identity disclosure option around the world. Wider discussions of queer tourism (e.g. Alexander, 2005; Binnie, 2004) focus on the consumption of sex. But lesbians denied access to assisted reproduction in their own countries constitute another kind of queer tourist. It is important to note of course, that the majority of women do not have access to the financial resources that this kind of international service entails. Indeed, Katarina and Elisabeth spent over €30,000 on assisted reproduction services in their efforts to conceive, an immense drain on their economic resources.

Irish clinics do not offer the possibility of donor identity disclosure. Although some participants had inseminated at the Well Woman Clinic in Ireland before it stopped providing DI, there is currently no clinic in the country openly advertising its services to lesbians. Such decisions are entirely at the discretion of individual clinics. One couple explored the possibility of importing sperm from the SBC with the option of donor identity disclosure. A gynaecologist was recommended to them by their sympathetic GP. Although the gynaecologist initially agreed to help them, he later changed his mind. This couple could technically still order the sperm and providing it was not deterred at customs, believed they could carry out the inseminations themselves.

However, it was unclear whether they would be able to import it successfully. In addition, as the success rates with frozen sperm are so much lower, they wanted to optimise their chances by arranging intrauterine inseminations with a doctor. In the absence of medical support, this proved impossible.

Discussions about donor secrecy can take a different form within lesbian parent families. Unlike heterosexual nuclear families, where DI can be concealed, for lesbian parents and their children the existence of a donor is immediately evident. Openness about donor insemination from the beginning of a child's life, combined with the deconstruction of biological and non-biological kinship may enable lesbian families to mark the significance of DI differently. Although lesbians who inseminated at a clinic acknowledged that having an anonymous donor may be a loss for a child, it was also understood that not all children are interested in their biological origins. It was hoped that children would recognise that DI was an indication of how much the child was wanted and welcomed and that this would temper any possible disappointment they might feel about not having access to information about the donor. Interestingly, two couples considered it beneficial not to be able to access contact information for a donor, because then the child was not faced with the difficult choice of whether or not to act on this information and attempt to contact the donor as an adult. They surmised that having a sense of closure from the beginning might make this reconciliation to donor anonymity easier.

Managing 'difference': Reflections on 'race' and ethnicity in lesbian parent narratives

In the context of donor insemination, biological characteristics, particularly appearance, become open to choice. Lesbians and heterosexuals can choose a donor who fits specific criteria – such as having a high sperm count, or 'matching' the appearance of the social father for example. Sperm banks potentially offer an overlap between the once taken for granted 'natural family' and consumer culture. Birenbaum-Carmeli & Carmeli (2002) argue that such commodification and choice may both challenge and reproduce hegemonic ideas about biological kinship.

The US HBO produced film 'If These Walls Could Talk 2' was released in 2000. It consists of three short films about lesbians in a US city, which take place in 1961, 1972 and 2000 respectively. The third story narrates the experiences of Kal (Ellen DeGeneres) and Fran (Sharon

Stone), a lesbian couple, as they plan to have a child together. After some consideration, they decide to go to a sperm bank. While discussing options from the donor catalogue, Fran (the planned biological mother) suggests '*Maybe we should think about having an ethnic baby. Ethnic babies are so beautiful!*' Both Fran and Kal are white, with blonde hair and blue eyes. In this instance, 'ethnic' refers to non-white. Kal objects to this statement, not on the grounds of its troubling commodification and construction of 'race', but because they had already agreed that the donor 'would look like me'. Since she will not be the biological mother, this implies choosing a donor who also has blonde hair and blue eyes.

This screen representation of lesbians choosing donors from a sperm bank, presents a picture of white middle-class women commodifying ethnicity. The film is problematic on a number of counts and clearly many of its features reflect an American context, including the easy access to sperm banks that this lesbian couple experience. What struck me most when watching it however was that the discourses it conveyed were not reflected in the interviews I carried out with lesbian parents in Sweden and Ireland. In fact, ethnicity was not treated lightly in the way it is depicted in the film. All but one participant in the study was white. Given the cultural contexts, two societies that have been ethnically relatively homogenous until fairly recently, potential donors were usually white and ethnicity was not reflected upon. However, there were exceptions to this.

A black heterosexual friend of one white Swedish couple offered to act as a donor. There were several reasons why they decided not to accept his offer, including their preference for a gay male donor and the fact that they felt he would not be as committed to parenting as they would have liked:

> So we just found that we would prefer to have a gay man...and he was also from Africa and we were afraid that he might move back to Africa and...you know, if we would have a little brown baby, we would like the baby to have a father who is black to relate to and if he would move to another country, to Africa or wherever, we wouldn't have that. So that was one thing and also he had oh five children already so he was a nice man but not a very good father, we knew that, so we didn't think so but that was why, why we decided not to take him.
> – Malena, Swedish participant

In this case, the interviewee articulated the importance to a mixed race child of having access to a black parent. This possible donor was rejected because of the possibility that he might not be as involved in parenting as they would like and might move abroad, leaving the child without a black parental figure to relate to. In the interview, Malena expressed concern for such a child's sense of identity and belonging and recognised that there would be a need for this child to have a parent who would understand their situation. Choosing a donor from a different race was not a possibility that was treated frivolously, or as an aesthetic tool.

Irish participants also described similar situations. One participant, who is not originally from Ireland, had already discussed the possibility of a black male friend acting as a donor for herself and her partner. Their relationship broke up before they started inseminating. In her next relationship, she raised the possibility of this same man being a donor, given the fact that he had agreed earlier. Her partner who is Irish was strongly opposed to this however:

G: [on suggesting her black friend as a donor]...and Ciara was like James [potential donor]? And I was like yes I think he's wonderful, he's [...] a good friend of mine and she goes James is black [laughs] and I said really?

R: So why would James being black be a problem?

C: Well I mean you'd issue number one that this was something Gillian had done without me, so this you know, so you've number one that whole thing. Then you've number two you know, we're going to be living in Ireland more than likely you know. And it's difficult enough dealing with the gay issue in Ireland, without having a child that's half black, half white, and lesbian parents, you know...but...I certainly wouldn't go to a sperm bank and have a blonde haired blue eyed, kind of, I wouldn't do that.

– Ciara and Gillian, Irish participants

In this instance, the discourse articulated is slightly different, in that there are broader references to the social context of racism in Irish society. The child's experiences of growing up with lesbian parents are considered to be a difficult situation, one that would be compounded by vulnerability to racism in the context of being raised by two white women. At the same time, she was keen to distance herself from a eugenic desire for a particular type of child, as evidenced by her remark about sperm banks and 'blonde haired, blue eyed' donors. The potential donor's association with her partner's previous relationship was another factor that contributed to her rejection of him as a possible donor. In this case, the donor would not have been living in Ireland and would not have been able to play a large part in the child's every-day life. Ciara was eager to communicate an anti-racist politics later in the interview and her thoughts on donors and 'race' were informed by an awareness of racism. Nonetheless, her preference for a white donor consciously incorporates white privilege into the construction of her family form.

The discussion of 'race' and donors articulated by these two couples, echo wider policy initiatives regarding 'matching' adoptive children to adoptive parents. In the UK for example, there is a strong emphasis on placing children in homes with adoptive parents of a similar racial and ethnic background. This arises from reports that minority ethnic children experienced difficulties being raised by white parents, who were not always able to offer sufficient support and understanding, no matter how well-intentioned. The same concerns informed lesbian parents' thoughts on having a mixed race child in the absence of an active father.

There are numerous indications that there has been a rise in racist attacks and harassment in Ireland coinciding with economic prosperity and wave of inward migration. Racism has always been a feature of Irish life – see the experiences of Irish travellers for example – but it has become particularly vociferous as in recent years (Lentin & McVeigh, 2002). Concerns about racism were not unwarranted, as one Irish family's experiences highlighted poignantly. An Irish lesbian couple, Joan and Barbara, were raising a mixed race son in a rural Irish environment. Although their son had many friends, he had been exposed to considerable hostility. As a result, they were contemplating emigration:

> J: Yeah the worst that Owen [son] would have got here when he was younger, when he was a baby, ten years ago or whatever would be oh what a lovely suntan you've got, you know. But now he gets called nigger
>
> B: By the other kids
>
> R: So he is facing a lot of abuse
>
> B: Dead serious, dead serious, yeah it's horrible. It is very difficult for him which is why we'd be better off out of the country.
> — Joan and Barbara, Irish participants

As described in an earlier section in this chapter, Joan and Barbara had belonged to a network in the UK that involved numerous donors who would donate sperm to lesbians attempting to conceive. Interestingly, their group of donors was diverse in terms of race. The decision not to restrict donors to white men was a conscious choice reflecting a commitment to an anti-racist politics. They viewed it as important not to exclude a donor on the grounds of race and to be open to raising a mixed race child.

In cases where a donor was to be involved in a child's upbringing, the main goal was to find a man with whom it would be possible to come to an amicable arrangement about visitation and negotiating parenthood. On the other hand, if women were attempting to conceive through a sperm bank, the issue of ethnic and racial identity and other factors was more complex. Katarina, a Swedish participant, expressed her thoughts about this in the following way:

> I want the child to look like us just because to save it from all the questions he will not have any answer to. If I chose brown eyes for example the child will not look like any of my relatives and he or she will always be reminded about a father he will maybe never know. But that's not so important any more for me as it was in the beginning. It's just a strange situation that we have to choose anything and we want to make a choice that we believe today is less problematic. If I had chosen a known dad for my child I wouldn't care at all what colour he might have as long as he shared a lot of my values and was a nice person.
>
> – Katarina, Swedish participant

Several participants expressed a preference for someone with a similar appearance to the biological mother, because it would be easier for the child if they did not have to face questions about where they got their brown eyes from, if their two mothers had blue eyes for example. This attempt to manage physical traits demonstrates an awareness of the role of physical resemblance and similarity in communicating relatedness. It also represents a further dimension of the 'best interests of the child' discourse.

In choosing a donor from a clinic, women have a variety of options concerning appearance, age, profession and so on. Overwhelmingly, women's main concern was that the donor had a good medical history and high sperm count. The ability to choose physical characteristics in this way was also experienced as new and not entirely comfortable, as the above quote from Katarina illustrates in her reference to it as a 'strange situation'. Participants' narratives reveal the complexity of choices around finding a donor and constructing family forms that will ensure their children's well-being. They accomplished this not through the denial of difference, but by actively acknowledging social norms and expectations. They were aware that their children might face difficulties in society by having lesbian parents and were eager to protect their children from potential homophobia. In relation to having a donor of a different 'race', participants who discussed this option were open to the possibility. One couple viewed it as part of their commitment to an anti-racist politics, others considered that in such situations children would benefit from contact with the donor in order to ensure support and confirmation of their identity in a racist world. It is also the case that lesbians can make decisions about a donor's race in ways that reaffirm and utilise white privilege. Lesbian participants' narratives nonetheless reveal an active awareness of difference and diversity and this is incorporated into their understandings of themselves and their families.

Alternative conceptions 'The Hard Way'

Not all pregnancies were the result of insemination. Some lesbians have never had, or wanted to have, sex with a man. However, many lesbians have experienced heterosexual relationships prior to coming out. It is also the case that some lesbians choose to have sex with a man sometimes. This might be a brief encounter or relationship after developing a lesbian identity, which may not change that identity in any way. The myriad complexities of sexuality are such that choice of partner cannot be presumed to delineate identity. Nonetheless, for many lesbian women, the prospect of conceiving a child through intercourse is an impossible option. This is often considered an unacceptable route to pregnancy for a variety of emotional, practical and ethical reasons. Sex without desire and/or sexual intimacy with a donor, were not possibilities that most participants could contemplate. Unprotected casual sex carries obvious health risks. In the context of a committed relationship, sex with a man for the purpose of conception may constitute infidelity. In addition, as already indicated, there was a marked preference for a known donor among participants and this is not necessarily facilitated by a casual encounter. Furthermore, sex is laden with emotional significance for many people and becoming pregnant through casual sex with a stranger is not an easy option for lesbians because of the personal meanings invested in sex, sexuality, identity, power and choice.

Although the overwhelming preference among participants was for alternative insemination, four Irish lesbians and one Swedish lesbian either attempted to conceive or became pregnant through intercourse. This was a voluntary encounter in four out of the five cases. Discussions about alternative insemination did not take place in Ireland until later than in the UK or the USA. There were no networks of women discussing insemination or how to find a donor until the early 1990s. For one Irish participant, the most practical way of becoming pregnant seemed to be through sex with a man. She had previous experience of heterosexual relationships and did not find the option physically difficult or emotionally distressing. Her partner was aware of this and it was not an issue in their relationship, or for her personally. The encounter took place prior to any major public awareness of AIDS and so the context of sexual health debates was also different:

> I think yeah if there had been a different kind of cultural environment in Ireland it might have been different, also because I had had a whole kind of heterosexual past if you like, it wasn't that difficult for me to think well this is a possible route and it might be more efficient than another route, even if I'd had those options clearly out there, you know what I mean [...] whereas I know that for other women that I've spoken to about it, that would have been an incredibly difficult thing to consider. But it didn't feel that difficult to me and also I had kind of you know [...] like I was a teenager in the '60s and sort of sexual revolutions and you know I suppose casual sex at some level was not really a forbidden, I didn't have a major ideological problem with it at the time and em it was kind of a, a pre kind of the whole AIDS issues and that way around, so it's just mixtures, but particular kind convergence of things at the time, I know now with other women, the whole issue around AI [artificial insemination] and what's available and that kind of end of things is much more on the agenda now here for women. I'm sure I would have looked at it differently.
>
> – Eithne, Irish participant

Another Irish participant, Clodagh, had a one-night stand while travelling abroad and became pregnant as a result. The encounter had been a casual and unplanned one and was probably not something she would have given much thought to afterwards, except for the resulting pregnancy. There was no way of tracing the biological father. In her case, she decided to go ahead with the pregnancy, reasoning that if she had an abortion, she would probably not get around to planning a pregnancy in the future.

> I suppose the reason I went through the whole thing and I had him was that it was you know, it had happened, a lot of people would pay a lot of money to be in the position I was in and I reckoned if I didn't go through with it then that would be it I would never have a child, so.
>
> – Clodagh, Irish participant

Clodagh felt somewhat relieved that the father could not be contacted, because she had witnessed difficulties among friends with fathers of unplanned pregnancies. In her view, if the man had not wanted the pregnancy, it would be difficult to stir his interest in the child. Although she was concerned that her child might develop a fantasy about her father, she also felt that raising a child alone prevented potential problems in terms of trying to persuade a biological father to share responsibility for the child:

> C: I wouldn't even be able to find him, you know, so it wasn't even a decision, it was just the way it was, maybe it was for the best actually.
>
> R: Why do you think that?
>
> C: I know women who have children whose fathers were around, these would be gay women, but whether they were or not, men if, I think, if they're not, if they never wanted a child to begin with, you'll never get them interested, it'll just be a constant battle. I know women who have court cases, all this kind of stuff and at the end of the day, it just, no matter, if they take the father to court and get the maintenance and all the rest it's just not worth it, between the hassle and the, everything. Most fathers are absent with the mothers I know, you know, and when they do appear back in the child's life, which is whenever they want to appear [laughs], they just mess it up for everybody [...] and in most cases it seems to be like that, and when I see all that happening, I think well okay she doesn't have a father that I can tell her about, but she doesn't have someone coming in and messing up her life either. I don't know, we'll have to see how it goes as the years go on, because an absent

father is always a brilliant one [laughs], is another side of it to a child you know.

– Clodagh, Irish participant

Clodagh's views are typical of the distinction between biological and social fatherhood articulated by many Irish participants. A biological father was not necessarily a positive presence in a child's life, whereas for Swedish women contact with and knowledge of biological fathers was important for children's well-being. This distinction between biological and social fatherhood among Irish participants constituted a critique of masculinities and a de-construction of biology and parenting. It did not reflect a negative view of men generally.

As already illustrated, the process of finding a donor can be a long and difficult one. For one Irish interviewee, her search for a donor proved unsuccessful and she became increasingly desperate. She was a co-parent to a child with her partner and attempted to become pregnant by the same donor. However, he then moved abroad and she was forced to begin her search again. She found another donor whom she began inseminating with and then he also emigrated. Her renewed search proved unsuccessful. Finally, she had a one-night stand with a casual acquaintance, which did not result in pregnancy. This event caused problems in her relationship with her partner, who was very upset that she had attempted to become pregnant in this way. In the end, she never conceived a biological child, although at this point in her life she felt reconciled to this and no longer had the wish to become a biological parent, particularly as her child grew older:

And then he left the country, so. And [...] the powerlessness in not being able to find a donor and that kind of thing you know, you found one and then he'd be around for three months and then he'd go away you know and wasn't available on the night you were ovulating anyway and looking around here and asking people and just coming up with no, no, no, no all along. Really I didn't find anybody here who was prepared to be a donor for me or for anybody else and that became, oh just the sense of just em, the, not having any power you know, and so, I did end up going and fucking a bloke, and that was like a big issue between Jean [partner] and I, because I had done that and she didn't like that at all.

– Catherine, Irish participant

As the above quote indicates, the sense of powerlessness and lack of control around finding a donor were a recurring theme for many women. The difficulty of finding a suitable donor was intensely frustrating and added to the stress of the process of attempting to conceive.

One Swedish participant asked a close heterosexual friend of many years to be a donor. She felt awkward about asking him to provide semen through masturbation and as they happened to be together on the day she was ovulating, decided to have sex with him instead. She became pregnant immediately. When referring to the method of conception, she said: '*I did it that way, the hard way.*' Although she initially felt comfortable with her decision, it proved difficult to resolve with her partner however and took a toll on their relationship, although this eventually passed.

> I don't think he would have liked that [insemination] and for me it was, he's like a, he's a very nice person I mean he is very easy to be alone with and he's eh, it was not a big deal for him and I felt very comfortable with him so I, I mean it would be, I would feel embarrassed if I should ask him just to well you have to and I said okay go for it, but I mean it was very hard in the relationship [with her partner].
>
> – Birgitta, Swedish participant

None of these encounters in any way changed these women's sense of themselves as lesbian. Although they chose to have sex with men, it was seen as a one-off event, in one case for pleasure and for the other three women it was with the explicit intention of becoming pregnant. In these latter cases, intercourse appeared to be the most practical means available at that time.

The last Irish participant who did not conceive by insemination, Dymphna, became pregnant as a result of rape. She did not initially tell anyone about the assault and did not report the crime. Due to her distressed state in the immediate aftermath of the assault, it did not occur to her to take the morning after pill. The realisation of her pregnancy came as an enormous shock. She informed her family and friends that she was pregnant when she was in her second trimester and her condition was increasingly obvious. Dymphna described her emotional state for the duration of the pregnancy as one of denial and did not attempt to obtain any prenatal care until close to the birth. Although she is pro-choice, she decided to continue with the pregnancy and raise the child. Despite persistent curiosity on the part of her family and friends, she has kept the details of the conception to herself. Dymphna is however, concerned about what to tell her son in the future. She is reluctant to reveal the truth about how she became pregnant to him, not solely because it would be difficult for her to discuss, but because she is concerned that the knowledge would adversely affect him or that he might feel guilty about causing her emotional pain by virtue of being born. Raising her child without a father has made her feel more confident about the possibility of having an uninvolved donor should she choose to have another child in the future.

The diverse circumstances of conception among participants are illustrative of the wide range of strategies undertaken by lesbians who wish to embark on parenthood, particularly in the face of legislative limitations that may hamper their efforts. However, a previously unexplored aspect of lesbian parenting concerns unplanned pregnancy, which is often assumed to be impossible for lesbians. As the case of Dymphna illustrates, lesbians are also vulnerable to rape, which may result in a pregnancy. Unlike Dymphna, who did not have any choice in the matter, some participants in this study chose not to conceive by insemination. In addition, one participant conceived accidentally as a result of a one-night stand. This latter case highlights the relatively hidden phenomenon of sexual encounters which may not correspond to popular conceptions of a particular sexual identity, but which also do not challenge or conflict with that identity on a personal level. The variety of narratives and experiences reveals the complexity of considerations informing reproductive decision-making among lesbian parents.

Conclusion

Lesbian reproductive decision-making is largely characterised by immense effort and discussion. Indeed, for lesbians planning parenthood, every step along the path to pregnancy and parenthood requires a radical rethinking of notions of parenting. For a small number of participants parenthood was an unplanned event and the option of abortion was given serious consideration. The fact that some lesbians experience unplanned pregnancy is a deconstructive notion, challenging fixed categorisations of sexual identity and highlighting all women's vulnerability to sexual violence.

This chapter explored the influence of social and institutional contexts in shaping reproductive choices available to lesbian women and their responses to legal and cultural constraints. Lesbian parents in this study created new family constellations within the context of broader cultural ideologies of motherhood, fatherhood and kinship. In both Sweden and Ireland, 'blood ties' are usually considered an intrinsic part of what constitutes a family. Sweden has a particularly strongly coded form of biological fatherhood, which is reflected in social policy and practice. The gender equality initiatives of the 1970s emphasised a model of participatory fatherhood. Sweden's radical innovations concerning families and social policy are marked by a commitment to gender equality based on a construction of the family around a nuclear family model. This does not reflect the variety of family forms in existence, particularly among lesbian and gay families, where there may be as many as four active parents. Reproductive decision-making among Swedish lesbian parents reflects broader cultural norms concerning biological and participatory fatherhood. However, there are myriad ways in which these ideologies are reinscribed in new forms in lesbian families. The preference for gay men as participatory fathers reflected a commitment to queer community and a more subversive masculinity. Although men do not contribute to families simply by their presence, in lesbian parent families participatory fatherhood was developed in ways that were seen to be of benefit both to children and their lesbian parents.

Among Irish lesbian parents, the history of control of women's bodies was continually undermined through their discursive emphasis on choice and creation of new paths to parenthood, which enabled them to develop families maximising their security as custodial parents. The lack of recognition afforded unmarried fathers in Ireland is often interpreted as a sign of male oppression in Irish life. In fact, as the discourse of custody concern articulated by Irish lesbian parents indicates, the particular ideology of parenthood underlying Irish guardianship legislation is intended to apply only to certain kinds of parents and is implicitly heteronormative with its emphasis on married family life as the 'best' family form. Not all women have equal protection before the law and mothers who transgress the boundaries of normative womanhood may be penalised. Legislation assumed to confer certain rights to women is of no benefit to differentially situated women (such as lesbians) if it is not implemented within a context of commitment to equality. Irish participants' discourses reflected their view that the law does not protect lesbian parents. Participants in Ireland therefore found new ways of circumventing their legal vulnerability, while retaining their preference for a known donor. The genealogy of motherhood in Irish society provided these women with a strong sense of self-confidence in their ability to create supportive, nurturing environments for their children without the involvement of active fathers.

Despite dramatic cross-national differences regarding whether or not donors would play an active parenting role, lesbian parents in both countries preferred to be able to provide their children with the identity of the donor. This is perhaps unsurprising since, as Freeman & Richards (2006: 70) argue, 'the concept of paternity can be understood as providing a lynchpin of western kinship systems which are structured around notions of marriage, blood relations and patrinlineal descent'. The relative importance based on knowledge of paternal origins cross-nationally also echoes wider developments regarding kinship and biotechnology. Freeman & Richards (2006) also point out that the rise of DNA testing as a means of establishing blood relationships highlights the relative 'geneticisation' (Peter & Bunston, 2002), 'biologization' (Franklin, 2001) and 'medicalization' (Finkler, 2001) of family practices and identities.[4] Thus, biological paternity is seen as constitutive of personal identity. This is illustrated in laws in Sweden and elsewhere (e.g. the UK), that require the identities of donors to sperm banks to be disclosed to resulting offspring after their eighteenth birthday. The discourses of paternity among Irish and Swedish lesbians thus reflect a wider societal emphasis on knowledge of paternity as necessary to constructions of selfhood. In both countries, this was generally seen as in the best interests of the child, although in Sweden it was also often described as a child's 'right' to know.

Challenges to heteronormativity take a different form in different contexts, at least in part because heteronormativity itself varies according to context. It is therefore more precise to discuss a plurality or multiplicity of *heteronormativities*, rather than invoke a notion of heternormativity as a homogenous concept. Clearly, heteronormative practices and assumptions are manifested in diverse ways according to the cultural context in which they occur. Swedish women's decisions to involve donors must be viewed within the context of a history of gender equality constructed as a shared project among women and men and the promotion of participatory fatherhood. While Swedish women could be interpreted as reinforcing an ideology of fatherhood as necessary to parenting, multiple parents challenge the centrality of the nuclear family. A preference for gay men is another way in which dominant notions of the family were subverted and reinscribed within these families. They further utilised shared parenting in ways that were personally advantageous. Decisions by Irish lesbians to create particular family forms are a reflection of their agency and creativity within a largely unsupportive social context. Their former access to sperm banks within Ireland due to the lack of legal recognition of lesbians and ability to use the situation of unmarried fathers to their advantage illustrates a creative disruption of the heteronormative assumptions underpinning Irish social policy. This pioneering generation of Swedish and Irish lesbians are creating families despite considerable obstacles. The ways in which lesbians envisage parenting possibilities is influenced by wider discourses of 'the family' as well as social and institutional limitations. Heteronormativities are diverse and variable across space, place and time. Reproductive decision-making among lesbian parents cannot therefore be understood independently of the contexts within which it occurs. In the next chapter, the significance of context will be explored further, with an analysis of the everyday spaces of lesbian parenting.

4
Queering 'Public' Space

Sexual identity is not simply a private issue, as the legal regulation of sexual practices, relationships and possibilities illustrates. Multiple measures render 'public' space heteronormative, including contexts where parenting may be enacted, such as hospitals, schools and neighbourhoods. Parenthood is supported within clearly heteronormative parameters. The prohibition of services such as assisted insemination for lesbians is indicative of the highly regulated nature of this realm. Lesbians who embark on parenthood, like heterosexual parents, encounter new social networks and institutional contexts. Becoming a lesbian parent also necessitates coming out in new environments and presents particular dilemmas. The lack of awareness about lesbian parenting and homophobic attitudes were detrimental to participants in this study, who were unsure of a supportive response from service providers and others as a result. This uncertainty provided a stressful edge to everyday life. Their experiences within a diverse range of contexts forms the basis of this chapter, in which the heteronormative construction of various spaces is considered.

Bell & Binnie (2000) have been critical of family based approaches to sexual citizenship. They argue that the central concern with partnership and marriage potentially constrains the limits of queer experiences and subjectivities within a heteronormative framework. Similarly, Judith Halberstam argues that 'Queer uses of time and space develop in opposition to the institutions of family, heterosexuality, and reproduction, and queer subcultures develop as alternatives to kinship-based notions of community' (2003: 1). On the one hand, I think Halberstam is accurately pointing out the potential for queer spaces to provide an alternative to a heteronormative life course model and she is correct in highlighting the heteronormative aspects of parenthood politics. However, there is a sense in which this argument leaves lesbian parents in a no-person's-land between the subversions of queer communities on the one hand and apparent heteronormativity of parenthood on the other. This perspective also assumes an assimilation/transgression dichotomy, which I argue is inadequate for exploring lesbian parents' experiences. So in this chapter, I am less interested in assessing the extent to which lesbian parents subvert or reinforce spatial norms, but rather the consequences for those who live outside heteronormativity and how they negotiate this. Gabb (2005) explores some of the spatial dimensions of lesbian parenthood and concludes that the difficulties faced by lesbian parents in wider society reinforce the centrality of their homes as a space of difference. But I would add that becoming a parent necessitates coming out in new spaces, such as schools and daycare. This chapter will address the implications of this and the agentic strategies adopted by lesbian parents.

The literature on gender, sexuality and space has often focused on the queer commercial scene and metropolitan life more generally (Ingram *et al.*, 1997; Fincher & Jacobs, 1998; Collins, 2006). This chapter therefore represents a departure from much previous research in this area with an exploration of lesbian parenting experiences in everyday contexts. It addresses some of the consequences of spatial exclusion for lesbian parents, as illustrated by participants' experiences on the path to parenthood. The strategies participants developed to protect themselves and their children in child-centred contexts such as daycare and schools are also explored. In addition, participants' integration into neighbourhood communities in metropolitan, small town and rural contexts are analysed and offer new understandings of rural queer identities. The discursive constructions of space within the research illustrate the heteronormative understandings of 'the family' pervading many everyday environments and the potential for lesbian parents to queer(y) such boundaries, thus disrupting spatial identities and discourses.

Gender, sexuality and space

Duncan (1996: 137) points out that sexuality, like gender, is also 'often regulated by the binary distinction between public and private'. Just as men and masculinities are traditionally associated with 'public worlds', women and femininities have often been confined to the 'private', or domestic sphere. Gender relations have involved the normalisation and perpetuation of these spatial relegations. Similarly, homophobic rhetoric which purports that homosexuals should not 'flaunt' their sexuality, invokes a spatial narrative of heteronormative social relations. She notes that arguments supporting the confinement of homosexuality to the 'private' realm, assume that heterosexuality is only present in private spaces. This ignores the ways that heterosexuality is evident within the public arena. The institutionalisation of heterosexuality within everyday life means that all social interactions are negotiated via heteronormativity. The term 'public space' is arguably contradictory, given that many people are excluded from such spaces on the grounds of age, disability, gender, 'race', sexuality and so on. The heteronormative coding of particular spaces is manifested in diverse ways, for example through advertising and policy. Social institutions such as museums may only offer 'family discounts' to heterosexual nuclear families. Similarly, 'family' travel rates may be denied to lesbian parents and their children. (Both these examples were mentioned by participants in this research). Queer communities have resisted the heteronormative coding of space by various means. Celebrations of queer identities that take place in 'public' domains are one obvious example of this resistance. The hegemony of heteronormative sexuality in the streets of major metropolitan areas has been challenged by activities such as LGBT Pride parades and Mardi Gras (Johnson, 2005). Thus, queer activists have both asserted a claim to 'public' space and revealed the extent to which such space is normatively coded as heterosexual (Bell & Valentine, 1995a; Ingram *et al.*, 1997). Valentine (2001: 221) suggests that the increasing visibility of gay men and lesbians within metropolitan areas 'reflects the growing confidence of sexual dissidents to assert a claim to sexual citizenship.'

The fact that the presence of hegemonic or marginalised groups can shape the identity of a spatial location, highlights the interconnectedness of spatial and other identities. Sexual identities may be produced within particular spaces – for example a person may be interpreted as lesbian or gay in a specific spatial context such as a gay bar, or may only feel comfortable being openly lesbian or gay there. Thus, spatial visibility has operated as a means of communing and establishing solidarity and has therefore played an important role in the development of LGBT equality movements. In addition, space is also produced through the performance of identities. This is evident in instances where the performance of lesbian or gay identities in traditionally heteronormative environments can 'queer' those spaces, one of the functions of LGBT Pride parades in city streets. Similarly, the performance of heterosexual identities within queer spaces can alter the coding of that space. Spatiality refers to the dynamic nature of this interaction, whereby identity is actively shaped in particular places, as opposed to a conceptualisation of space as a passive terrain upon which identity is inscribed.

Beyond the queer metropolis

The majority of empirical work on queer sexualities has focused on queer experiences in metropolitan areas.[1] More recently, the implicit urban/rural binary of much of this work has been critically addressed. Phillips & Watt (2000:1) argue that all sexual identities and discourses, whether hegemonic or liberatory, are grounded in a spatialised notion of centres and margins. They support this argument with reference to Foucault's work on the history of sexuality, which they suggest has 'a hidden geography: the legal, medical, religious and other institutions, which discursively constitute and regulate sexualities, are concentrated in geographical and political centres' (i.e. metropolitan centres). They further argue that in equality struggles, metropolitan cities are seen as the centre of the regulation and liberation of sexualities. This has led to the empirical neglect of 'in–between' or liminal spaces on the margins of sexual geography. In their view, de-centring sexualities from metropolitan centres can be critically transformative by destabilising the spatial dichotomies informing theoretical and empirical understandings of queer experiences.

Bell (2000) argues that non-metropolitan queer experience within these localities has been depicted as virulently homophobic, in contrast to popular representations of the rural as 'idyllic'. Halberstam (2003) also points to this spatial dichotomy within work on queer sexualities. Authors such as Bell & Valentine (1995b) earlier highlighted the limited structural services and facilities (entertainment venues, support groups, safe sex information) and 'basic resources' (such as LGBT media and books) available to support queer lifestyles in most rural communities. Weston (1998) offers a similarly bleak view. She argues that the urban/rural dichotomy is central to the construction of lesbian and gay identities, whereby the 'Great Gay Migration' to urban areas reflects a quest for community. In addition, she suggests that the anonymity associated with urban environments is less inhibiting than the closeknit nature of many rural communities. Valentine (2001) notes however that lesbians and gay men can develop spatially disparate communities through telephone helplines, newspapers and the internet, which may help counteract problems of isolation and lack of information.

Knopp (1998: 172) argues that queer experiences beyond the metropolis are potentially undermining of the hegemonic power order,

especially if they are organised around other marginalised axes of identity. In contrast to the gay urban (particularly white, middle-class and
male) sex radical, he suggests that queer working-class, non-white,
non-urban and female identity is less easily assimilated into hegemonic
interests within British society. Gay white middle-class men can be
accommodated within unequal power relations where 'their critiques
of the class system, urbanisation, and possibly even patriarchy' can be
undermined 'by labelling them as hypocrites (for indulging their privilege) or 'eccentrics' and tolerating them'. While Knopp's argument
potentially downplays the oppression experienced by white middle-
class gay men, it does highlight the various spaces of privilege that this
group occupies, thus offering a reading of their multiple locations
within the 'matrix of domination' (Hill-Collins, 1990). His work also
emphasises the diversity of queer experience and different situatedness
of queer actors. Despite this evident range of experience, previous work
on gender, sexuality and space has largely focused on the gay commercial scene in urban locations, one of the most visible manifestations of
queerness. This chapter explores a rather different terrain – the everyday spaces of parenthood and how lesbian participants negotiate them.
Their endeavours illustrate the heteronormative construction of diverse
spaces and the ways in which spatial identities can be destabilised by
lesbian parents. This is also revealing of wider discourses of 'the family'
that pervade the everyday spaces of parenthood.

Queer spatiality in Ireland and Sweden

The spatiality of lesbian parenting has evolved differently in the two
countries. The criminalisation of male homosexuality in Ireland and
the campaign for decriminalisation in the early 1990s, provided Irish
gay men with a public identity. For Irish lesbians, no such identity
– albeit a criminalised one – existed in the public arena. Irish lesbians
were therefore outside the law and at the same time rendered invisible
by lack of official recognition (and condemnation). According to Walshe
(2000: 477) 'This lack of an official identity for Irish lesbians can be
seen as something of a mixed blessing, with little cultural visibility but
a greater freedom from prosecution and a consequent imaginative
freedom and openness, and this is reflected in the writings of contemporary Irish lesbians'. He suggests that this different negotiation of
public space led to differences in literature produced by Irish lesbians
and gay men. While Irish gay men, he argues, have tended to be more
circumspect in their representation of sexual Otherness, Irish lesbians

have 'occupied a different literary space', one which is 'often more radical and subversive but less widely known' (2000: 477). It is perhaps therefore unsurprising that despite a flourishing Irish lesbian literature, lesbian parents in Ireland rarely congregate as a group, even in alternative, 'safe' spaces. There was no support group for lesbian mothers in Ireland when fieldwork took place, although one previously existed in Dublin. (However, one such group has since been established outside the capital.) Lesbian parents are visible at queer events, such as Pride parades and for example the 'Lesbian Lives' conference held in UCD in 1999. (The theme of the conference that year was 'kinship'). In addition to support groups, lesbian parents in Ireland have developed particular spaces for themselves – the annual 'Women's Camp' being the most notable example of this. This camp takes place over a two week period during the summer and is organised on a co-operative basis by volunteers. It is a significant gathering place for lesbian parents and their children in Ireland and offers a chance for them to meet similar families. Despite these important instances, lesbian parents nonetheless do not appear to constitute a politically organised social movement in Ireland at this time. This may be due to the constraints on leisure time imposed by parenting. It also appears to be strategic on some level – in order to protect their families, they must safeguard themselves from widespread homophobia by maintaining a low profile in Irish society. Recent campaigns around same sex marriage in Ireland have however explicitly referred to lesbian and gay parenting in their political agenda and so lesbian parents are gradually achieving more visibility.

In stark contrast, lesbian (and gay) parenting has been far more visible in Swedish society, in both political and media debate and popular culture. This is often attributed to the introduction of registered partnerships for same-sex couples in 1995, after which lesbian and gay parenting issues became the most blatant legislative example of LGBT discrimination. Cultural representations of lesbian and gay parenting include images by renowned Swedish photographer Elisabeth Ohlsson. She incorporated two pictures of lesbian couples who embarked on parenthood in her famous series 'Ecce Homo'. In this photographic series Christ is depicted as a gay man. The first photograph shows a real-life lesbian couple, one of whom is heavily pregnant, receiving a syringe from an angel – a parallel with the biblical scene whereby Mary is informed by the angel Gabriel that she is pregnant.[2] The next photograph shows the infant 'Jesus' with his two mothers and two fathers – a lesbian couple and a gay male couple. This exhibition attracted widespread attention in Sweden and abroad. In addition, Pride Week in

Stockholm has a designated family day every year, with special events catering to lesbian and gay parents and their children. The national organisation for lesbian and gay equality, RFSL, has organised several conferences on the topic of lesbian and gay parents and their children. They have also run numerous 'parenting' courses for LGBT people contemplating parenthood. Clearly, lesbian parents occupy far more visible – although still often separate – and politically organised spaces in Sweden. However, while the existence of alternative spaces may serve an important function, the majority of parenting experiences take place in everyday contexts, such as hospitals, daycare, schools and neighbourhoods.

The path to parenthood

Consequences of spatial exclusion

At the time the research for this book was carried out, lesbians were prohibited from accessing particular services in Sweden, such as medical assistance with artificial insemination by a donor (AID) and other reproductive technologies, including in vitro fertilisation (IVF). It was also difficult for Irish lesbians to access these services openly. Thus, fertility clinics and other places of service provision are coded as heteronormative spaces and new reproductive technologies (NRTs) become part of heteronormative imaginaries.[3] There were numerous consequences of this exclusion. As already outlined in the previous chapter, lesbian participants were forced to travel abroad for these services. In addition, some participants were deterred by the prohibitive cost and effort of this endeavour and opted to become co-parents instead. Susanne, a Swedish participant, did attempt to identify the source of her inability to conceive with a basic infertility investigation. She and the donor informed doctors that they were attempting to conceive together. While they did not lie outright and say they were a heterosexual couple, they did not reveal that they were gay. The prospect of lying to medical staff, in combination with the invasive nature of further fertility treatment, made Susanne decide not to persist any further with her efforts. Eventually her partner became the biological mother of their child:

> We had these clinical examinations and I did some x-rays and anyway the next step was an operation, laparoscopy and that's quite, to me it's quite a large step and we somehow stopped there and we were talking, discussing and I felt that my drive [...] wasn't big

enough for that step [...] and also there's legal difficulties in Sweden anyway, you're not allowed to do IVF, it's difficult to say now afterwards whether I'd have gone through the whole programme if it had been legalised [...] Maybe I might have, but we were kind of lying every time that we entered the clinic and eh I don't know.

– Susanne, Swedish participant

During fieldwork, I also interviewed an Irish lesbian, Bridget, who had attempted to become pregnant, but eventually gave up after several years of unsuccessful inseminations and has remained childless.[4] She was unwilling to seek a medical consultation, as she assumed doctors would be unhelpful towards a lesbian in her situation. As a result of medical policy that confines services to heterosexual couples, both these women were unable to undergo intra-uterine insemination (IUI). This is a simple procedure performed by medical staff, which involves the placing of semen closer to the cervix and thus maximises the chance of conception. Like Susanne, Bridget was also concerned that fertility treatment would involve invasive procedures. Clearly, their experiences are not isolated cases. In addition to those participants in this study who experienced fertility problems, there are probably many other Irish and Swedish lesbians who have been unable to conceive and denied the possibility of adoption or affordable fertility treatment. This group of women – lesbians who are unsuccessful in their attempts to become pregnant and/or parents – is a largely hidden population. Their efforts are invisible, unless they manage to adopt or become parents with a partner.[5]

A small number of Swedish participants also disclosed that in desperation, they posed as heterosexual in order to access services such as in-vitro fertilisation.[6] The case of Anita is particularly poignant. She and her partner were in a registered partnership and were attempting to conceive with a gay male friend of theirs, Sven. Anita had fertility problems and needed IVF. She and her partner Ingela describe what happened when the doctor looked at her records and realised that she was in a registered partnership with another woman:

A: Then the next time she [doctor] met me, just me and her and then she said I must ask questions about your social status because [...] she found out in the papers that I was living with a woman and then I had to say that well I lived with a woman in the past and now I lived with Sven

I: And you had to say you were bisexual

A: [...] yes she said because you know it's forbidden if it turns out that you're a lesbian and [...] she looked in my eyes and said I want you to be honest now okay and I said yeah [...] and I had to look into her eyes and I hated it because I had to lie and I said of course you want the truth and the truth is I'm bisexual, I have had an affair with a woman for many years and then I met Sven, blah blah blah. Shit and I felt it was, it was horrible, I hated it. But at the same time I hate, I'm forced into this thing because I can't do anything else and I need this help to understand what's happening with my body [...] It's been very hard, and I hate to play this role thing, because I'm always honest.

– Anita and Ingela, Swedish participants

Anita found her infertility very difficult to accept emotionally, as she herself was adopted and had long been curious about experiencing biological motherhood. As it was not possible for her to be open about her sexuality with staff at the clinic, she also felt unable to avail herself of the counselling services attached to the clinic, despite grappling with complex emotions around her infertility. Given that for lesbian and gay people, the act of coming out means asserting and claiming the right to an identity, the experience of posing as heterosexual was also painful for her, as it forced her back into the closet, a position she thought she had relinquished in her life. This act of denying her sexuality and her relationship to Ingela, in addition to being unable to use the counselling services, further compounded the trauma of infertility.

In this context of exclusion from reproductive services and technologies, home insemination constitutes a form of resistance. However, for those participants who chose the clearly 'low-tech' route of home insemination with a known donor, the restricted possibilities for medical consultation and advice also occasionally created difficult scenarios. Although the 'turkey baster' is a recurrent feature of alternative insemination in popular culture,[7] it is in fact a rather awkward size for this purpose. A smaller syringe is more appropriate given the relative volume of semen involved. Participants in this study typically used a needleless syringe for insemination. Occasionally straws and a speculum were also deployed to optimise the possibility of conception. While there is a considerable literature on alternative insemination (e.g. Pies, 1988; Pepper, 1999; Mohler & Frazer, 2002) and participants were aware of how to perform this straightforward procedure, accessing the materials necessary – such as syringes – occasionally proved difficult. A lack of familiarity with the utensils themselves and how to obtain them, resulted in uncomfortable situations for several participants. As it was not possible to ask their doctor openly for information – who would possibly not be familiar with lesbian home insemination in any case – they were forced to rely on word of mouth or helpful friends for advice. An Irish couple, Ciara and Gillian, were advised to use a cow syringe by another lesbian couple who had conceived by alternative insemination. Ideally they would have liked a doctor to perform the insemination (preferably IUI) in order to maximise the likelihood of success, but this was not possible. They acted on the advice regarding the cow syringe, although they found the process of insemination uncomfortable and difficult:

> G: We actually looked into going to the doctor [to perform insemination] [...] and there was nobody to do that here, there was nobody who could do that.
>
> C: It was Úna [friend] who put us in touch with her friend in [county] and they said, what was it they said, use a cow syringe and oh Christ
>
> G: I'll never forgive them! [laughter]
>
> C: [...] God we nearly killed ourselves but anyway they were the start of Hilary [daughter] and that's where it went from there.
> – Ciara and Gillian, Irish participants

While this was a humorous topic during the interview, it is also illustrative of the potential problems to which this lack of access to medical support can lead. Both Ciara and Gillian were well-informed about this topic, but had no familiarity with syringes, which caused problems in terms of accessing and choosing an appropriate kind. Similarly, Katarina, a Swedish participant, ran into difficulties when attempting to find a syringe for insemination. She was aware that appropriate ones were available for free at local pharmacies. Unable to disclose the fact that she wished to obtain a syringe for the purpose of insemination, Katarina was forced to provide an alternative reason for the purchase. She therefore told the pharmacist that she needed one to give her child an injection (the most common reason for obtaining a free syringe). However, she did not realise that the syringes came in different forms. The pharmacist asked what medicine her child was taking, in order to determine the correct type. Katarina then replied 'I don't know', at which point she understandably felt extremely foolish. She e-mailed me afterwards to describe the incident:

> 'I said "I don't know" when she asked me what type of syringe I wanted. They are free at the pharmacy but they have different kinds and that made me [feel] really embarrassed and confused because I didn't know that. I felt so stupid when she asked because it's a syringe to give a child medicine and she asked me what medicine I should give my child. And I don't know?!??? I didn't [...] tell her the whole story but she solved my problem by saying "you better try the basic one" and it turned out to be right.'
>
> – Katarina, Swedish participant

These latter two examples illustrate how lesbian parenting remains to some degree an 'underground' activity, in that participants cannot be entirely open about their plans to become parents in all contexts, regardless of whether they actually require medical help or not. The denial of basic medical consultation and information resulted in numerous stressful situations that could not be anticipated by participants. It therefore exposes their vulnerability in contexts where appropriate services are restricted to heterosexuals. This exclusion occurs across various modalities of space, manifested in diverse contexts such as pharmacies and in the imagined spaces of NRTs.

Educating the 'caring professions'

In addition to problems encountered in becoming pregnant due to exclusionary practices, many participants reported numerous difficulties with staff in prenatal and antenatal care contexts. Uncertainty about the consequences of disclosure regarding their sexuality was a cause of concern. Numerous interviewees described feeling stressed about outing themselves to potentially unsupportive staff. On the whole, participants found members of 'caring professions' to be sympathetic and helpful. However, midwives and doctors for example often had little or no experience of dealing with lesbian parents and participants frequently found themselves in the position of educating personnel, both as to the type of treatment that they required and in terms of correcting problematic assumptions about their families. Participants reported feeling somewhat drained by this aspect of their encounters with service providers, in addition to facing the challenge of embarking on parenthood. One Irish participant, Evelyn, resented having to challenge her midwife's ideas about family forms and father-absence within their family, particularly as they pertained to her son. The midwife in question ostensibly attempted to be cognizant of diversity in family forms, but nonetheless made reference to 'fathering and mothering' at the end of their prenatal course, without acknowledging that not all families consist of a father and a mother:

> She [midwife] [...] would work hard at being very politically correct but she did a bit of a wobbly at the end of it, where she forgot, at the course, talking about fathering and mothering and whatever. She rang up out of the blue [...] and the next thing was something about and who is going to play the fathering role in our relationship and I was like, what, you know, where are you getting off. So we kind of, I had to bring her through all of that, you know, which I resented having to do [...] She had never met Cormac [son] [...] and she had decided that he needed a lot of controlling or whatever, kind of fatherly heaviness or whatever. But anyway so [...] that certainly rubbed up the wrong way in terms of having to deal with her issues around our family.
>
> – Evelyn, Irish participant

The difficulties of participating in prenatal courses as a lesbian couple or single lesbian expectant mother, were a feature of several Irish accounts. Course providers often assumed that all participants were heterosexual. Although they reported some awareness of issues pertaining to lone mothers, lesbian parents appeared to be a relatively unknown phenomenon. This lack of support exacerbated participants' concern about the possibility of exposure to homophobia, not only from course providers, but also from the other people attending the courses.

Swedish participants also reported similar difficulties among midwives and other medical personnel in terms of a lack of familiarity and awareness of their family form. They were often the first lesbian expectant parents that staff had encountered. Again, the issue of educating staff arose:

> We've had to do some educating because I mean, like the midwife we went to before Alexandra [daughter] was born [...] actually we asked her have you come across two mothers before and she said oh yes she said [...] and then it turned out it was ten years before wasn't it, just once and she still remembered it and she was not,

educated a little bit and the same has been with people at the hospital and it's always like that.

– Ingela, Swedish participant

However, in contemporary Sweden there have been some improvements in service provision in recent years, often as a result of queer activism. In Stockholm, there is even a midwife who is recommended by the national organisation for LGBT equality, RFSL, as someone working in this area who has particular expertise regarding lesbian parents.

Assumption of heterosexuality

The conflation of pregnancy with a heterosexual identity in myriad contexts was a recurring feature of Swedish and Irish accounts. This illustrates the role of space in shaping identity – for example, a woman giving birth in a hospital is assumed to be heterosexual. For many participants, the recurring assumption of heterosexuality was depressing and served to make them more aware of their marginalisation and therefore vulnerability in society. Mairéad, an Irish participant, was a single mother who found hospital questions about her 'husband' or 'boyfriend' – never 'girlfriend' – tiresome:

> At the hospital they were saying do you want to call your husband. I said I don't have a husband, do you want to call your boyfriend, I don't have a boyfriend [...] and if they had said do you have a girlfriend, but there was just that and I think I was feeling very vulnerable, I was in pain so I was very like oh bother all of this bother all the straight people like all these questions, questions, questions [...] because I'd had nine months of this you know and em and I was tired of it you know, tired of it all.
>
> – Mairéad, Irish participant

These questions could also be experienced as alienating by solo heterosexual mothers, but it is interesting that for Mairéad acknowledgement of her lesbian identity was important. As pregnancy was so strongly associated with heterosexuality, biological mothers in both countries experienced a negation of their lesbian identity in many contexts as a pregnant woman. Unlike co-parents, whose lesbian identity becomes apparent in the assertion of parenthood (which is itself continually contested), biological mothers in this study found that their sexuality was rendered invisible by pregnancy. Stina, a Swedish participant, experienced feelings of frustration similar to those articulated by Mairéad regarding the assumption of heterosexuality because of her impending motherhood:

> But it was also that people seeing me as pregnant thought I was heterosexual once again. So all these people who didn't know me, okay I couldn't go in the streets screaming I'm a pregnant lesbian but it was disturbing [...] and I wanted people to know that also a lesbian can be a pregnant woman, so when I got the opportunity I always told people in some way that I was lesbian too, that was very important to me.
>
> – Stina, Swedish participant

If the biological mother was automatically categorised as heterosexual, her partner – the co-parent – was often assumed to be a helpful friend or relative. Participants who did not wish either to lie about their sexual identity and relationship, or marginalise the role of co-parents, were forced to continually challenge this interpretation of themselves as heterosexual. Swedish participants tended to be more direct and open when communicating with hospital staff and expect both partners to be treated as equal parents, whereas Irish participants emphasised the importance of equal access, such as extended visiting hours, rather than acknowledgement of their relationship or parental role.

The confusion about understanding that participants and their children represented a lesbian family form illustrates the ways that families are invariably interpreted through a heteronormative lens. For example, the supportive midwife of a Swedish couple, Katarina and Elisabeth, recorded that Elisabeth (the co-parent) was a 'mother' in their medical records. Minutes after Katarina gave birth, a new nurse on duty asked her if Elisabeth was 'the mother'. Katarina was nonplussed by this question and asked her to clarify. In an interesting attribution of motherhood to biogenetic substance, the nurse then explained that she thought Elisabeth was the egg donor. She had read their journal and interpreted the reference to Elisabeth as a 'mother' in this way. Despite having just endured a protracted and difficult birth, Katarina had to come out to the nurse and explain that she and her partner were a lesbian couple who had conceived a child by insemination.

The failure to acknowledge co-parents could be a source of pain to couples in both countries. This was a common theme of participants' accounts regarding medical emergencies, including miscarriage. In these distressing circumstances, hospital staff often appeared unaware or unwilling to acknowledge their status as lesbian couples. Participants themselves did not always feel capable of illuminating staff on this point, in what was a medical emergency scenario. This exacerbated an already emotionally difficult situation:

> My experience in the hospital wasn't great at all in terms of Maeve's [partner] involvement when I was miscarrying, they didn't really understand or accept or whatever the fact that she was my partner. I don't think they quite got it [...] so that was very hard.
>
> – Gráinne, Irish participant

> When we went to the hospital [...] especially one older male doctor [...] we told him that we were both mothers but he didn't want to see me like a mother, he wanted to see me like Margareta's [partner] friend. And we didn't take that discussion then but it doesn't feel good [...] I will have to fight in some situations I think.
>
> – Linnea, Swedish participant

Swedish couples were more likely to press for an acknowledgement of their partnership status, as illustrated by Linnea's comment '*I will have to fight*', above. In contrast, Irish participants tended to 'choose their battles', occasionally prioritising a helpful and less stressful service over communicating their lesbian identity. For example, an Irish couple, Caoimhe and Aisling, chose not to mention their lesbian identity in the context of a hospital childbirth. While Caoimhe was present throughout the birth, she was ostensibly there as the 'birthing partner', rather than co-parent:

> In the hospital I was [...] her birthing partner, I wasn't her partner do you know what I mean or I wasn't the mother or the husband or whatever, I was just her birthing partner and they didn't know our relationship so every now and again you just for peace's sake you just say nothing but that doesn't make me feel that I'm less because you know like instead of getting involved in a situation that you don't want to be slightly embarrassed or you don't want Aisling [partner] to be embarrassed or you know you just go with the flow you say look I'm a friend I'm here to help her with the baby so but that didn't make me feel less excited or part of it because when I was ringing my friends they were all congratulating me. These were nurses I just wanted them to do a job, I didn't need them to recognise me.
>
> – Caoimhe, Irish participant

In this sense, Irish participants' accounts of their interactions with relevant personnel appeared to be characterised by a greater degree of self-conscious distancing on the part of participants, than seemed to be the case among their Swedish counterparts. This was a strategy that Irish participants adopted in order to deal with a heteronormative context that was potentially unsupportive at a time when their main priority was to access a particular service. In this particular case, as Caoimhe indicates in the above quote, her personal understanding of herself as a parent was not undermined, as she received sufficient validation from friends and family – in other words her parental identity was made visible and supported in alternative spaces and contexts.

Homophobic discrimination and heteronormative expectations

In addition to a lack of awareness of lesbian parenting in general, participants who were open about their identity as lesbians occasionally encountered active criticism of their life choices. For example, the midwife who attended Maeve, an Irish participant, during childbirth communicated her disapproval regarding Maeve's family form. The birth was unusually long and there were complications. The midwife was unsupportive of Maeve in this context as a result of her homophobic opinions:

> I felt there was one [midwife] that was a bit moralistic [...] she was giving out to me about pushing [...] I'd been pushing for hours and I was getting very tired [...] no matter what I was doing I couldn't push him out [...] she [midwife] was tired and stressed but there was a touch, just a touch moralistic about it, this shouldn't be happening anyway, you know lesbians.
>
> – Maeve, Irish participant

Gunilla, a Swedish participant, found nursing staff behaved in overtly homophobic ways after she had given birth. She had difficulties breastfeeding and many nurses were uncomfortable being alone with her, so were reluctant to help. She and her partner described this experience:

> G: The personnel who were working there, not all of them but some of them
>
> H: They didn't want to go into you
>
> G: No they didn't want to come into my room
>
> H: As if she was going to rape them
>
> – Hanna and Gunilla, Swedish participants

Another Swedish participant, Ulrika, encountered homophobia when she attempted to get help for the severe postnatal depression she experienced. Although her GP was very helpful and supportive, she was feeling particularly distressed one evening and in desperation phoned a helpline:

> When I was really bad I felt like I'm going to hang myself or throw myself out of the window or something [...] and then when I called to this helpline, this nurse who was answering, she was really really homophobic and [...] she almost dropped the phone when I told her that I was living with Annika [partner] and I felt like this you know, I really needed help and she asked with really, she was so you know scared or upset or whatever, so she almost screamed 'and where is the father' you know and like, and I said he is, I know who he is and he is here and all this but he can't help me with this. And then she just said that you should have thought of that before, she said to me. She was really a pain in the ass, really. After that phonecall I felt like I'm going to jump, I felt so bad.
>
> – Ulrika, Swedish participant

In addition to the general lack of awareness and prejudice that participants encountered, there were countless instances in which particular spaces were clearly inscribed in heteronormative ways. For example, hospital hours gave special privileges to visiting fathers, rather than co-parents. Although all participants who gave birth in hospital were able to negotiate the same access for co-parents, the prospect of having to do so was a source of anxiety prior to giving birth. Participants were concerned that they would encounter homophobia and resistance in response to their efforts to ensure that co-parents had the same hospital visitor hours automatically awarded fathers. Furthermore, in a Swedish context, hospital policy conferred donors with special privileges that birth mothers did not always find appropriate or desirable. Åsa, a Swedish participant, recalled that the donor visited her every day when she was in hospital and was insensitive to the fact that she wanted more time and space for herself and her partner. As he was the father, he was entitled to these lengthy visits, despite the fact that she had not had a relationship with him:

> He didn't announce, it was just suddenly he'd stand there in the door and I was trying to sleep and I was bleeding and the milk was...and he just came in and sat down for hours and talked about other things, his private life and...I didn't have the strength, he wasn't that close to us. He was the father to her [child] but he wasn't that

close to me, he wasn't my husband. [...] But because he was the father to her he was always welcome and [...] you [partner] should be the one who is always welcome and he should have this special time of the day when visitors come. [...] The hospital didn't do wrong but it made a little bit of a problem because it was a very strange family, they didn't know how to deal with it. They tried to be nice.

– Åsa, Swedish participant

Another problem encountered in a hospital context concerned recognition of partners as next-of-kin. There is no formal recognition of lesbian and gay partnerships in Ireland, thus all lesbians and gay men in relationships are vulnerable to exclusion from the decision-making process regarding their partners in contexts such as medical emergencies. This occasionally featured in participants' accounts. For Irish participants, there was no possibility of being recognised as their partner's next of kin. One couple attempted to redress this, albeit unsuccessfully:

G: You tried to put me down as your next of kin as well but there was difficulty with that.

M: There was a difficulty with that, wasn't there? And I wouldn't give them another name. That bit at the end, we refused to give them a name. Because legally you're not recognised as next of kin, so I refused to give them a name.

– Gráinne and Maeve, Irish participants

In Sweden, due to legal recognition of co-habiting or 'sambo' relationships and registered partnerships, for those couples who had children after the introduction of these laws in 1988 and 1995 respectively, co-parents could be identified as next of kin. Nonetheless, one Swedish couple in a registered partnership reported that medical staff did not keep the co-parent informed of her partner's condition after she was rushed to hospital with complications and given a caesarean section. Fathers are allowed to attend this operation, but staff did not offer her this option. In addition, she was not asked if she would like to touch their child, who was placed in an incubator in intensive care. She was in a state of shock as a result of her partner and child's illnesses and the emergency nature of the operation, thus it did not occur to her at the time that physical contact with their child might be possible. The treatment she received highlights her vulnerability as a parent in a context where she was not legally recognised. Even when, as in

Sweden, partnership status was legally recognised, the heterosexual nuclear family model is so ingrained that co-parents could nonetheless be excluded from important scenarios, such as attendance at the birth of a child by caesarean section.

While participants reported many instances where medical and other staff were supportive and open, the fear of encountering homophobic reactions in a variety of contexts, including hospitals, was a stressful experience. Participants did occasionally experience overt hostility and discrimination. However, encounters with institutions were more generally characterised by a lack of awareness concerning lesbian parent families. Thus participants were forced to educate staff – an onerous task – while simultaneously seeking their services.

Child-centred contexts

Openness for the sake of the child

Upon becoming parents, participants faced new dilemmas of openness. In addition to asserting their status as lesbians and parents, they had to identify the best ways to protect their children from discrimination. All participants, without exception, stated that it was important to be open about their family form for the sake of their children. Rather than children bearing the burden of telling people about their parents' sexual identity, participants themselves disclosed the relevant details to extended family, friends, neighbours, school staff and so on. For many participants, parenthood involved new sets of relationships with heterosexuals, such as their children's friends' parents and thus extended their social networks. While being 'out' may have been important prior to parenthood, it now held a new significance and simultaneously involved negotiating coming out in unfamiliar spaces.

> You can be openly gay but only live in the gay community and you think that you are open, open, open, but really you are not, because you're just [...] dealing with people that are gay too [...]and I think now [...] we cannot hide, never, I mean if you want to do it sometimes, you cannot do it because of the children, because I can never deny myself in any situation when I have children, never. I have to be strong and I have to all the time be aware of what I'm saying about me and, because I want them to be open about it. I mean if you, if I, if I'm gay and I don't have children, then I can meet somebody and I can say okay I'm not going to say anything this time. Just they can ask do you have a partner and I can say yes and they

don't know if it's a man or a woman but they probably think it's a man and then I don't care, but I never do that anymore, never.

– Birgitta, Swedish participant

I think I've come out more as a lesbian since I've become a parent [...] I think it's important for us to be open because I think it's important for her [daughter] [...] and I have been more open, it's just has been a more natural progression for me to be more out since Danae [daughter] was born because em I suppose I, it's not that I'm closed up, but I'm more private I suppose and I suppose I would pass for straight or I had passed for straight I think [...] but em I suppose in my work circles it wasn't something that occurred to people a lot you know [...] So em, it's just been, I have been a lot more public and a lot more out and more people now of my colleagues and throughout the whole [industry] sector in Ireland you know, know about Danae and about you know our family, now.

– Eimear, Irish participant

In child-centred contexts such as daycare and schools, participants reported engaging in similar practices of informing staff about their particular family form. Rather than simply disclosing the information and relying on staff to deal with any relevant situations appropriately, they then had to explain how they became parents, the identities of all the parents and the possible implications for their child of having lesbian parents in the particular context. All participants were pro-active about protecting their children in school situations, although the nature of this protection took various forms. A strong discourse emerged among Irish participants regarding the choice of a suitable school for their children to attend. The majority of state-run schools in Ireland have a Catholic ethos, unlike in Sweden where schools are run on a secular basis. Among Swedish participants, it was taken for granted that their children would attend a local school. In contrast, Irish participants often made special efforts to locate a multi-denominational school for example, or any school perceived to have a more tolerant environment and greater relative awareness of family diversity.

The interactions between participants and daycare or school staff in both countries also took a different form. While Swedish parents made it explicitly clear to the relevant parties that they were lesbians raising children, Irish participants in couples emphasised their equal roles as parents, rather than their sexuality as lesbians. This relates to a rejection of normative scripts of coming out, reflected in the broader LGBT rights movement in Ireland, where an indigenous approach to equality struggles is particularly salient. It reflects a cultural mode of communication, whereby meaning is created with what is not said, as much as what is directly expressed.[8] This does however enable people to avoid confronting the potential implications of the information being communicated. This is clearly highlighted in the case of Eithne, an Irish participant, who described how she and her former partner would attempt to identify a sympathetic person within a daycare or school establishment to discuss 'the situation' with:

> In a nursery situation or a school situation it was a question [...] of deciding maybe who we thought would be a good person to kind of establish the situation there, you know [...] and maybe it's to a certain extent it's a cop out, you know like we would say co-parents and you know this is the child and here we are and all the rest of it, we wouldn't necessarily talk about lesbianism and this that and the other, we'd let them deal with whatever they were going to deal with about that, or make whatever assumptions, but present them with the situation as it pertained to Ciarán [son] if you like em, and in some ways maybe people found that easier, you know, maybe they didn't think about, although you know after a period of time they did, but you know maybe they didn't even have to go there at some level and we maybe allowed them not to, if they chose not to.
> – Eithne, Irish participant

In contrast, Swedish participants felt less constrained in encounters with institutional staff. Hanna and Gunilla, Swedish participants, provided a vivid illustration of educating daycare personnel about how to treat their family. They described how they challenged staff at their son's daycare to acknowledge their family form. When a child began daycare, it was standard practice for a sign to be put up on the wall with the names of his or her parents. The staff initially put Hanna's name and that of Olof, the biological father, but did not include Gunilla or Johan, the co-parents. When Hanna and Gunilla complained, the staff obligingly added Gunilla and Johan's names, however they placed Hanna and Olof together and Gunilla and Johan alongside one another on the sign, as if they were heterosexual couples. When they complained again, the staff made yet another sign, this time with Hanna and Gunilla's names on one side, Olof and Johan's names on the other and their son's name in the middle, thus acknowledging the parental status of all four parents and their relationship to one another. The staff were helpful and open to suggestions, so Hanna and Gunilla were disappointed when they failed to acknowledge Tomas's status as an older brother when their second child was born. When a younger sibling is born, a sign is also displayed to indicate that the older child has a new sibling. The daycare workers were unsure as to whether the birth of their second child was to be acknowledged or not. As both Hanna and Gunilla were biological parents with different donors, staff were also unclear about the fact that they were brothers:

> G: And now we have taught the person at the daycare centre how they should treat us because it was the same when Daniel [younger son] was born, when other kids get their sister or brother they put up a sign saying congratulations Tomas has a brother, but when Daniel came that sign didn't come up

> H: And I was very disappointed and I said to them immediately why don't you put up a sign that Tomas [older son] has a little brother

> G: [...] They didn't know if it was okay to do it or not because they didn't know exactly how we wanted it or if it was a secret or something like that and we said no it's not a secret and everybody should know and we are not at all a secret and Daniel is Tomas's little brother even though I'm not the biological mother and he has two other biological parents than Tomas has but he is my kid too so we had a long discussion there and they understood that they had made a mistake and there was not bad feelings about that but it was nice to have this discussion.
> – Gunilla and Hanna, Swedish participants

Irish participants could also challenge daycare/school staff, particularly in situations where a child was in need of information and support. Thus, although the difference between Swedish and Irish participants' discourses regarding emphasis on the sexuality of the parents was a general pattern, there were exceptions. Not all Irish participants exercised reticence on this point and could also choose to educate staff when the need arose:

> D: Well of course he announced to all of them how he was born with a syringe and everything.

> J: He just talked about having a donor

> D: And what's a donor and how does that work and blah blah blah and omigod. And so the teacher nearly had a heart attack [...] She said it all to Julie [partner] and what should I say and what should I

do and Julie just gave her the sentences to say and she said them so
it was, at least they talked to us about it.
                                        – Deirdre and Julie, Irish participants

Another strategy reported by Irish participants (but not Swedish) was
to participate in school activities and become a valued volunteer. In
this way, they protected their children within the school environment
by establishing good relations with staff and becoming an integral part
of the school community:

> I also got very involved in the school itself which meant that I had
> good relations with the teachers and staff [...] I did work for the school
> so I mightn't have bothered doing all of that and [laughs] all that time,
> if I wasn't trying to make sure that his [son's] situation in school
> would have been positive but it was important to me that it was.
>   – Eithne, Irish participant

Thus, Irish participants actively sought out the most supportive environment for themselves and their children, which highlights the generally heteronormative nature of most child-centred spaces. In contrast,
Swedish participants were less constrained in their attempts to queer
existing environments.

Safeguarding children

Several participants referred to difficulties for their children at school that
originated not from the staff or other children, but from the parents of
other pupils. For example, some parents were uncomfortable with their
children becoming friends with the children of lesbians and/or spending
time at a lesbian family home. One Swedish couple remarked that they
had always told their children that they could fall in love with a boy or a
girl when they grew up. However, when their small son announced that
he was in love with another boy in his class, the parents of the boy in
question appeared quite uncomfortable. Participants generally encouraged the development of friendships between their children and children
with parents who seemed unconcerned about their family form.

While all participants described their children as being very proud of
their families and two mothers and even, in some cases, boasting about it
at school, there was some indication that the level of openness that Irish
children exhibited changed with age. Although the number of children
over 12 was very small (n = 2), Irish participants reported that their children tended to be more reticent about having lesbian parents as they
became older. This was interpreted as the development of a clearer under-

standing of the marginalisation of lesbian parents in society and also as part of a teenage endeavour to cope with change, difference and their own developing sexuality. Participants however respected their children's right to decide whether or not to disclose this information. This was not a feature of Swedish participants' accounts, although this does not foreclose the possibility that their children may similarly become more inhibited with age. This reticence on the part of children was manifested in several ways – for example by inviting fewer friends home, or only friends from primary school who had always known about their family. One Irish co-parent who returned to Ireland with her partner and child after some years living abroad commented on the change in their son in Ireland:

> He's [son] having a very difficult time with us being lesbians here, which he didn't have in [abroad], it wasn't really an issue for him. You know all his friends came round to the house, they knew we were partners, we could be sitting cuddling on the couch, they could come in and play whereas here I'm some kind of auntie and it's a huge insult but you know he, I have to accept, I have to give him permission to be how he needs to be, to adapt to this culture [...] I can understand that he finds it hard but it doesn't stop it hurting me. I am not his mother here and I hate it.
>
> – Rosemary, Irish participant

Swedish parents could also experience marginalisation as a result of their child's negotiation of the wider world. Unique to Swedish participants in this study was the creation of special names for co-parents, such as nicknames or a term such as 'extra mamma'. These names constituted a function in addition to a term of address. Thus, a child might refer to both parents by saying *'I have a mamma and an extra mamma'*. However, such appellations were not understood or validated when used by children outside of their intimate circle:

> From the beginning, it was mamma and malla [nickname] and that felt equal, sort of, and then it was, she started to call me Malena because no-one knew what malla was outside, in the society, so that was where she learned that, she began to understand [...] when she said malla, no-one understood, what's that.
>
> – Malena, Swedish participant and co-parent

All participants emphasised the important role openness about their family form played in their children's well-being. However, this was often communicated differently by participants in both countries. In child-centred contexts, Swedish participants were more likely to assert their identity as lesbians, in addition to parents. In contrast, Irish participants made considerable effort to locate and establish safe spaces for themselves and their children. They defended their role as parents, rather than highlighting their status as lesbians. However, these patterns are not absolute – many Irish parents did highlight their lesbian identity and some Swedish participants were more reticent. What these general differences illustrate is the perceived degree of social and institutional support and cultural forms of communication in two national contexts.

The queer metropolis and beyond: urban/rural landscapes

Participants often commented that having a child opened up new arenas for meeting heterosexuals, such as mother and child groups for example. However, neighbours and family of origin also related to them in a different way, a child providing common ground upon which to establish a rapport. Irish participants frequently emphasised their efforts to locate supportive neighbourhoods, more so than Swedish interviewees. This resonates with Irish participants' attempts to identify appropriately diverse/supportive/aware schools, a concern that was not expressed by Swedish participants. It would be reasonable to assume that lesbian parents are concentrated in urban areas, given that metropolises are usually associated with greater tolerance towards queer people. However, only one third of Irish participants lived in Dublin and half of Swedish participants in Stockholm, the two capital cities. The majority of the remaining participants lived in small towns or rural areas.[9] While urban areas were seen to provide a more open-minded environment, rural spaces were also perceived to have particular advantages.

For some Irish participants, financial security played an important role in establishing protection from neighbourhood harassment. Despite this, rural Irish participants were generally from the lowest income brackets in the study. However, they were usually embedded in alternative communities where a lesbian identity was supported. Swedish participants articulated a perception of rural neighbourhoods as less tolerant, although they reported positive experiences overall. Participants in both countries often described the countryside as a nicer environment to raise a child, with fresh air and nature activities all around. The lower cost of living in the countryside also facilitated a better lifestyle for their families. Some Irish participants were located in alternative subcultures for whom rural landscapes represented a retreat from what one participant referred to as the 'rat race'.

Escaping harassment in Ireland

Several Irish participants had experienced verbal and other harassment in residential neighbourhoods prior to becoming parents, often from local youth. This informed their decision to move to areas where they might be less likely to experience such difficulties. These were typically more middle-class/affluent neighbourhoods. Concern for safety and freedom from harassment could even inform participants' decisions to become home-owners, as this was considered to provide further protection against potential problems, such as eviction by an unsympathetic landlord for example. A homeowner status would enable them to become more embedded in a neighbourhood in ways that would facilitate the creation of supportive relationships with neighbours and police. One Irish couple, Karen and Orla, experienced repeated harassment over time, including having stones thrown at the windows of their rental home. Ultimately they decided to move to another neighbourhood where they bought a house:

> K: Because of the kind of harassment that we experienced where we were living and because it would be so insecure to go ahead with a pregnancy as a lesbian couple in rented accommodation somewhere like [town] where it's small and your landlord will probably hear about it or know about it, it did also affect our decision to buy.
>
> O: Yeah because we were thinking like Jesus if we had a baby now and all this stuff being thrown at the windows you know.
> – Karen and Orla, Irish participants

Although I specifically enquired about instances of harassment, there were no similarly violent examples reported among Swedish participants, who did however refer to verbal harassment and other discrimination. Nonetheless, such violent incidents undoubtedly occur in Sweden, as Tiby's (1999) research shows.[10]

Knopp (1995) has suggested that non-urban (and other marginalised) queer identities may provide a more challenging location from which to interrogate both critical notions of queer and hegemonic power relations. However, it may also be the case that other facets of privilege are invoked to counteract hostile environments. For example, one Irish couple attributed their freedom from harassment to their economically privileged status, which enabled them to be considered 'eccentric' but nonetheless socially acceptable:

> We live here, we're in the country, in this area if you're not in an estate you're rich and that's it and we're eccentric [...] and you can get away with it once you build that fac[,]ade around yourself here. Otherwise you can forget it. I mean I wouldn't live here in any other way. But we find people are incredibly nice to us, we have good friends, straight friends, local people, who are very keen on us and who are prepared to accept us at face value, who will come into the house and come to parties and do all that.
>
> – Joan, Irish participant

In this case, their 'difference' as lesbians was mediated by their wealth, a privilege which they recognised and actively utilised to secure protection for themselves and their children. Although financial security was sometimes perceived to act as a buffer against harassment in Ireland, many Irish participants did not have substantial disposable incomes, often as a result of choosing to work part-time. Working shorter hours enabled them to spend time with children and reflected a political commitment to a less materialistic lifestyle. These participants usually lived rurally, where living costs were lower and they could participate in alternative communities (often lesbian) that were supportive of difference. In contrast to an urban/suburban environment, rural areas could also offer freedom from the inhibiting gaze of neighbours:

> I wanted to live in the country and I always wanted privacy and that would have been important in terms of being lesbian you know the freedom to go out into the garden and hug Bronagh [partner] or whatever without being overlooked potentially like, that was important.
>
> – Muireann, Irish participant

In the above excerpt, Muireann identifies the urban environment as more constraining and does not draw on notions of urban anonymity so central to other queer metropolitan narratives (e.g. Weston, 1998). This is an intriguing characterisation of life in the countryside, as freer from the constraints of densely populated urban living. However, it also constructs the metropolis or urban spaces as hostile, rather than emancipatory. This may indicate that Irish urban environments are less supportive of non-heterosexuals than urban contexts in many other nation-states. However, it may also suggest that the claims to emancipation that constitute the liberatory narrative of the metropolis in so much of queer theory are in fact exaggerated.

Socialising in the neighbourhood

Irish participants described other strategies utilised as a means of self-protection when interacting with new non-LGBT acquaintances in a variety of contexts, including neighbourhoods. One of these was an assertive demeanor that prevented people from expressing overt hostility:

> I probably wouldn't make it very easy for somebody to be expressing some kind of overt homophobic stuff at me in the normal course of events, em, I think.
>
> – Eithne, Irish participant

> I would be more prickly like that style you know, my attitude to people who are going to be any way funny is like come off it, probably throw them out of it [laughs]
>
> – Sorcha, Irish participant

This approach was necessary in the face of potential hostility and was developed when living openly as a lesbian, prior to becoming parents. More common among participants however, was a strategy of confident self-presentation. By self-confidently and unapologetically disclosing their lesbian identity, participants felt that they neutralised other people's responses. Presenting their sexual identity as something uncontroversial and unproblematic, was perceived to evoke a similar reaction from those around them:

> I suppose that I just have the mentality that if I don't have a problem with it then other people don't have a problem with it. If I don't go in there feeling defensive or you know imagining that people are going to feel this way then they tend not to.
>
> – Síle, Irish participant

Thus, Irish participants actively and continuously 'manage' and negotiate their identities in diverse spaces. Although previous research has focused on the emancipatory scope of urban spaces (in contrast to the constraints of rural life), many Irish participants presented an intriguing vision of life in rural Ireland. Rather than 'escaping' to a big city, they actively chose to carve out lives for themselves and their children in the countryside. An awareness of homophobia and the need for support shaped their choices concerning place of residence. Financial security played a more important role in suburban and urban areas.

Integrating communities in Sweden

Swedish participants articulated concern about perceived conservatism of rural and small town communities, compared to the apparently more tolerant metropolis of Stockholm. However, their experiences in these localities were generally very positive. Participants were often surprised by the acceptance they experienced in rural communities. Although lesbian parenting was typically a new concept or neighbours had never personally met a lesbian parent before, they usually became accustomed to the idea quickly and remained friendly:

> M: This is a small society really and I go to this group for mothers and their babies, we [...] just meet to have coffee and they are also really nice and they are a little bit surprised but at the first meeting they get used to the idea.
>
> L: That's not a big thing, the big thing is to have children and talk about that
>
> M: [...] I think in general people are very friendly, I'm surprised.
>
> L: When they get to know you they see that you are just like everybody else, not so strange.
>
> – Margareta and Linnea, Swedish participants

In the above excerpt, Margareta and Linnea present an image of themselves as 'just like everybody else', unlike the 'rich eccentrics' of Joan's narrative earlier. In this way, developing relationships with neighbours, particularly through the shared experience of parenthood, enabled lesbian parents to become familiar as individuals, rather than just representatives of a minority group. In contrast, the rich eccentric strategy actively utilises the concept of difference in order to render lesbian parents outside compulsory normative categorisations and standards.

Participants themselves occasionally invoked notions of sexuality based on an urban/rural dichotomy. Metrosexuality was associated with sexual freedom, where rural sexuality was constructed as conventional and unaware of alternative sexual practices:

> They [heterosexual neighbours] don't know, they don't realise that I have other experiences than they, that I know everything about

fistfucking, [laughter] that they don't even know exists. And that [...] I have another background and other experiences and [...] I can feel that, that if I tell something about my life before the children, they would be very very shocked because they are very, here in [town], more than in Stockholm for example, much more [...] conservative people.

– Sofie, Swedish participant

Although Sofie's comments may invoke a caricature of rural heterosexuality, they illustrate the continuing importance to her of her lesbian identity. For Sofie, urban environments provide greater possibilities for awareness and acknowledgement of her lesbian 'difference', which she desires. The sense of community she experiences with her heterosexual neighbours is partly a result of the elision of difference between them. In this sense, urban environments represent a link to a sexual imaginary that she identifies with and that holds a certain symbolic significance.

Similar to Irish participants, many Swedish interviewees referred to the importance of conveying self-confidence about their sexuality, which offset any potentially negative reactions. Asserting their sexuality as self-evidently unproblematic constituted a self-protective measure. However, the most effective means of defending themselves and their children was through the strategy of openness, as already outlined in the previous section on child-centred contexts. This highlights the centrality of a discourse of openness in a Swedish context, where it constitutes both a self-conscious protective strategy and political goal.

Conclusion

The active negotiation of space is a recurring theme of participants' narratives. Heteronormative spatiality was evident in myriad contexts. Participants utilised a diverse range of strategies to disrupt and challenge this coding of space. This occurred in a variety of modest ways embedded in the ordinary practices of parenting. Irish participants often sought out particular spaces that they perceived as more supportive of lesbian parents. Swedish participants were less constrained in their range of spaces and were more likely to access whatever was available in a given locality, rather than choose a location/space as a potentially more tolerant place. While all participants stressed the importance of openness about their families for their children's sakes, Swedish participants openly asserted a lesbian identity as part of a politicised discourse, in which being 'out' constituted both a means of protecting their children and a rights-based strategy. In contrast, Irish participants were more reticent on this point and fought for equal recognition as parents, rather than acknowledgement of lesbian identity. Thus, their experiences of particular spaces were more often characterised by barriers to relationships/intimacy, compared to Swedish participants. This was a general pattern of participants' accounts, rather than an absolute difference: some Irish participants were quite confrontational in their method of coming out, while some of their Swedish counterparts chose to be less direct. Nonetheless, this did form a notable difference between the two samples and reflects the general perceived level of social and institutional support. In addition, it is also perhaps illustrative of cultural forms of communication. Ireland is a cultural context where direct verbalisation is less common, rather meaning is created by complex allusions or elucidations. The normative script of 'coming out' is often viewed as an international import in a postcolonial context where an indigenous LGBT movement has particular significance.

A spatial analysis marks a shift in emphasis from marked bodies (lesbian identities) to the ways in which heteronormativity is constructed within particular spaces. This enables a consideration of power dynamics that problematises heteronormativity, rather than an evaluation of the success or 'lack' thereof, with which lesbian subjects negotiate space. Common to both contexts was the construction of heteronormative spatial identities. This was manifested in policies such as hospital visiting hours and discursively by the frequent interpretation of lesbian parents as heterosexual. The experiences of participants in this study suggests that much could be done to improve awareness of lesbian parenting issues among service providers in for example medical and educational settings.

Recent work on gender, sexuality and space goes beyond addressing geographical and physical boundaries and exclusions, to an examination of the construction of spaces themselves. Thus, lesbian parents' experiences of spatiality can be understood as part of a wider moment in which heteronormative spatiality is often destabilised and occasionally reconstituted. This queer(y)ing of 'public' space enables a reconsideration of debates within the literature on gender, sexuality and space, which have previously focused largely on the experiences of white urban gay men. As this research study illustrates, an integration of 'domestic' spheres – in this case the everyday spaces of lesbian parenting – contributes to queer spatial analysis, particularly from a gender perspective. In addition, the emphasis on visibility in previous work on lesbian and gay spaces is perhaps less applicable to a consideration of lesbian parents' daily life. A more diffuse and transitory conceptualisation of lesbian parenting spatiality appears more appropriate, given the relative absence of spaces specific to lesbian families and the locatedness of their familial practices within other arenas. The fact that lesbian parents are often invisible to 'other' onlookers in everyday parenting contexts, does not render those spaces less important in the shaping of their subjectivity as lesbian parents.

Finally, in this study participants offer new queer readings of rural spaces from the perspective of rural inhabitants. Much queer theory has been premised upon an urban/rural binary in which the rural is implicitly pathologised. However, some rural participants in this study offered an alternative vision of the rural as a potentially less constrained space than urban locations, challenging metrocentric notions in previous work. Lesbian parents deconstruct the heteronormative spatiality of myriad everyday contexts, therefore destabilising particular spatial identities.

5

Negotiating the Biological 'Tie': Identity, Power and Difference Among Lesbian Parents

If the lesbian mother is at once 'icon and conundrum' (Weston, 1991: 169), what of the 'non-biological co-parent', whose parental status is even more contested? Rohrbaugh (1989: 157) refers to her as 'a shadowy figure'. In the previous chapter, we saw that her identity as a parent is frequently challenged in wider society. Certainly in legal terms, there is generally little or no acknowledgement of her existence. Recent studies of lesbian parenting have highlighted the egalitarian practices of many lesbian parents who share the responsibilities of household labour and childcare equally (e.g. Sullivan, 1996; Dunne, 1998a). The literature on queer 'families of choice' (Weston, 1991; Weeks *et al.*, 2001) has emphasised the alternative basis of families that are not organised around 'blood ties'. However, relatively little attention has been paid to the implications for equality and kinship formation of the differential legal status of lesbian couples with children where only one partner has any parental rights. Participants in this study gave a variety of reasons for choosing to be/becoming a 'biological' or 'non-biological' parent. What then were the consequences of this difference? If two women plan and raise a child together, but only one of them is accorded any legal recognition, is this difference understood as a power imbalance and if so, how is it negotiated? Aside from the legal advantage/vulnerability, are there any other ways in which couples articulate difference associated with being a biological or non-biological parent as manifested through the lived experiences of parenting? Are the meanings attributed to motherhood/parenthood different/contested in this family form? Do lesbian parents and their children utilise alternative kinship appellations for biological and non-biological parents? In this chapter, these questions are explored with reference to reproductive decision-making, the symbolic interpretation of biology, the

110

nomenclature of parenting, family constellations and the break-up of couple relationships. The myriad possibilities for the disruption and reinscription of heteronormative assumptions regarding the role of biology in parenting will be explored.

Lesbian parenting: reinventing cultures of relatedness?

It has long been acknowledged that a distinction between the biological and the social is intrinsic to constructions of kinship in many European and American cultures. Schneider (1968) questioned the centrality of biology, or nature, to American kinship and argued that biological 'facts' were merely cultural interpretations. According to Edwards & Strathern (2000: 159) 'It is arguable that what makes twentieth-century English kinship, and its Euro-American cognates, distinctive is precisely the division and combination of social and biological facts'. These 'facts' are understood not as foundational categories, but rather as culturally contingent and variable.

Carsten (2000) questions any prior analytic distinction between the 'biological' and the 'social' in studies of kinship. In deploying the term 'cultures of relatedness', rather than kinship, she endeavours to consider comparatively ways of being related that do not 'rely on an arbitrary distinction between biology and culture, and without presupposing what constitutes kinship' (p. 5). She further argues that the infinite (re)combinations of these two elements – biology and culture – is the basis for the dynamic potential of Euro-American cultures of relatedness. This in turn has implications for an epistemology of relatedness and reproduction. In view of Carsten's arguments, we may consider whether lesbian and gay kinship creatively recombines the elements to which she refers.

Kath Weston's classic work suggested that kinship in lesbian and gay communities was centred around choice rather than blood ties. Thus, many lesbian and gay people, ostracised by or alienated from their families or origin, create new kinship networks consisting of friends, lovers and ex-lovers. Schneider (1997) later argued that in an American context, many lesbians and gay men form kinship networks that may contest the norm, but in which the norm is always the point of reference. Thus, '"culture" is indeed the "hegemonic discourse"' (p. 273). In response, Guitiérrez (1997) crucially points out that the term 'American' needs to be critically interrogated (particularly in terms of ethnicity), before claiming any one particular cultural discourse as '*THE* hegemonic one' (p. 280).[1] Schneider's suggestion that lesbians and gay men's kinship narratives are defined in relation to normative discourses of kinship, rather than independently of them, remains valuable when an under-standing that there are multiple possibilities for sites of normative discourses is retained.

In a consideration of debates about the 'uniqueness' of lesbian and gay kinship, Hayden (1995), in a groundbreaking article, suggests that lesbian parents utilise the same symbols of kinship as heterosexuals, but that they are reconfigured within these family forms. Thus, (hetero)-normative ideologies of 'the family' remain the reference point for arguments in favour of the legitimacy of lesbian and gay family con-figurations. She highlights two important ethnographies from the west coast of the U.S. to illustrate her argument – Weston's (1991) work on 'families of choice' and Lewin's (1993) work on lesbian motherhood. Weston (1991) argues that lesbian and gay kinship is distinctive because of the decentralisation of blood ties, whereby friendship or 'love' and choice become a defining characteristic of kinship. Hayden points out that for Weston, gay and lesbian 'chosen families' do not constitute mere derivations of, or substitutes for, a traditional view of kinship based on heterosexual relations, 'rather they are distinctive in their own right' (p. 41). In contrast, Lewin (1993) suggests that for lesbian women, 'motherhood' becomes a defining characteristic of identity that elides the 'difference' of lesbianism. I would add however that Lewin's focus on primarily lone parents, most probably influenced these findings. Both ethnographies have informed debates about the potential for distinctive kinship formations among lesbians and gay men.

In Strathern's view the 'families we choose' thesis exposes the dimen-sion of choice that is also present in heterosexual kinship through 'the detachment from blood families implied' (1993: 196). Many lesbians and gay men may experience hostility and ostracism from their families of origin and create new families of choice with friends. In other words, 'blood ties' are also constructed, rather than based on so-called 'facts of nature'. An integration of these insights is particularly salient for a con-sideration of lesbian parenting couples, where one partner is a biological (and therefore legally recognised and recognisable) parent – and one partner is not, or rather is continually defined in terms of her 'lack', as a 'non-biological/non-legal' (and therefore perhaps invalid) parent. As Hayden notes, in an American context this partner is 'doubly excluded from the realm of kinship', as she is neither a legal spouse, nor a bio-logical parent (p. 49). Many Swedish participants in this study were regis-tered partners, a status similar to heterosexual marriage, which however at that time denied all parenting rights possibilities such as adoption and access to new reproductive technologies. Nonetheless, this legal recognition of the co-parent as a partner, did perhaps go some way to endorsing if not her role as a parent, at least her existence as a partner.

The literature on lesbian and gay kinship has generally ignored the *combination* of biological and non-biological status *within* the family (particularly in the case of lesbian couples parenting together), although Hayden's (1995) work is an important exception in this regard. A consideration of this dynamic within 'the family', is not meant to suggest that lesbian couples with children necessarily constitute a new 'nuclear family' form. Indeed, as we have already seen in Chapter 3, the involvement of donors in Sweden challenges the model of two parents and one home implicit to the traditional nuclear family structure. Rather, the purpose here is to explore the meanings attributed to biology and consanguinity within these families in all their diversity. Hayden (1995: 50) suggests that the ways in which lesbian mothers in an American context attempt to 'rectify' the 'asymmetry' of differential biological status is an indication of the salience of the 'blood tie' to American kinship, even in a context where traditional dominant articulations of kinship are apparently resisted. In her analysis, unlike 'chosen families', where the centrality of biology as the basis of kinship is undermined, lesbian couples with children invoke articulations of biology that emphasise its 'diffuse' quality, as opposed to constructing it as a monolithic category. Thus, 'Far from depleting its symbolic capital, the dispersal of the biological tie seems here to highlight its elasticity within the symbolic matrix of American kinship' (p. 45).

Although lesbian parents themselves may negotiate the meanings of these symbolic signifiers in different ways, it is interesting to consider how researchers have utilised categorisations of lesbian motherhood that exclude co-parents. Lewin (1993) framed her comparative research on lesbian and heterosexual motherhood in the United States as work on 'single mothers', despite the fact that approximately 25 per cent (n = 20) of her sample were lesbian participants who planned and embarked on parenthood with a same sex partner.[2] In the first stage of her research, she looked at women who became pregnant in a heterosexual relationship. For the next stage of her study, she researched what she termed at the time 'intentional single mothers' – women who conceived while single or in a relationship with another woman. Lewin (1993) clearly outlines her reasons for constructing this latter group of lesbian mothers as single mothers.[3] At the time of embarking on her research, the lesbian baby boom was in its infancy and it was a strategic way of constructing lesbian motherhood in a hostile political context. Certainly, in legal terms, they were technically identified as single mothers. It is nonetheless striking that co-parents are entirely excluded from the categorisation of 'lesbian mothers' in her analysis. It is only in more recent writings and research that co-parents' parental status is acknowledged, although it remains relatively unexplored. This relative marginalisation of co-parents in academic work is a further indication of the 'taken-for-granted' parental status of lesbian birth mothers, compared to their partners.

Legal recognition of co-parents has been particularly problematic to achieve, as in most European countries the law still retains a nuclear family model, whereby a child has one mother and one father, or a maximum of two parents. New reproductive technologies have challenged this categorisation with the advent of possibilities such as sperm and egg donation and surrogacy. The legal regulation of heterosexual couples and same gender couples availing themselves of these technologies are clearly different. If a married heterosexual couple in Sweden or Ireland chooses to conceive via a sperm donation, the social father is legally acknowledged as the second parent. Lesbian couples who conceive by the same method are unable to gain legal recognition of the co-parent in Ireland. This situation has recently changed in Sweden. However in these cases the lesbian couple must be in a registered partnership (unlike heterosexual couples) and the biological father must be either unknown or willing to rescind all parental rights. As most donors played an active parenting role in the families in this study, this is clearly not reflective of many lesbian parenting arrangements in Sweden. Nonetheless, this recent legislative change represents a welcome first step towards acknowledging the rights and obligations of co-parents. Although this possible legislative change was under discussion when I was carrying out fieldwork in Sweden, it was not passed in parliament until after fieldwork had concluded. These interviews therefore took place with women who did not yet have that possibility – although all appeared optimistic that the law would change within the near future.

Numerous sociologists have pointed to the ways individuals are constantly constructing and reconstructing their intimate relationships (e.g. Giddens, 1992; Heaphy *et al.*, 1999). In this chapter, the possibility that lesbian parents reinvent and expand notions intrinsic to normative definitions of kinship, such as 'biology', are explored. The fact that only biological mothers were legally recognised in this research study is also addressed in terms of how this difference in legal status was negotiated by participants. Malone & Cleary (2002) argue that 'The attributes of harmony, adjustment and equality that pepper reflections on the lesbian family are modern heirs to a number of fantasies of "being one". The fantasy of "one" marks traditional heterosexual images of love and family' (p. 274). In this way, they argue, power and difference within lesbian parenting families are ignored or overlooked. Most participants' parenting experiences in this study are characterised by kinship arrangements in which children are raised by 'biological' and 'non-biological' parents. An explicit consideration of the status of biology in these families, will therefore enable an exploration of the dynamics of power among lesbian parenting couples. The ways in which kinship is delineated in these families potentially de/re-constructs or substantiates heteronormative discourses regarding the significance of biology and parenting, reinventing or reinforcing hegemonic kinship discourses in complex ways.

To be or not to be: a birthgiving mother

Prior to conducting fieldwork, I anticipated that the biological status of parents would be a sensitive issue in terms of a related power imbalance among couples. For my first 'couple' interview therefore I initially met with Viveka, the biological mother, independently of her partner Susanne. Viveka was also in the apartment while the interview with her partner took place. During the course of the interview with Susanne, the co-parent, I observed that the couple continually reminded one another of incidents which they might individually have temporarily forgotten. Furthermore, it appeared that the issue of a biological relationship with their child was something that they had addressed openly and at length between themselves. This was apparent in all the interviews and the biological status of parents was not usually a sensitive topic. It was however a more painful issue for participants who had experienced infertility, but even then the implications of this were discussed with their partner prior to insemination. This reflexive awareness of biology and parenting was a recurrent theme of interview narratives. The assumption that partners would feel inhibited about discussing biological 'difference' in parenting in front of one another, failed to take account of parenting as a shared enterprise.

For many participants, the choice about who would become a biological parent was really a decision about whether or not to experience pregnancy and childbirth. This was often a point of straightforward agreement among couples. In fact, a striking characteristic of the sample was the relative ease with which this reproductive division of labour was allocated. Among many couples in both countries, there was a clear distinction between who wanted to experience pregnancy and child-birth and who did not. Almost 40 per cent (n = 11) of all co-parents interviewed, expressed a clear and persistent wish **not** to experience the physical aspects of childbearing. The reason most frequently arti-culated for this complete absence of inclination to be a birth mother was a fear of the pain associated with childbirth. This was often a source of amusement to the couple when recalling this aspect of the reproductive decision-making process:

R: And was it difficult to decide who would be the biological mother?

N: No that was the easy part! [laughter] We didn't even discuss that! [laughs]

R: [To I] You didn't want to?

I: No I'm terrified of being pregnant and then to go through the delivery and oh god I didn't want that, I wanted a child so this is good.
– Nina and Ingegerd, Swedish participants. Nina is the biological mother.

C: Well my mam had warned us never to let me have a baby

A: Because she doesn't have a very high pain threshold!

C: They know me so well!

A: I'll have to go again [laughs]
– Caoimhe and Aisling, Irish participants

Interestingly, this discourse concerning fear of childbirth featured equally powerfully among Swedish and Irish accounts. This is perhaps sur-prising, given that Sweden has a strongly institutionalised role of the midwife in prenatal care and childbirth, a factor associated with increased control on the part of the birth-giving woman (Kitzinger, 1992; Romlid, 1998; Wrede, 2000). In contrast, childbirth in Ireland is traditionally regulated by obstetricians and the 'active management of labour' model is influential in policy and practice.[4] The discourse of fear of childbirth articulated by participants in this study perhaps suggests that more could be done in both countries to cater to women's concerns about pain relief and empowerment during childbirth. However, these findings may also suggest that women find insufficient comfort in prevailing discourses – some of which were expressed by birth mother participants in this study – such as 'you forget the pain', when contemplating an undoubtedly difficult physical process.

What is also striking about these accounts is that for co-parents (and indeed for many birth mothers), consanguinity was not a priority. Social parenting represented the most meaningful connection for them personally as a parent. Rather than explicitly desiring a biological or genetic relationship with a child, co-parents expressed a desire to have a child in their life and for a social parenting role. In this context, I use the term 'birth mother', as it was specifically discomfort about this aspect of the reproductive process that featured in co-parents' accounts. Consanguinity may not have been important, but it was not objectionable in the way that giving birth was:

M: I never wanted to be a biological mother, so.

R: Why was that?

M: Well I'm terribly afraid of delivery that's one thing and I never really wanted it. I'm fine with raising a kid, living with one. Having one biologically, that's not important to me.

> – Mia, Swedish participant and co-parent

Geraldine [partner] was definitely, wanted to have a child and I was definitely wanting to be a parent. But I never had any intention of being the biological mother I had no desire to you know be the one to carry the baby.

> – Aoife, Irish participant and co-parent

Some birth mothers took on the role of pregnancy and childbirth simply because it was the only option if they wanted to have a child, given their partner's fear of childbirth and of course the practical difficulties regarding adoption, including legislative prohibitions. Sofie, a Swedish participant had no particular preference for becoming a biological parent, but her partner was adamant that she could not face pregnancy and childbirth herself. In referring to her decision to be the birthgiving mother, Sofie said: '*It was not something she* [partner] *could even consider!*' This is not to suggest however that birthgiving mothers were under duress to take on this role. Participants were agreed that if both partners had shared a fear of childbirth they would not have embarked on parenthood at all, as adoption was not a possibility at that time. Nonetheless, in cases where one partner was unable to have children, occasionally the more reluctant partner did become the biological mother. However in these cases, participants described their initial reluctance to take on this role in terms of a lack of enthusiasm rather than a more intense revulsion or fear at the prospect.

Another reason articulated by some co-parents for not wanting to be a birth mother, was a perception of pregnancy as violating a sense of control. One birth mother laughingly described her partner's personal resolve not to become pregnant, as dread of her body being 'colonised'. This perception of pregnancy as a compromise to bodily integrity arose in several interviews:

> I just didn't have any internal desire to actually have a baby growing inside me, I didn't, I don't know what that is whether it's just a control thing you know but I didn't.
>
> – Aoife, Irish participant and co-parent

> B: I always have known that I don't want to be a biological mother. I don't know why, I just feel that that's not for me. I want children but I don't want to have something in here growing and coming out well, no. So it was not a problem for us at all.
>
> R: Are you frightened of the physical pain?
>
> B: I don't know, I mean to have something growing inside you, it feels like oh, ugh!
>
> – Beatrice, Swedish participant and co-parent

It seems unlikely that these concerns about bodily integrity and physical pain in childbearing are unique to lesbian women. It is surely the case that many heterosexual women share these feelings. However, unlike lesbian couples they do not have the option of becoming a parent with a partner who is willing to carry out this part of the reproductive process.[5]

This discourse regarding the pain of childbirth was also articulated as a *gendered* concern. Many co-parents articulated their fear in terms of a gendered embodied identification with a birthgiving woman. Katarina and Elisabet, a Swedish couple, described this phenomenon. Katarina laughed as she recalled an incident that occurred after they watched a video about giving birth at their prenatal course. Afterwards, Elisabet, the co-parent, turned to Katarina, who was pregnant at the time and

said soberly: 'My God, you really have *hell* in front of you, you know!'
In describing her feelings at the time, Elisabet explained:

> E: Well I think that's a woman issue, because I'm not thinking about Katarina giving birth when I'm in there [watching film]
>
> K: No
>
> E: It's more like I'm thinking about me giving birth! [laughter] I feel omigod, I will never go through that and I'm feeling like, poor you! [laughs]
>
> – Katarina and Elisabet, Swedish participants

Several co-parents mentioned that feelings of distress when witnessing their partner in extreme pain during childbirth, in combination with their own anxiety about that pain, made the birth a less than pleasant experience. It is probably the case that many men also find it upsetting and experience a sense of helplessness when witnessing a partner giving birth. Indeed, in Kearney *et al.*'s (2000) comparative study of fatherhood in Sweden and England, many respondents referred to feeling shocked at the degree of pain their partners endured during childbirth. However, the narratives of co-parents in this study suggest an added dimension of embodied gender identification. Clearly, this is not something that all women experience – certainly female doctors and nurses do not necessarily identify more with the pain of female patients in childbirth due to a shared gender for example and this embodied gender identification was not a universal feature of participants' accounts. However it did occasionally emerge in interview narratives and not always in a purely imaginary or empathetic way. One Irish participant for example experienced physical symptoms similar to some of those her partner was undergoing while giving birth:

> M: Actually Eileen's breasts got sore and perineum and vagina swelled and everything at the birth, so she came out in sympathy with me!
>
> E: I did yeah, I did I was in a ferocious state.
>
> – Mary and Eileen, Irish participants

Mary and Eileen were raising Eileen's two children from a heterosexual marriage and another child who was conceived by AI in the course of their relationship. Eileen's symptoms may be related to her experience of having given birth herself, in addition to an embodied gendered sense of identification with her partner, where these dimensions are understood as mutually implicated.

Hanna, a Swedish participant, developed serious complications during her pregnancy and went into labour early in the third trimester. The birth was treated as a medical emergency and carried out by caesarean section. She felt that she had missed out on some of the pleasures of pregnancy because she experienced it for a relatively short time and also of the birth, because she was barely aware that it was happening. This initially left her with a strong desire to experience a second pregnancy, but these feelings receded during her partner's pregnancy:

> I was very sad and disappointed over that [personal experience of pregnancy and birth] so then I thought for a long time that I wanted one more kid, but then when Gunilla [partner] got pregnant, I was so close in her pregnancy that I felt like it was my pregnancy because I felt her stomach and I slept beside you and I was so close all the time and I was the first person in the delivery room and I was all the time so near so I got very satisfied and so I felt like no, it's not necessary to have one more biological kid and a pregnancy for me because it was such a nice experience with Gunilla.
>
> – Hanna, Swedish participant

In this quote, parenting is emphasised as a shared experience in the context of a couple relationship. The biological mother/co-parent is not simply another woman, but an intimate partner. Hanna's emphasis on this closeness and parenting as a shared experience also served to reinforce her role as a parent.[6]

The very small number of couple relationships consisting of two birth mothers is not a simple reflection of the reluctance, already described, of many co-parents to become a birth mother. Some co-parents (n = 5) intended to become a birth mother at some point in the future. Indeed, several have gone on to do so since fieldwork took place. Age was another consideration that also influenced women's decision not to be a birth mother. Several participants considered the health risks too great to risk a pregnancy, in which case the younger partner took on that role. In addition, some women (n = 5) experienced fertility problems which prevented them from becoming a birth mother, as a result of which their partner began inseminating instead. These factors are broken down in the following table.

Table 5.1   Reasons for co-parent status among participants who did not plan future insemination

	Co-parent because of fear of childbirth	Co-parent because of age	Co-parent because of infertility	Future birth mother	Other reasons	Total
Swedish	7	1	3	4	1	16
Irish	4	3	2	1	2	12
Total	11	4	5	5	3	28

This table does not include participants who were both a birth mother and a co-parent. Former partners involved in parenting who did not participate in interviews (Swedish n = 5 and Irish n = 1) are also not included. In these cases, interviews took place with the birth mother. Other reasons given for co-parent status included a combination of factors such as age, health and having already had children in a previous heterosexual relationship or the break-up of a relationship prior to the participant becoming a birth mother.

Infertility

In five cases, participants who wished to be a birth mother discovered that they had fertility problems. Although the realisation of infertility was often traumatic, it did not necessarily become a source of tension between the couple. The factors influencing difficulties in resolving this included the importance placed on having a biological or genetic connection to a child. Overall however, participants emphasised their strong desire to have a child in their life, rather than a longing for a bio-genetic 'tie':

> I tried to get a child myself and [...] we tried for two years and we didn't succeed. And I don't, I'm not sorry about that in any way because I'm happy enough with Torsten [son] so that's how I conclude that it was not in a reproductive way, more a family, a social wanting. Because I don't mind that Torsten is not my biological child, it doesn't mean that much to me and I really tried to think about this [...] how is it, do I trick myself or don't I and [...] it doesn't matter because I feel that Torsten is my child as well in every way, so.
> – Susanne, Swedish participant

Susanne also referred to her relationship with both her step-parents, to whom she was very close. She did not distinguish between them and her birth parents, a factor which also influenced her reconciliation to an inability to become pregnant. Again, the desire to be a parent was articulated in terms of becoming a social parent, rather than having a bio-genetic relatedness with a child.

Catherine, an Irish participant, experienced fertility problems as the result of a life-threatening illness. For her, becoming pregnant and giving birth represented a validation of her health and thus fertility complications were particularly difficult to accept. In contrast, her partner conceived easily and quickly, a source of envy on Catherine's part. She referred to her own infertility, in contrast with what she termed her partner's 'super-fertility', as a sensitive issue between them. Thus, power, fertility and embodiment were connected in complex ways – being a birth mother was meaningful because of what it would symbolise in relation to her health status. This is an illustration of the diversity of factors that could influence the symbolic role of biology in parenting.

Similarly, Anita, a Swedish participant who was adopted at birth, was influenced by these circumstances in her desire to become a biological parent. She had an excellent relationship with her adoptive parents and did not express any interest in making contact with her birth parents until well into her adult life. She became particularly curious about the relationship between a biological parent and child and was very excited at the prospect of embarking on parenthood as a birth mother. The knowledge of her infertility was devastating. After a long and unsuccessful struggle to become pregnant, her partner, Ingela, volunteered to inseminate. Unlike Anita, Ingela had initially been less enthusiastic about parenthood, but gradually came round to the idea. She conceived after just one insemination. Anita described her mixed feelings of joy and pain when this occurred:

R: How did you feel when Ingela became pregnant?

A: Em, well since I had still these grief feelings. I mean I was so sad from the [failure of insemination].. at the same time I was happy but I didn't know how to handle it. Neither the grief for me nor these feelings. I mean when we made Wilma [daughter] it was a very good day, it was really, the four of us were very happy, we were happy to meet again and happy with the way we did it [...] we were in an apartment in Stockholm, we took the train in the early morning and we were talking first, we were sort of excited all of us and then we thought we'll just give it a try and see what happens and that, I was a very, part of that because I just put a lid over my other feelings and then I mean the guys in the apartment, they were first in there and then we were standing outside [...] and I was happy, sort of part of it.

– Anita, Swedish participant

Still struggling to come to terms with her sadness as a result of her own infertility, her partner's attempt to conceive was difficult for Anita emotionally. In her account, above, the conception is constructed as a group process and she emphasises her role among the parents (Anita, Ingela, the donor and his partner) in creating their child. She appropriates generative power when she refers to the day when 'we made' their daughter. However, her pleasure at participating in this process is enabled by 'putting a lid over' her feelings of sadness at her personal inability to conceive. She refers to her difficulty at handling all these different emotions simultaneously. Despite this, her subsequent relationship with their child helped her to overcome feelings of loss at not being a biological parent. It was often apparent that becoming a co-parent helped to alleviate distress caused by infertility and that longings for a biological child faded after time spent loving and caring for a non-biological child.

Sara, a Swedish participant attempted to become pregnant for two years and finally conceived via IVF. However, she miscarried, at which point her partner began inseminating and later gave birth to their daughter:

But when Bodil [daughter] was a couple of months [old], one evening I was thinking about this, oh I also wish that I could have one biological child for myself. It went through my head once and we talked about it but then it was gone and now I know I thought so, but I don't anymore [...] She is my child as much as she can be and if we also get the adoption,[7] it will be equal [...] I feel her so much as my child that I can't imagine another way.

– Sara, Swedish participant and co-parent

Eimear, an Irish participant had tried to become pregnant for some years but was unable to conceive and eventually her partner gave birth to their child:

If I weren't with Sorcha [partner] I would still not be a parent you know so, you know there was a compromise on my part and I still got a lot from it you know which you know more than makes up for that sadness I feel for that personal thing that I would have liked, so..

– Eimear, Irish participant and co-parent

Co-parents who were unable to conceive often referred to their delight at becoming a parent and feelings of good fortune that this was possible because of having a female partner. However this does not mean that the decision to change over to a partner for insemination was always easy to accept. Even if the consensus was that it was important to be a social, rather than a biological parent, the decision for one partner to abandon the prospect of being a biological mother and for her partner to begin inseminating instead required some time to adjust to. Karen and Orla, an Irish couple in the study, were attempting to conceive. Although Orla had been trying to become pregnant for some time, no pregnancy was forthcoming. They referred to the assumption on the part of friends that they would simply swap places and that Karen would begin inseminating immediately. However, as Orla stated *'you can't just switch'*. Both were determined to try every possible avenue for Orla, before beginning a process of accepting that she was unable to conceive. Difficulties in accessing fertility treatment (as already outlined in Chapters 5 and 6) exacerbated the distress associated with infertility.

This ubiquitous myth: biological relatedness and parenting

All participants identified as parents, regardless of biological relationship to their children. This does not mean however, that the biological relationship between birth mothers and children was ignored or viewed as entirely insignificant. Although participants were equally involved in parenting, a belief in a special or unique mother-child relationship based on the experience of pregnancy, occasionally emerged. Participants for example often referred to a birth mother's ability to wake up as soon as a child began crying, or even immediately beforehand. This 'special connection' was seen as particularly or only apparent during a child's infancy and breast-feeding periods.

I think you feel something towards a child that you've given birth to that is different from a child that you haven't, or the child responds differently to or something, I don't know, I don't know what it is. And I might be wrong, but I just can't believe that that nine months counts for nothing immediately. I think it does get much less influence as time goes by but I think it you know, it takes time for that to fade you know.

— Emma, Irish participant and birth mother

I think you can never come away from the fact that when you've carried a child there's also something else in it which for example, the only thing I can say is, and I think that's very very normal is that and I know most parents have that thing during night-time and all this, with children waking up all the time, I know fathers and mothers have the same thing, the mother wakes up, it doesn't take one second and she doesn't need to cry or anything, I just wake up straight ahead if there's just a noise though she's not in our room or anything, I think that goes very deep inside yourself because you had her in your, carried her and everything [...] I think that's something very special that can never ever be taken away or anything.

— Åsa, Swedish participant and birth mother

This awareness of a child's physical needs was not shared by all birth mothers however. For example, Sinéad, an Irish participant, is rarely woken by external noise and slept through most of her son's night feeds. In the morning, Sinéad would have no memory of these nocturnal interruptions and would often comment with wonder on his ability to sleep for long periods of time. Her partner had children from a previous heterosexual relationship and Sinéad had been curious to see if she felt a particular 'fine tuning', or special awareness of her biological child's needs. However, this never developed. In contrast, her partner, the co-parent, woke immediately upon hearing his cry:

Sinéad would sleep through half the breastfeeding. She would go to bed, she would wake up in the morning and say that baby was brilliant, and I'm going he woke at two and four and six [...] but she slept alright, not even disturbed by him [...] I would wake, I've always woken at the first sign of a child's cry. So I was very tuned into that anyway. Sinéad just never needed to get tuned in, no need, and she wouldn't have done anyway. I think the child would have gone through the night as a necessity, he just would have been a very hungry baby when she woke up.

— Rosemary, Irish participant and co-parent

So for this couple, the roles reported by some other couples were reversed and having given birth did not provide a special awareness of a child's physical needs. Nonetheless, Sinéad did find that being a birth mother was significant in one way. Having co-parented her partner's children from a heterosexual relationship since their infancy and identifying strongly as their mother, she was surprised to find that she experienced a 'genetic connection' with her birth child. While she loved all three children equally, she found that the marked physical resemblance and similar mannerisms she shared with her son held a particular resonance for her. The physical similarity between Sinéad and her son, is made meaningful precisely because it represents a particular ideation of biology:

S: I think what surprised me was the genetic connection [...] from the minute Turlough [son] was born and I saw this nose, this O'Reilly nose it was just like oh shit you know he really is mine, you could pick him out in a crowd! [laughter]

R: He always looked very much like Sinéad

S: And I'm the image of my father and this floored me, you know. And seeing Turlough, there was one point where Turlough was three and he was reciting this poem for my father and it was like, it was like going right back there and being in that place. And looking like that, it was very very strange and the poem was one that [...] was about whole generations going past, but it was also a children's [poem], it was one of those ones. So it was kind of meaningful for all three generations and this kid was three saying it and I can remember being that kind of child and knowing that these were children's words, but there was, I can remember being in that space, so that was very very strange and just seeing him doing things in the same ways, which I didn't have with David and Christopher [partner's children from previous relationship]
– Sinéad and Rosemary, Irish participants

Many co-parents also invested in the notion of a special connection between a birth mother and child for at least a period of time, usually immediately after birth and during the breastfeeding stage. Numerous participants referred to children turning initially to the birth mother for comfort during the breastfeeding stage because *'she was the one with the breasts'*. Not all participants experienced this and those who did said that it changed when the child was weaned. For some co-parents the weaning of the child therefore represented a new stage in their relationship as a parent. Both Niamh and Eva in the following quotes describe their occasional feelings of frustration as the non-breastfeeding parent.

> I would have felt with Cormac [non-biological child] well this breast-feeding lark especially when I, two and a half years down you know I'm not sure how much more I can hack this where every time Cormac cries he wants Evelyn [partner] because of the breastfeeding. But it peters out and it switches and it has been through different times.
>
> – Niamh, Irish participant

> But sometimes I get [...] not jealous but sometimes I feel like I want to be a part of it more [...]I can feel a bit outside, but it's just now in the beginning and I know that it's going to be different when Regina [partner] is not breastfeeding anymore.
>
> – Eva, Swedish participant

However, this notion of a particular physical connection between a birth mother and child was often presented as a positive concept which was to be acknowledged, rather than viewed as undermining of the co-parent. In this way, co-parents emphasised their personal sense of security in their role as a parent. Rather than equality being depen-dent on 'sameness', difference could be acknowledged without being threatening. This perhaps draws on or emulates a hegemonic kinship discourse dependent on sexual difference, thereby legitimating the lesbian parents' culture of relatedness:

> And I think that's a nice thing, I have no, I think that's a good thing. I don't feel you know envy or jealous or anything. I think that is something to celebrate I think that's a really nice special thing I wouldn't like to take it away at all because that's the fact of the matter, he was inside Aisling [partner] for nine months.
>
> – Caoimhe, Irish participant and co-parent

While some participants referred to the significance of a biological or genetic relationship, this was not a universal feature of accounts and is not to suggest that all birth mothers in the study felt an immediate connection with their children. In particular, where the pregnancy was unplanned or reminiscent of an earlier traumatic experience, as was the case for several Irish participants, such feelings of 'connectedness' took some time to develop. Dymphna, an Irish participant, became pregnant as a result of rape. She referred to being 'in denial' about her condition for the majority of the pregnancy. Thus for example she did not receive any prenatal care until the final trimester. The birth itself was a particularly difficult one and it took some time before she felt 'connected' with her child:

> D: Because I was so in denial about being pregnant and everything, when he was born, the bond that so many people said oh when you have a child and the bond will be there
>
> R: It wasn't?
>
> D: No, no [...] it took some time, yeah a few months at least. But not to say that I didn't care for him or you know but I just, I guess there was something in me that wasn't connected so therefore I couldn't connect to him in the way that I would have liked to.
>
> – Dymphna, Irish participant

Nicola, an Irish participant, had given a child up for adoption 20 years previously and found that giving birth again brought back memories of this difficult time earlier in her life. She described her 'bond' with her younger child as a 'strong feeling' that took several weeks to develop. In her view, her feelings for her younger child developed at a slower pace because of the emotional trauma surrounding the adoption, which she also considered to have played a role in the complications she experienced in the second childbirth:

> N: It [emotional bonding] took about four weeks. I think that was because of having adopted a child and just having been quite traumatised
>
> R: You mean it brought that back to you?
>
> N: Yeah I think that's why the birth sort of went a bit wild. Then obviously there is a bond, but before it sort of really kicked in, it took a while. I was thinking what am I doing and then you know it just gets stronger and stronger [...] it's just such a strong feeling.
>
> – Nicola, Irish participant and biological mother

Another Irish participant, Clodagh, became pregnant unintentionally after a casual sexual encounter. As the pregnancy was unplanned, it took some time for her to feel comfortable with becoming a mother and developing what she viewed as particular manifestations of 'attachment' intrinsic to parenthood. These were feelings that she had recently begun to experience:

> But I have to say in the last few weeks, I've really started having these attachment things and it's probably only now, a year and a half old, I just think my god if something happened to him, it would take me a hell of a long time to recover, whereas I think it was over my head a little bit before that.
>
> – Clodagh, Irish participant

Another birth mother in this study referred to her partner 'engaging' with their child much more quickly after the birth, because she herself was so exhausted after a long labour that she did not have the emotional energy to do so. It appears likely that these experiences will resonate with those of heterosexual women who come to terms with motherhood in unplanned circumstances. These latter accounts, which refer to trauma, uncertainty about becoming a parent, and physical exhaustion challenge cultural myths of an automatic, universal and unwavering bond experienced by all birth mothers for their biological child. The circumstances and experience of childbirth affect women's emotions and identity with respect to parenting, which may be complex and conflictual.

The concept of an essential, unchanging and universally experienced maternal 'bond', remains a persistent and ubiquitous myth. This is not to undermine or deny the powerful emotions experienced by many women in pregnancy or childbirth, rather the diversity of narratives is a reminder that these responses are also mediated by context. This does not make them feel any less 'real', but does suggest that responses can and do vary and this needs to be acknowledged, rather than pathologised. Clearly, as has long been acknowledged in the case of heterosexual adoptive parents, a non-consanguineous relationship can be the source of powerful emotional relationships and a biological relation does not guarantee any form of connection. What is perhaps interesting about these accounts is that while hegemonic discourses of motherhood are often articulated, they are undermined equally as often. These hegemonic discourses can also be realised in ways which challenge singular meanings of concepts such as 'biology', as the next section illustrates.

'I Try to Push My Genes into Him': co-parents and the attribution of bio-status

Participants occasionally described incidents where attribution of biological relationship between co-parents and children was seen to validate their parental status. This illustrates the pervasive importance of biological status as a symbol of parenthood. While a birth mother's parental status was assured by virtue of giving birth, in contrast the recognition of co-parents was more contested. Participants recalled instances where a co-parent's parental status was affirmed by presumption of a biological contribution:

> Actually when Karl [son] was a baby [...] my cousin's wife asked what colour were his eyes, and we said yeah he has brown eyes, yeah sure you have both brown eyes she said. And then she started to laugh because she knew [laughs] what she was saying and we just took it as okay she has accepted us as parents.
>
> – Elin, Swedish participant

> It's interesting sometimes because she's really like me, she doesn't look like me at all but sometimes her personality, she'll say things or do things a little bit like me and I kind of laugh or sometimes at the school I'd collect her or whatever and people would say, when they didn't know [...] oh she's the spit of you[8] and I used to think that was really funny because she doesn't look remotely like me.
>
> – Aoife, Irish participant

Another co-parent and Swedish participant, Eva, emphasised that she played a larger role in her child's life than the father. She articulated her relationship to her child in terms of passing on physical characteristics as well as personality traits, which she referred to however in biological terms:

> E: I try to put a lot of personality into him [laughs], as much as I can, you know I try to push my genes into him [son].
>
> Rg: He's got your
>
> E: My eyelashes
>
> Rg: Eyelashes, yeah. He has got Eva's! [laughs]
>
> E: But I think it's important, if you see that he carries your genes, it's for the self feeling, especially for Mattias [donor] who doesn't, is

not such a part of Alfred [son] yet. I'm such a big part of, I'm more
a part of Alfred's life than Mattias is.
    – Eva and Regina, Swedish participants. Eva is the co-parent.

The deployment of biology as a discursive strategy in claiming her
place as a significant person in her son's life, illustrates the continued
centrality of biology to understandings of kinship. However, in this
case biology is understood not solely as biogenetic substance, but as a
symbolic reflection of a close caring relationship her contribution to
her son's upbringing. Interestingly, Eva emphasises the more central
place she occupies in her son's life, compared to his father. This is particularly notable as the father in this case was very involved and at the
time of the interview, visited the child daily. Eva asserts her position
as a primary carer, 'pushing her genes' into him by social contact.
The father's position, while that of a biological parent with regular
contact, is nonetheless constructed as the outsider in the family unit.
Thus, whereas the birth mother's parental status is taken-for-granted,
this may be less so for donors/fathers in the context of the couple
relationship.

Participants' attempts to redress power imbalance relating to differential legal and biological status expanded the symbolic deployment of
biology as a symbol on several levels. The attribution of biological
status to co-parents reinscribed the centrality of biology to understandings of relatedness, but biology was also invoked by co-parents and
others in complex discourses to validate their position.

What's in a name? The nomenclature of kinship

In a Swedish context, the possibility of adoption has recently become
available to lesbian couples in a registered partnership, whereby a co-
parent can obtain legal recognition. This is known as 'närstående'
(literally 'nearstanding') adoption, or adoption by a person with a close
relationship to the child. The issue of what to call the 'second parent'
is a complex one. The apparent ambiguity of her role is illustrated
by the variety of terminology used to refer to her in the academic
literature. For example, much of the literature originating from the US
uses a variant of the term mother: a 'non-biological mother' (Benkov,
1994; Nelson, 1996), a 'co-mother' (Muzio, 1999) and the 'Modern
Other Mother (MOM)' (Sullivan, 2001). The classic children's text by
Lesléa Newman (1990) refers to the lead character's 'two mommies'.[9]
Other authors refer to her as a 'co-parent' (Schwartz, 1998), and a

'non-biological parent' (Kenney & Tash, 1992). Similarly, there were various options utilised by the participants in this study.

Having read the academic literature and socio-cultural accounts that tended to invoke a 'two mothers' model, when embarking on fieldwork I anticipated that participants in Sweden would tend to use the term 'mother' to describe themselves. However, in interviews many co-parents referred to themselves as a 'parent', rather than 'mother'. Although they identified strongly as a parent, the term 'mother' was most often used to refer to the birth mother. This was usually a way of communicating who carried out the physical aspect of childbearing, rather than to signify a differential caregiving role. Consider the following quote from an interview with Sara, who distinguished between herself and her partner. She described herself as a 'parent' and her partner as a 'mother':

R: Do you think there's any difference then, between a mother and a parent?

S: ...well the difference is that I didn't give birth. That's the only difference. But I'm not a parent in the way a father is a parent, I don't think so at least, I don't want to be it, that way, I, I'm just neutral parent. [laughs]

– Sara, Swedish participant and co-parent

Although Sara identifies as a parent, rather than mother, she does so while rejecting the inhabitation of a male parenting space. Hayden (1995) argues that 'For women with a clear and gendered agenda for lesbian motherhood, its promise is deeply bound to the existence of a second female parent, who is neither downplayed nor de-gendered. She is not a father substitute, nor is she a gender-neutral parent; she is clearly another mother' (pp. 46–7). The excerpt by Sara above supports Hayden's (1995) claim that lesbian co-parents challenge heteronormative constructions of the family by not claiming a male space. However, whereas in an American context she suggests that this is achieved by both women appropriating the term 'mother' as an identity, in this research many co-parents described themselves as parents, rather than mothers. Despite refusing the title 'mother', Sara clearly differentiates between herself and a 'father'. A 'mother' is someone who gives birth. But this is a complicated claim, as it seems likely she would support a heterosexual adoptive woman's status as 'mother', rather than 'parent'. So perhaps the claim to a motherhood identity also rests on the number of mothers available. Or do these families represent a new 'culture of relatedness'? For Sara, this semantic difference delineates the different role in reproduction played by her partner. She does not appear to invest any other importance to it. But by distinguishing between themselves in this way, there is an investment in this difference, although what this may signify is open to interpretation. In Sara's interaction with schools, doctors, friends and extended family for example, she clearly presents herself as a parent and introduces their child as her 'daughter'. Is this less radical than a two mothers model referred to by Hayden? I would argue that it is indicative of the earlier stage of the lesbian baby boom in Sweden than in the US, where particular scripts for this family form, including the nomenclature of kinship, are less established, rather than clearly representative of a less destabilising approach to kinship. This is not to suggest however, that they will necessarily follow a trajectory resulting in the predominance of a 'two mothers' model – which already exists among some couples in the study – but may either forge new identities or frameworks, or evolve traditional formulations.

Participants also emphasised the importance of making things 'as easy as possible' for children, whose way of describing their family might be misunderstood or ridiculed. In these cases the child would initially call the birth mother 'mom' or 'mamma' and the co-parent by her first name or some variation. The child could make their own decision about this as they got older, but in the meantime it was considered easiest for the child to use terms that fitted into the dominant discourse of one mother and one father.

> Well basically he's not going to call Caoimhe [partner] mammy as well because we think it might be a bit confusing at the early stages. Like later when he's older he might decide to call her that.
> – Aisling, Irish participant and biological mother

> When she becomes three maybe she wants, maybe she says now I want to say mamma Sara and mamma Åsa instead. And that's fine because then it's her decision but we want to make it as easy as possible for her as long as she can't sort of, with language, explain what she wants.
> – Åsa, Swedish participant and biological mother

As Strathern (1993: 160) has observed, 'it is an axiomatic tenet of Euro-American kinship reckoning that everyone has parents in the biological sense, whether or not one knows who they are'. This hegemonic discourse was both incorporated into and contested in participants' narratives. An Irish participant, Eileen, had children from a previous heterosexual marriage and was a co-parent to a child with her same sex partner. She described her personal identity in relation to their child as that of a mother, but wanted their child to call her by her first name and to call her partner 'mommy':

E: I see myself as a mother.

R: OK, but you want her [child] to call you Eileen, not mother.

E: Yes, because I think it's important that she knows who her mother is.

R: OK, so what's the difference?

E: I don't know, but I just, because I'm a mother myself before Fiona [child] came along and I know how important it was for me that I was recognised as being a mother [...] so when Mary [partner] wanted to have a baby I knew how important it was for her and I think it's important for Mary to be the mother.

M: You're contradicting yourself there.

E: I know that but I mean I do a lot of mothering things, but I'm not her mother, biologically I'm not her mother.
                                      – Eileen and Mary, Irish participants

For Eileen, rejecting the name of 'mother' as a personal designation served two functions. In addition to communicating information about the identity of the birth mother to their child, it was a way of providing her partner with the space to claim 'recognition' for 'being a mother'. This was not something she viewed as undermining of her place in their child's life or as illustrative of different roles in everyday caretaking. Rather it encapsulates the complexities of navigating traditional notions of family within a context where they are reconfigured. In reference to this point, Mary, who had no objection to Eileen being called mother, commented:

I dunno like sometimes I think Eileen's a bit contradictory because she's like I'm Fiona's mum but I want her to know who her mother is and I think life is like that sometimes we have contradictions or things we haven't quite sussed out and sometimes like it sounds funny you know.

– Mary, Irish participant

This example suggests that clearly defined categorisations are not always appropriate or even desirable. Indeed, in the interviews when I asked participants about this delineation of names, contradictions often emerged which participants were comfortable with. When responding to my questions about naming and identity, participants struggled to articulate complex standpoints. While the spectre of a social/biological distinction that is a socially constructed dichotomy was clearly raised, the complex meanings attributed to new and old terms constructed in the interview narrative illustrate the process of the interview as a 'joint production' (Valentine, 2002).

A Swedish co-parent, Lisa, made the same distinction as that outlined by some participants above – she called herself a 'parent' and her partner 'the mother'. She considered her relationship to their child to be different from her partner's, although this difference was not reflected in financial contribution or carework. In Lisa's view, the question of her place in the child's life was constructed as problematic or unknown by society, but would be easily worked out between herself and the child over time:

I mean there is a difference, it's not that em it's not two mothers, it's a mother and you know another person that, I think that my relationship with Astrid [child] will be something else, but I don't think that it has to be complicated necessarily [...] in the beginning when it was more abstract you know [when] she [partner] was still expecting I'd be thinking what will my role be and, but then I think that my role will be quite uncomplicated because we are living together so you know we're going to get to know each other in a very natural way and it's more society that is asking like what is your role and [...] I don't think that she [child], perhaps when she'll be five or so, people are going to ask her and then she's gonna start thinking, asking questions, but but em, I think that instinctively she's not going to have a problem with my role.

– Lisa, Swedish participant and co-parent

In this excerpt, Lisa constructs a distinction between public and private domains. In the family realm, her relationship with her child and 'role' are unproblematic, but outside 'the home', her child may encounter questions about who, or what, Lisa 'is'. This demonstrates the difficulty of forming a new kind of relatedness in the context of a society where kinship is clearly delineated along the lines of a social/biological distinction and heteronormative family form.

However, some co-parents considered it very important to be identified as 'mother'. Anita, a Swedish participant, was very upset by the absence of a new name for herself on the birth of her daughter. Initially she was to be called Anita and identified as a second parent, whereas her partner was the 'mother'. After some time however, they decided that this was an unnecessary distinction and chose to call themselves both derivations of 'mother'. For Anita, being two mothers represented a more radical alternative than one mother and an 'extra parent':

> After the baptism ceremony we were sitting and everyone had a name, a new name, like grandmother or grandfather blah blah blah and I was Anita you know. When they were talking about me with Alexandra [daughter], there was one mummy and one Anita and I didn't accept that. I got so angry, upset, sad. I was crying a lot because I felt I'm not an Anita, I'm a very important person to her so of course I should have a name. But instead of having mother and mother for Alexandra it was mamma och [and] mamsan[10], we made it.
>
> – Anita, Swedish participant

For Anita, a new name conferred a particular status as a parent. The lack of a clear name undermined her parental role. The title 'mother' validated her place in their family. However, most co-parents appeared unperturbed on this point. Swedish women were more likely to use the terms mother, father and 'extra parent' than Irish women, but often also deployed alternative strategies in signifying the co-parent's role as a parent, for example with surnames.

Last names were also a point of discussion. In most cases, the child had the birth mother's last name, but there were exceptions. Some Irish and Swedish participants used a double-barrel name with both female parents' last names, or the co-parent's last name was used as a middle name. Several Swedish participants took their partner's name upon becoming registered partners – in one case the co-parent's name – and some Swedish couples created an entirely new name for themselves and their children:

> So we took a brand new name. And [new last name] is the name of the place where my mother grew up [...] it's kind of emotional that

my children have the name from my side of the family, as we don't have this legal or biological connection we have this, this connection. We have the same name and it's the name from my side of the family. It felt important and I definitely wanted to have the same name as my children to make this connection.

> – Beatrice, Swedish participant and co-parent

This is an example of a creative strategy for overcoming the power imbalance resulting from the non-legal recognition of co-parents. By using a last name that originated from the co-parents' family background, she appropriates generative power and establishes her place figuratively in their children's 'lineage'.

Interestingly, unique to Swedish participants was a reference to the creation of a new name specifically for co-parents by children, based on a version of their first name similar to 'mamma'. So for example, if a co-parent's first name was 'Susanne', she might be called 'Sussa' by the child. Among participants with older children, naming rested on terms that children preferred to use themselves. Particularly where children were very young, it appeared that many co-parents were still establishing what they would be called and particular denominations often changed or developed over time. Children frequently played an active role in this, by deciding themselves what they wanted to call their parents. Many participants emphasised their children's agency in deciding how to describe their parents and what names to use to refer to them:

> It wasn't anything that we had decided, they decided to call to me mamma and her Ylva [co-parent] and when they talk about her they call her their extra mam, in Swedish 'extra mamma'. Some, someone called it medmamma [co-mother], but we say extra mamma, or they have invented it.
>
> – Elin, Swedish participant

> Some of them [child's friends] go 'how come she calls you her mom and Geraldine [partner] her mom?' So I say because she's got two moms so I think a lot of the time I tend to use that more because I'm used to explaining to the other children and it's also how Lorna [daughter] describes us.
>
> – Aoife, Irish participant

Overall, Irish participants were more likely to both be called 'mom' or by their first names by children, whereas Swedish participants used the terms 'mom' and another term for the co-parent. This may be related to the norm of having involved donors in Sweden, reflective of reproductive decision-making that more strongly retains elements of a one mother, one father vision of parenthood. Among Swedish participants with involved donors children often had a last name from their father as well, illustrative of his parental role. This was occasionally described as a concession to the donor, particularly if he was not a residential parent.

> He has his father's name and Eva [partner] has her name and I have my name [...] I wanted that because if I put my name on him then Eva gets more out [excluded] and when we were thinking about this I thought that the one who is most outside, that's the father. So because of that he got his father's name so he shall be more in.
>
> – Regina, Swedish participant

This example suggests that power may reside primarily with the mother and co-parent in a Swedish context, as usually the primary carers and residential parents. While the donor/father is perhaps marginalised, the co-parent's relative power however derives from her status as a partner, in addition to carer.

Although birth mothers could claim the term 'mother' unproblematically, for co-parents this was a more complex negotiation. While the term mother is interpreted in a conventional sense as the person who gives birth, the relational meanings attributed to this term rarely differ from those of the co-parent. Even when a 'special bond' during breastfeeding and infancy was endorsed, this was viewed as something that faded over time. As the previous discussion illustrates, there were no clearcut categorisations here and certainly naming practices changed and evolved over time, particularly as children got older and themselves 'named' their parents.

Lewin (2001: 660) refers to lesbians 'who eschew the normalising nomenclature of kinship' as a challenge to normative understandings of lesbian life stages. I would argue that it is not simply the abandonment of categories that is of interest in a context where lesbian parents are struggling for legal rights. Rather, it is the creative reformulation of these categories that has much to reveal about contemporary relatedness. The expansion of kinship terminology to encompass non-biological relationships constitutes a resistant discourse. The dynamics of nomenclature in lesbian parent families suggests that naming and identity follow complex trajectories that may both repudiate and confirm heteronormative discourses of the family. It is the unstable and self-conscious nature of this dynamic that gives rise to new understandings of the content of these terms.

Sharing and caring: challenging an exclusive motherly 'niche'

The automatic conferring of motherhood to biological mothers was a striking feature of interview accounts. Thus, birth mothers potentially had the power of choosing whether to share parenting with a partner or not. This was illustrated by birth mothers' assertions of their partners' parental status, a claim not made in reverse by any of the co-parents. Whereas the co-parents' role had to be continually reiterated, that of the birth mother was taken for granted. Some birth mothers commented reflexively on their awareness of a need to include co-parents in parenting:

> I breastfed him for about six months so there was that kind of bonding that Caoimhe [partner] wouldn't have been able to have as well. But I'm very conscious of things like that, that I wouldn't want Caoimhe to feel left out and you know she's as much say, like I wouldn't have the last word, if I feel like what she said makes more sense well eventually I'll say okay [laughs] but you know things like that, I'd be very conscious that I wouldn't want her to feel left out and that it's as much her child as mine.
>
> – Aisling, Irish participant

> I'd say I've been very very much aware of, since she was born, how important it is to let Sara [partner] in all the time. It's like when she was born in the hospital, I gave Bodil [daughter] to Sara straightahead and she actually had her more in the hospital than I did, just to sort of, to show to her, because I, I've thought about it a lot during my pregnancy that I thought that just that time in the hospital when she's actually, or we thought it was a boy, when he's actually out, that's the time when it's really going to be important that I sort of prove to Sara that it's her child as well, that I don't just take a, breastfeed her and she's mine. I've thought about it a lot and it's very very important, just these first few days sort of, that I give her to Sara and let Sara be with her as much as possible and eh to make her feel that she's really a parent.
>
> – Åsa, Swedish participant

Gabb (2002) when referring to the birth mothers in her study of lesbian motherhood in the Yorkshire region, UK, states that they often 'jealously guarded "special time" such as child(ren)'s bedtime routines, seeing them as "quality time" which they did not want to relinquish, similarly Mother's Day. Such routines were always associated with 'birth mothers' and underpinned the "birth mother"-child "bond".' (p. 1). While this is undoubtedly related to the fact that her sample consisted largely of lesbian step-families, where children were conceived in a previous hetero-sexual relationship, it is notable that I did not encounter many examples of such overt 'ownership' of mothering work/traditions in this study. Although a small number of participants referred to occasions when birth mothers had exhibited a sense of possessiveness around being the primary carer, these incidents seemed to be rare. If anything, participants appeared delighted to share parenting with a partner, which is perhaps illustrated by the very small proportion of lone parents in the sample.

Among Irish participants, one couple unusually divided carework along a full-time breadwinner and full-time caregiver model. However, it was the birth mother who decided to return to work when their child was one month old, whereupon the co-parent became the full-time carer. In the following extract Gillian, the biological mother, reflects on people's expectations that she might feel 'concerned' about her partner Ciara being the primary caregiver:

> I think people respond not to whether you're close or what you look like or, it's how you behave and in the context of this situation Ciara [co-parent] behaves much more like the mother than I do, people are kind of going Gillian, is she concerned or whatever and I'm like no Ciara is much better at this sort of thing than I am and I think the fact that I was the biological mother was purely that I was willing to do it and that we were on a trajectory where we were doing it and everyone was really happy and I was really happy about it and I had a really easy pregnancy so there was never a point where I thought oh this is a ter-rible decision, this is stupid. And I also never thought oh I'm going to stay home and take care of this child because there was no way!
>
> – Gillian, Irish participant

In this excerpt, Gillian invokes a traditional understanding of the mother as a primary carer and notes that her exclusive motherhood status is undermined by the fact that her partner performs this role. For Gillian, becoming a biological parent had been an enjoyable, rather than a nec-essary aspect of parenting. She did not find her partner's decision to take on a more traditional mothering role threatening. In fact, I fre-quently noted the openness participants seemed to exhibit towards their children and the large extended kinship networks surrounding them. A striking aspect of these families was the number of people involved in raising a child. In addition to a biological mother, there were different constellations of family forms, including a female co-parent, biological father, male co-parent and the extended biological families of all these parents. There were also the close friends and 'chosen kin' of lesbian and gay friends. One participant for example referred to her son's many 'lesbian aunties'. I was struck by how open and generous participants were with their children, welcoming other people's involvement. A friend of a couple who participated in the study, was in another room caring for their child during the interview. Afterwards she commented on exactly this point, remarking that she enjoyed how unpossessive the parents were of their child, welcoming friends' involvement. Interestingly, inviting more parents into a child's life necessitated relationships with their kin as well.

> I really like the feel of it, instead of us, me feeling very isolated like in a very traditional nuclear family type structure, like I think I'd hate, you know me, I think I'd feel that's too tight. Whereas I like this, how broad it is, I like how many people are involved in his [son's] life and, you know, in terms of like three families involved in his life, just a lot of people sharing an interest and love of Seán [son], you know. So it feels very broad you know, and broad enough for him, just love and affection and attention and diverse you know, different ages, male, female, lesbian, gay, straight. I love the whole diversity of what's in his life and I think that's very extended and I think it's great, I love it.
>
> – Maeve, Irish participant

> G: We really love them [fathers] as friends and they are really near friends to us now and if something happens we always call them
>
> H: And we help each other if we have a hard time or something like that and their parents are also very involved in our kids, both Jens' and Albert's [fathers] parents are very involved in our kids, just the same as my mum and yours. So we have to relate to this big family you know. But mostly it's positive, it's very positive.
>
> – Gunilla and Hanna, Swedish participants who parent with two active fathers

However, contact with extended families occasionally presented challenges. The involvement of donors in Sweden could raise specific difficulties for co-parents, who were potentially more marginalised in a family that already consisted of 'one mother and one father'. For example, some participants referred to difficulties in having co-parents acknowledged by the donor's parents, who treated the two biological parents as a kind of couple:

> Some people, they saw Mattias [donor] and Regina [birth mother] as a couple, straight people did. Mattias' parents, they saw Regina and Mattias as a couple, they didn't see me as an equally big part of this thing. That's what I felt you know, they didn't say it you know, but that's how I felt when we visited Mattias' parents.
>
> – Eva, Swedish participant

In addition to instances whereby co-parents were not acknowledged by biological grandparents, co-parents' families of origin occasionally exhibited a certain ambivalence in 'claiming' their non-biological child as a grandchild, although this usually changed over time. As 'grand-parents' got to know a child, a strong affection often developed on both sides:

> There were tensions as I say around, at the beginning, with my family around whether they'd [children] be part of the family or not but that evaporated once they knew them if you see what I mean. It was all about, are they really blood relatives, which of course they're not.
>
> – Deirdre, Irish participant and co-parent

While negotiating kinship with extended families presented chal-lenges, it was overall viewed as a very positive aspect of participants' lives. The openness to having many people involved in a child's life, may have contributed to relieving the burden of care among inter-viewees, who often had large resources of friends and family to help out in practical terms. The isolation and feeling of being overwhelmed associated with first-time motherhood or parenting small children was no doubt ameliorated as a result.

'It's My Child': Power and vulnerability in relationship break-ups

The writing of a 'moral contract' was common practice between parties during pregnancy. Such contracts outlined the parents' (including fathers where appropriate) agreements about the sharing of custody, carework and the financial costs of raising a child and also indicated who they would like the guardian(s) to be in the event of the death of the biological mother. These signed documents technically have no legal standing but could theoretically be used as a statement of intent in the event of a break-up or the death of a biological parent. Should a biological parent die before a child reached adulthood, her extended family, or the donor, could fight for sole custody.[11] The practice of writing these contracts is an interesting example of the reflexive nature of egalitarian politics within these families. Parenting in the absence of legal recognition of one primary parent, meant that partners were forced to acknowledge not only the legal vulnerability of the co-parent in the event of bereavement, but also the possibility of breaking-up at some point in the future. All participants, when discussing these kinds of preparations were certain however, that they would not have embarked on this arrangement without complete trust that the biological parent would not attempt to use their legal status as sole parent against them.

In the following table numerical data concerning custody arrangements among participants after a relationship ended is presented:

Table 5.2   Custody arrangements after the break-up of a relationship

	Biological mother primary residential parent	Shared custody – 50/50	Co-parent primary carer	Total
Swedish	6	1	0	7
Irish	2	2	0	4
Total	8	3	0	11

Despite the common practice of writing a contract together during pregnancy, the legal vulnerability of co-parents was poignantly highlighted in these cases. The higher numbers of biological mothers retaining primary custody after separation does not reflect an unwillingness on the part of most co-parents to share custody more equitably. Rather, it illustrates the biological mother's decision-making power on this point. Nonetheless, participants on the whole reported being on good terms with their former partners, although for those who had more recently parted issues remained to be resolved. Numerous writers have documented how former lovers remain close friends and become part of 'chosen kin' networks in lesbian and gay communities (Weston, 1991;

Weeks *et al.*, 2001). Certainly, this appeared evident in several cases, where former partners continued to parent together and maintained an intimate friendship.

For example, Niamh and Evelyn, an Irish couple, not only decided to continue living together after their relationship ended, they went on to have another child. They continued to share financial resources and had recently bought a home together. The reason given for this arrangement was that even though their relationship as partners had ended, they wished to retain the same practical care and kinship arrangements. Evelyn described this when she said: *'We continue to function as a family, but we're not a couple'*. Evelyn was the birth mother of their older child. Their second child was born to Niamh 18 months after their relationship ended. The fact that they had considered the possibility of not staying together forever before having their first child, had been helpful in negotiating the ending of their relationship as partners and forging a new life together as parents:

> Because you know you just don't end up sort of like a heterosexual couple where you're having a child and you sort of haven't thought about the possibility of what will happen if we don't stay together. So I suppose from that we had actually thought about it and we had sort of at least had a thought that you know, if we should, that should happen, where we have been ourselves, em, or what would we have wished for Cormac [son], you know, in the middle of that, if we did, if we did split up. And I suppose that in some ways was a guiding, it was a guiding point for us.
>
> – Evelyn, Irish participant

Another participant, Malena, was a co-parent whose relationship with her former partner, Annika, ended when their daughter Karolina was two years old. Six years later, at the time of the interview, she regularly went on holiday with Annika, Karolina, the biological father and also Annika's current partner. In addition, Malena had another long-term relationship with a woman called Rakel after she broke up with Annika. When her relationship with Rakel ended, Karolina continued to see Rakel on a regular basis. Although she shared custody of Karolina and remained on good terms with Annika, her former partner, the separation had made Malena painfully aware of her vulnerability as a co-parent. In the months immediately following their break-up, Annika said several times during arguments 'It's my child'. Her legal status remained a source of concern even though she now felt reasonably secure that Annika would not exploit this:

> In a way, I mean, it is, just to know that I don't have any rights, makes me kind of nervous sometimes, because I have to behave, otherwise Annika [former partner] could always say, okay I don't want you anymore, leave me and my child alone and I couldn't do anything and she could do it if she wants to, she has that power and that makes me afraid and nervous sometimes, I mean I don't think she would, but just knowing that she could is scary.
>
> – Malena, Swedish participant and co-parent

Not all participants were equally clear about the role they would play in their children's lives after the breakdown of a relationship. This is at least partly attributable to changing discourses about lesbian parenting with LGBT communities over time. Agneta, a Swedish participant, had two children in a former relationship. These children were among the oldest in the study. Both she and her former partner were biological mothers and their children were aged two and four years old at the time of the breakup. After their separation, Agneta began to doubt for a time whether she wanted to play a full parental role in the life of her non-biological child, but this passed. Her former partner, Selma, never doubted her parental status regarding both their children.

> Not from Selma [former partner], she has been very strong all the time but I think I had a period of my life when I was em not so sure, it wasn't like I didn't want her to be my daughter, but I wasn't so sure that our bond was so, was strong enough. I think I was a little bit confused. But now I think that, now it's no, she is my daughter.
>
> – Agneta, Swedish participant

On the whole however, co-parents emphasised their unambivalent sense of commitment to their children and vulnerability because access and guardianship were not legally secure. Catherine, an Irish participant, felt that she had stayed in a relationship with the biological mother of her children long after it should have ended, because of her feelings of vulnerability as a co-parent, with no legal recognition. She needed to wait until the children were older and actively acknowledging her place in their life, before she felt comfortable leaving the relationship and security of a shared residential home. The children now stay with her half-time. When the children were infants, she was seriously ill for a time and during that period of her life, wondered whether her presence in their early life would have any meaning for the children if she died. A biological mother's life and death might be a source of curiosity and affect children' identity as adults, because of the way in which motherhood is continually signified as a central relationship. However, as a co-parent she felt at risk of being erased from the children's lives because of dying before they were old enough to remember her:

> I think the thing is from the beginning, I would have been worried, especially when I was ill you know that I'd just die and they'd forget me anyway, that there wouldn't be the things there that would prop you up and support you in being mum and at the same time if we'd have split up when they were any younger you know, would that have been, would it all have been maintained. It wasn't till the actual children, I was sure of the children's own response, their own, assured in their love or whatever, that then that made me very different yeah, the choice you know, that you do have the choice of whether or not I am their mother in a way. They don't have that choice with Jean [former partner], but they do have that choice with me and so it makes it even more powerful if they do choose that.
>
> – Catherine, Irish participant and co-parent

In this above extract, Catherine constructs the biological tie as unquestioned and therefore powerful, whereas the co-parent's status is characterised by choice. However, biological mothers were also vulnerable in terms of non-recognition of co-parents, in that they could not assume that their former partners would continue to reliably fulfil parental responsibilities, for example financial contributions, in the event of a separation. Thus, power was not simply uni-directional and exerted by the biological mother 'over' the co-parent. Veronika, a Swedish participant and biological mother, had recently split up from her co-parenting partner, soon after the birth of their son. They were still coming to terms with their separation and trying to work out what role her former partner, Ingeborg, would play in the child's life. Veronika felt disappointed by the reduced role that her former partner has played in her son's life since their break up. Ingeborg visits once or twice a week to spend time with him, but does not contribute financially – she is on a very low income and therefore says that she simply cannot afford to pay any maintenance at this time. So Veronika and the father share the costs. Ingeborg's parents however see themselves very much as grand-parents and visit at least once a fortnight:

> I've asked her [Ingeborg] how it's gonna be and I've said that you are going to lose the contact with him, I think so, but then she gets very angry and says no I'm not, so let's just wait and see. It's hard to know what she is going to be to him. Before she was his parent, that was, I thought so, but now I don't know. It's really confusing.
>
> – Veronika, Swedish participant and biological mother

Participants' narratives concerning the experience of separation and negotiating custody emphasise issues of inequality and vulnerability. Although complete trust may be a feature of relationships, the realities of separation are a stark reminder of the power difference between co-parents and their former partners. Power does not reside solely with biological mothers however, who upon separation must also depend on co-parents to fulfil their obligations in the absence of a legal frame-work that requires them to do so. Nonetheless, after a relationship ends, co-parents are dependent on their former partner's goodwill to ensure regular contact with their children. Unlike biological mothers, a co-parent's place in a child's life is not continuously validated in society and is therefore more vulnerable to displacement.

Conclusion

The salience of biology to lesbian parenting discourses illustrates its continued importance to contemporary notions of kinship, even in contexts where the symbolic value of biology to concepts of related-ness is also undermined. Biology therefore becomes a signifier of a power imbalance between partners in parenting couple arrangements. However, the relative unimportance often ascribed to consanguinity in lesbian parenting desires, means that this power imbalance may be externally imposed (by researchers for example), rather than a necessary function of couple relationships where one partner is the biological mother. The potential undermining of the parental status of co-parents as a result of her non-legal status often fails to invalidate their relationships in the everyday practices of lesbian parents and their children. Power is certainly a feature of lesbian parenting nar-ratives, but it does not necessarily take the form of tension and con-flict with regard to biology in couple relationships that might be expected.

The appropriation of biology as a signifier of relatedness by lesbian parents suggests that 'substance' and 'code', or biology and the social regulation of kinship, are not simply distinctive arenas, but rather are made meaningful in relation to one another. The discrete and singular categorisation of biology and the law is challenged in a context where both elements may be discursively constructed in myriad ways. Contradictions and diversity in lesbian parent narratives suggest that biology, parenting and the law are concepts that may be invested with diverse meanings and mutually constituted in the complex terrain of cultures of relatedness. However, while lesbian parents may often reinvent and resist heteronormative concepts of kinship, alternative discourses regarding biology and relatedness are not exclusive to lesbian families. The concomitant changes in family patterns among heterosexual parents, for example the growth in step-families, are reflective of challenges to the centrality of biology in families across the spectrum of society. In addition, it is clear from the interview narratives that lesbian parents may also appropriate conventional discourses.

Understandings of lesbian and gay kinship as 'unique' versus 'conventional' echo discussions of the transgressive/assimilative potential of lesbian and gay parenting. As has been argued here, the complex intersections of context and identity require more nuanced analyses of lesbian parenthood. Rather than consider whether lesbian parents reinvoke heteronormative discourses of kinship in the creation of their families and family practices, it is more useful to explore the intersection of culture, politics and subjectivity that influence their choices, decisions and possibilities.

It will be interesting to see if the laws conferring potential legal recognition of co-parents in Sweden influence lesbian parenting discourses. Will second-parent adoption make any difference to the enactment of these relationships? While legal recognition is clearly both of political importance and a practical necessity for co-parents and their children, this research suggests that families are as much what they 'do', as what they are defined to be. The meanings attributed to motherhood are diverse and contested. There is no one universal mothering identity, although there are hegemonic discourses which can be acquired or repudiated. In negotiating the social regulation of kinship and the biological 'tie', lesbian parents highlight the socially constructed nature of these categorisations. The dynamics of sameness/difference with regard to lesbian parent practices and experiences will be explored further in the following chapter.

6
Challenging Heteronormativity?: Gender Flexibility and Lesbian Parenting

In a sense, this chapter is a return to the questions that this book began with, as it explores notions of sameness and difference in relation to lesbian parent families. As noted in Chapter 1, previous research on non-heterosexual families has largely focused on the children of lesbian and gay parents. The majority of this research has been used to refute homophobic myths about lesbian and gay parenting. Typically, these studies have concluded that there is little or no difference between the children raised in LGBT-headed families and children raised by heterosexuals. This research has been used effectively to counteract homophobic myths about these families and has been politically strategic. For example, it has been utilised in custody cases where an LGBT parent has been at risk of losing custody or access due to homophobic assumptions about their children's well-being. However, more recently researchers have been critical of the impulse in research to 'prove' that LGBT parents are 'just like' heterosexual parents. Firstly, it has been argued that this 'assimilative' research emerges (albeit understandably) from a highly defensive position that ultimately endorses heteronormative ideals by implicitly taking a particular version of heterosexual parenting as the normative standard against which all families should be judged. Secondly, this approach serves to deny positive differences that may exist between LGBT and other families. More recently, some authors have focused on such positive differences in the form of a 'transformative' model of lesbian parenting. However, this perspective has also been criticised for neglecting diversity in research samples. Another methodological criticism of both perspectives is that they draw on a positivist tradition in which gender and sexuality are treated as external variables that exist beyond discourse. Finally, I would argue that research in this area rarely addresses the role of the state in mediating lesbian women's possibilities for the equitable division of labour. In this chapter, I will examine these sameness/difference debates and problematise both assimilative and transformative models of lesbian parenting. These issues will be explored with reference to empirical material on the gendered division of labour and the pedagogical practices of gender in lesbian households.

The assimilative model of lesbian parenting

There is a long history of discrimination by the legal system against lesbian (and gay) parents. Typically, lesbians (and gay men) who came out after having children in the context of heterosexual relationships could expect to lose custody if challenged by their former heterosexual partner. Although the judicial system has improved enormously in this respect, it still remains a factor for many LGBT parents.[1] The concern expressed by many Irish participants regarding their potential vulnerability in a custody battle was outlined in Chapter 5.

In this context, the substantial body of research indicating that the development trajectory of children with LGBT parents is the same as children raised by heterosexuals has played an important role. Studies comparing children raised by lesbian and heterosexual mothers repeatedly find little or no distinction in the child's gender identity, sex role socialisation, or personal sexual orientation (see for example Golombok *et al.*, 1983; Tasker & Golombok, 1997). This research has repeatedly emphasised similarities between LGBT families and heterosexual families, and in some cases the superior performance of lesbian parents in terms of parenting, social support and family members' psychological adjustment. In Patterson's (1992) comprehensive review of outcome studies, she reported that children of lesbians rated comparably to children of heterosexual mothers on all measures of psychological adjustment, including separation-individuation, emotional stability, moral judgment, object relations, gender identity, and sex-role behaviour. The Swedish SOU commission report (2001: 10) also concluded that a lesbian or gay identity does not affect a parent's ability to provide children with a nurturing and caring upbringing.

There have been numerous methodological criticisms of many of these studies. Some of the research is based on psychological tests that are highly problematic in terms of their cultural and androcentric biases. Many studies have largely focused on children born into a heterosexual arrangement, which some have argued prevents the research findings from being generalised onto children born to openly lesbian and gay parents. Although they are supportive of lesbian and gay parenting, Stacey & Biblarz (2001) are also critical of the prevailing trends in research in this area, partly on methodological grounds. They argue that hetero-sexism has hampered the progress of research on lesbian and gay parent families. They suggest that there may in fact be many positive differ-ences between these and other families but that researchers have been afraid to acknowledge difference due to the prevailing homophobic social climate and that this is the reason for the proliferation of studies emphasising these children's similarity to their peers raised in hetero-sexual families. They point to findings indicating difference among lesbian parents' children that have been downplayed in research, such as departure from gender-based norms in adolescent sexual behaviour (Tasker & Golombok, 1997). It is their view, based on an assessment of the literature, that 'the sexual orientation of mothers interacts with the gender of children in complex ways to influence gender preferences and behaviour' (p. 170). They further argue that researchers are reluctant to theorise such findings. Interestingly, both positions – the homophobic/sceptic approach and the sympathetic 'rigorous' approach – rest on a positivist view of knowledge production and treat gender and sexuality as variables that are 'acquired' by children independently of discourse, rather than as sets of complex ideas and discourses in a post-structuralist sense (Hicks, 2005).

So how *is* difference theorised in research on lesbian families? Clarke (2002) argues that the there are four dimensions of difference that inform research and theorising on lesbian parenting. These perspectives con-struct lesbian parenting as: (i) no different from heterosexual parenting; (ii) different from heterosexual parenting and deviant; (iii) different from heterosexual parenting and transformative; and (iv) different from heterosexual parenting only because of oppression. The second category is exemplified by a publication from The Christian Institute in the UK (Morgan, 2002), which argues that having lesbian or gay parents is detrimental to children's well-being. The poster campaign accom-panying the publication asked 'If you died, who would they give your children to?' and was accompanied by a photograph of a gay couple, Barry Drewitt and Tony Barlow, who conceived twins via surrogacy in the US in 1999. The publication coincided with UK government dis-cussion regarding the revision of adoption laws to include same sex couples. This publication was soundly critiqued by Hicks (2005), whose edited volume (1998) containing personal accounts of lesbian and gay fostering and adoption was used by Morgan to substantiate some of her claims. Similar publications have been critiqued in academic circles for their anti-lesbian discourse and lack of academic rigour (e.g. Herek, 1988).

The fourth category outlined by Clarke (2002), which constructs lesbian and gay parenting as different from heterosexual parenting only because of oppression, argues that lesbian parents' difference is not chosen; rather it is socially imposed through oppression. According to Stacey (1996), the only difference between the children of lesbian and heterosexual parents derives 'directly from legal discrimination and social prejudice' (p. 135). However, this means that ultimately lesbian and heterosexual families are the same. These two categories are important in that they are illustrative of the widespread prejudice against these families, albeit in different ways. The 'different and deviant' approach itself constitutes a form of homophobic aggression against lesbian and gay families. The fourth model refers to the existence of discrimination. Nonetheless, the vast majority of academic research in this area falls into the first category of Clarke's typologies, supporting the claim that these children are no different from the children of heterosexuals.

This latter research has played a vital role in challenging commonplace homophobic assumptions about these families. The production of publications such as Morgan's (2002) by researchers associated with organisations that are ideologically opposed to LGBT parenting and that are produced at politically sensitive times, is indicative of the widespread prejudice that remains. It also illustrates the need for rigorous, informed research that can effectively counter homophobic myths and arguments with regard to LGBT parenting. Some of the authors of these studies have themselves called for new forms of research about LGBT parenting (e.g. Patterson, 1992; Kitzinger & Coyle, 1995) that go beyond assessing the well-being of children in these families.

What I have termed the 'assimilative' perspective, where the super normative performance of LGBT parents is emphasised, is clearly politically expedient. But it may also reinforce an acceptance of the ideal (hetero)norm against which all families must be measured, in terms of family practices and configurations. Queer theorists have placed considerable emphasis on the importance of subversion of heteronormative ideals. The idea that LGBT families are no different from any other family could therefore be interpreted as a failure, by conforming to heteronormative standards. Early lesbian feminist work critiqued the role of motherhood as a source of women's oppression (Firestone, 1971; Rich, 1976). More recently, feminist writers have begun to acknowledge and explore the complexity of women's experiences of motherhood, in both its positive and negative aspects.

However, lesbians who choose parenthood face a new form of criticism from within the LGBT community – they may be viewed as conforming to prevalent notions regarding the importance of biological kin and children to what constitutes a 'real' family (Warner, 1994, 1999). Weston's (1991) work in a US context suggested that lesbian and gay kinship is characterised by configurations where biological ties are decentered and choice, or love, becomes the defining feature of kin relationships. In a British context, Weeks *et al.* (2001), argue that LGBT people's kinship networks are increasingly characterised by an emphasis on choice, with friendship forming the basis of long-lasting relationships. Similarly, the existence of non-biological co-parents challenges biological ties as the basis for parenthood. Arguments for the distinctiveness of a lesbian and gay kinship system often privilege non-biological ties as the more radical queer alternative. While recognising that transitions to adulthood in Western societies are intricately bound up with a parenting role, in a context where LGBT parents are largely unsupported, lesbians who become parents are hardly conformist. Malone & Cleary (2002) suggest that this emphasis on 'families we choose' in recent postmodern literature may also be a reflection of 'America's obsession with individual voluntarism' (p. 280). Gabb (2002), who interviewed lesbian parents in the Yorkshire region of the UK, found that most of her respondents relied on biological kin and extended family support, as opposed to the 'friends as kin' model reported in other studies. This is an area that requires further exploration in research. Certainly, participants in my study often reported improved familial relationships upon becoming a parent, with children often acting as a 'bridge' between participants and their families of origin. This did not however mean that their biological kin were the only important participants in their family lives. One respondent for example referred to her son's many 'lesbian aunties'. Gabb suggests a move towards a notion of 'family as friends', rather than construct 'families we choose', as the more 'radical' kinship notion. The two concepts are not diametrically opposed; rather together they suggest the complexity of contemporary kinship networks.

Another critique of the prevailing research focus in this area is that it ignores the role of sexuality in these families, effectively de-sexing the queer, who becomes a 'safe', asexual parent (Warner, 1999). This perspective rests on a socially constructed binary between kinship and desire. According to this binary, 'kinship' (particularly state-recognised forms) is associated with heteronormativity and lesbian parents with children represent the social realisation of these values, whereas the radical queer resists all attempts at 'normalisation'. This is also often implicit in arguments made by queer activists opposed to lesbian and gay marriage for example. This dichotomy therefore renders lesbian desire within the family invisible and provides a prescriptive understanding of what constitutes resistance. As Malone & Cleary (2002) point out, previous research on lesbian and gay parenting that emphasises similarity between these families and heterosexual ones, does so 'in a manner that promotes an erasure of the internal **difference** within the family and by neutering the parents' (p. 283, bold added). Certainly the obsession with the effects of lesbian and gay people's sexuality on their ability to function as parents, invokes the spectre of the queer 'Other', whose 'dangerous' sexuality may damage the child. In particular, the conflation of a gay male identity with paedophilia in homophobic rhetoric is one illustration of this. It may be the case that lesbians are perhaps marginally more acceptable as parents than gay men due to the traditional relegation of women to the private sphere and the essentialist construction of womanhood as caring nurturing femininity. The denial of internal difference within the family fails to address the potential power differential between biological mothers and co-parents in lesbian-headed families, where only biological kin relationships are recognised by the state.

Sedgewick (1994) suggests that the contemporary lesbian and gay movement has theorised gender and sexuality 'as distinct though intimately entangled axes of analysis' (p. 72). To some extent, this has been a necessary strategy, exemplified through the assertion that a lesbian, *as a woman*, desires another woman; that a gay man desires another man *as a man*. This assertion has been important in the context of a history which collapses gender and sexuality as categories, suggesting that anyone who desires a man must therefore be feminine and anyone who desires a woman must therefore be masculine. Yet as she points out, recent strands of contemporary psychoanalysis that pathologise an atypical gender identification do so by distinguishing between gender and sexuality in much the same way as lesbian and gay movements have. She argues that one problem with this way of distinguishing between gender and sexuality is that while it deconstructs the necessary association between gender and sexual object-choice, it renaturalises gender. However necessary this assertion has been to challenge the idea that gender and sexual preference are indistinguishable, Sedgewick (1994) suggests that this strategy may for example leave the effeminate boy as the haunting abject – 'this time as the haunting abject of gay thought itself' (p. 72). This is because it reinforces a normative notion of gender as a particular masculine or feminine performance correlating to a particular sexed body. So for example an 'acceptable' gay man may be attracted to men, but remains a 'masculine' man. I would argue that butch/femme couples are often implicitly stigmatised in the assimilative discourse on lesbian parenting in much the same way that the effeminate boy becomes the 'abject other', as Sedgewick suggests. Taking a Butlerian approach to gender, whereby gender is not inscribed upon a prior sexed body, rather the sexed body is itself discursively constituted via 'acts of repetition', enables a consideration of gender discourses among lesbian parents that does not renaturalise gender.

While the assimilative approach has in many ways proved useful politically, it is also problematic. In addition to the reinforcement of the hegemony of heteronormative family ideals that it often provides, it relies on an erasure of sexuality within the family. This is not to deny that there may be overwhelming similarities between lesbian and heterosexual parent families. My intention is rather to problematise the recourse to normative performance as a discursive resource. The assimilative approach in research also downplays the possibility of these families engaging in challenges to heteronormativity that may be realised in unconventional discourses and practices. The next section explores this point further in relation to perspectives emphasising the transformative potential of lesbian parenting.

The transformative model of lesbian parenting

In contrast to the assimilative approach, a new model of lesbian parenting – the transformative model – has recently emerged. Research falling into this category suggests that not only is a lesbian identity compatible with effective parenting, but that lesbian and gay couples may be more likely to engage in family practices characterised by equality (Dunne, 1998a; Heaphy *et al.*, 1999); that in this way LGBT parents can be positive role models for all parents (Dunne, 1998a, 1998b); and that queer families challenge kinship systems based on biological ties (Weston, 1991; Weeks *et al.*, 2001).

Dunne's (1998a) work is perhaps the most well-known example of this kind of research. In a study of lesbian couples with children, she found that childcare and housework was shared equally among partners and that they found new alternatives for achieving this. Couples in her study chose to work part-time hours so that they could contribute equally to domestic responsibilities, rather than relying on a breadwinner/caregiver or dual-earner model. Numerous other studies

have documented findings similar to Dunne's regarding egalitarian practices among lesbian couples (e.g. Blumstein & Schwartz, 1983; Peplau &
Cochran, 1990; Kurdek, 1993). However, Dunne's research departs from
the body of work examining the egalitarian division of labour among
lesbian parents in two ways. Firstly, the methodology deployed in her
study is particularly appropriate for addressing the research question
– Dunne used time-diary studies, as opposed to interviews. Clearly time
diary studies are a more accurate method of ascertaining 'who does what'
in a particular household. The second departure of her study in the literature is her theoretical interpretation of her findings. She argued that her
results indicated that lesbian couples were less confined by traditional
gender divisions in relationships and that this facilitated a particular
creativity that could lead to more egalitarian family practices.

Some authors have expressed doubts about generalisations concerning the challenges to heteronormativity posed by lesbian and gay
parents. Hicks (2002) for example states: 'Whilst any challenge to the
heternormative and heterosexist order is to be welcomed, the idea that
all gay parents represent this and that their children acquire it is rather
utopian'. Lewin (2001) has also been critical of the notion that lesbian
and gay families are particularly 'queer'. She suggests that this illustrates the pointlessness of essentialised identities: 'The impulses that
move lesbians and gay men toward benign domesticity also animate
their psychic lives, and these are no different from those that shape the
emotions of nongay people[...]In the end, lesbian and gay love, family
life and domesticity are so dull that they barely fit the label "queer".
This very dullness is worthy of note, for it finally makes all essentialised identities the nonsensical creations of bigots' (2001: 661). This
perspective is interesting in that it could perhaps challenge the idea
that the sameness approach is purely assimilative – for Lewin, this
standpoint undermines the homophobic view that there are essentialist differences between lesbian and gay families and other family
forms. Nonetheless, it ignores the alternative possibilities of lesbian
parenting and the literature addressing this. I disagree with her assertion that lesbian and gay motivations to parenting and domestic life
are no different to those of heterosexuals – this may be the case, but it
has not been ascertained. It appears that the pressures that heterosexual women face, particularly those in long-term relationships, to
have children are not experienced in the same way by lesbian women,
who are struggling for social support for their parenting, rather than
against social pressure to become parents. Participants in my research
often referred to the assumption on the part of family and friends that

they would never become a mother after their coming out. Clearly, social expectations for heterosexual and lesbian women regarding becoming a parent are different.

Another potential problem with a normative model of lesbian parenting based on the transformative model, is that it may place even more pressure on LGBT people to be 'outstanding' parents. As a group that is already under scrutiny, they must not only be 'as good as' heterosexual parents, but even more 'perfect'. Similar to the assimilative perspective, this approach takes heterosexual families as the norm, thus implicitly reinforcing heteronormative hegemony. While not as blatant as a homophobic approach which construes LGBT families as inherently deficient compared to straight ones, there is nonetheless a potential for a more subtle heterosexist bias in research which promotes an upbeat view of lesbian families as ones that display their own unique strengths. It places these families under considerable pressure to live up to a particular ideal in order to justify their existence, rather than directly challenge the homophobic assumptions that suggest they are inadequate parents in the first place. Participants in my research referred to the scrutiny that they experience as lesbian parents – they are subjected to extra surveillance because society doubts their ability to parent effectively:

S: [...] being a lesbian parent, it also put some kind of higher pressure on the parenthood, because you really have to be a good parent when you are a lesbian parent, you have in a way to show them that we are really good parents, nobody tells us but it's something in our minds, we know that we, we have the eyes on us

H: All the time

S: people at the preschool, doctors and nurses, they have an extra eye for us. Are they really, and what about the girl, is she alright, you know? And it's something that they never say it, but we can feel that we have eyes on us and have to be good parents
                                        – Sara & Helena, Swedish participants

It is important to note that the transformative model of lesbian parenting is based on an egalitarian politics, as opposed to a conservative heteronormative model that delineates gendered divisions of labour or gender performativity along traditional lines. In this way, the transformative model renders heteronormativity visible by problematising gendered power dynamics. As the quote from Sara and Helena above suggests, many lesbian parents are aware of the 'extra eye' upon them. It appears that any non-normative parent, including lesbian parents, have to be not only as good as, but even better than heterosexual parents. One problem with utilising the transformative model as a political strategy is that if lesbian parenting only becomes acceptable on the basis of conforming to a particular egalitarian ideal, a double standard which takes heterosexual parenting as a 'right', in contrast to which lesbian parenting must be continually justified, remains.

In addition, a transformative-normative model can serve to silence the complexity of lesbian women's experiences of power and difference in relationships. As Malone & Cleary (2002: 274) point out, 'The ideal of equality masks issues of power and difference and seems to participate in dispossessing lesbians of any taint of untoward sexuality (any pleasure and danger that might invade the happy home)'.[2] This relates to the point made earlier about the desexualising or 'neutering' of lesbian parents. Butch/femme couples for example may become Otherised – either explicitly or implicitly – within this particular approach. Nestle (1992) and Munt (1998) have pointed out that butch/femme identities undermine the rigid distinction between heterosexuality and homosexuality. In addition, butch lesbians performing masculinity and femme lesbians performing femininity challenge the notion that a particular gender relates to a specific sexed body and 'opposite' sex desire. I would further argue that butch women who may act as masculine 'role models' for example can challenge conventional gender discourses in new ways. It is also important to note that butch/femme is a diverse category, incorporating a wide variety of behaviours and practices. A couple who identify as butch/femme do not necessarily engage in an unequal division of labour. While often implicitly construed as retrogressive 'unacceptable' lesbians by research favouring the transformative model on the one hand, butch/femme couples are also liable to be derided as the apotheosis of the heternormative system and as proof that lesbians do not follow 'more equal' trajectories in their personal relationships than heterosexuals. However, butch/femme may potentially subvert heteronormative discourses in complex ways.

Gabb (2002) raises some provocative questions regarding what she perceives to be prevailing trends in contemporary research on lesbian parent families. In contrast to previous studies whose research findings illustrated the egalitarian nature of lesbian parent families, she found quite different results in her research on lesbian families living in the Yorkshire region of the UK. Interestingly, childcare and housework were not shared equally among the lesbian couples in her study and biological mothers often 'jealously guarded "special time" such as child(ren)'s bedtime routines, seeing them as "quality time" which they did not want to relinquish' (p. 3). Clearly this is related to her research sample, which consists almost entirely of lesbian stepfamilies. Claims regarding the egalitarianism of lesbian stepfamilies in comparison to heterosexual stepfamilies have not been made in the transformative model literature. The egalitarian model claims based on previous research that she refers to predominantly originate from studies of families with children that are conceived in the context of an openly lesbian lifestyle. There were only three AI families in her study, with most children conceived in previous heterosexual relationships. Nonetheless, her research does raise an important point – that a lesbian identity does not necessarily guarantee equality in a relationship. I would argue that this point undermines essentialist accounts of lesbian experience – not all lesbian relationships are characterised by equality, any more than all heterosexual relationships are characterised by inequality. But this does not in my view invalidate the interesting insights regarding gender and sexuality that have been raised by Dunne (1998a) and Oerton (1998). Indeed, in her work Gabb does not attempt to undermine research findings in previous studies, but rather to argue for greater diversity in sampling frames.

Oerton (1998: 79) argues that 'virtually no woman escapes the processes and practices which constitute women (even lesbians) as having a **gendered** relationship to family and household work'. Taking the role of the housewife as a starting point, she argues that although analyses often assume that lesbians cannot be housewives, due to the absence of a male head of household, this approach is limited in that it ignores or disguises the caring and household work done by lesbians for family and kin. She suggests that lesbians, like heterosexual women, do work for their families and in their homes, and must be analysed as gendered subjects, rather than non-heterosexuals. The assumption that lesbians can be analytic subjects only in terms of their sexuality, obscures the ways in which sexuality and gender are interrelated. I would further argue that to ignore the significance of gender to lesbian experience is to render a construction of lesbians as Other, by reinforcing the notion that the category of woman is inherently heterosexual. This theorising of the interaction between sexuality and gender is an important development. The debate has shifted from the effect of gender on sexualities, to the influence of alternative sexual identities on constructions of gender. When applied to the area of lesbian and gay parenting, this theoretical shift transforms the kinds of research questions formulated about queer families.

The ways in which lesbian couples negotiate parenthood may be quite distinct from many heterosexual couples. Unlike many heterosexual parents, lesbians who choose motherhood are raising children in the context of relationships where dichotomous gendered parenting scripts are potentially reconfigured, if not absent. As the current wave of lesbian parents building families are a pioneering generation, they may be less constrained by normative ideologies. The construction of new family forms reflects the interaction between wider societal scripts and the creative potential of pioneering families. Malone & Cleary (2002: 274) suggest that 'Isn't queering really the moment when a norm is not exactly repudiated, but rather subverted – if not ironically (as in Butler), then through being realised slightly askew? If so, this would mean that we take up gender and sexualities with lesbian families differently'. In the following sections, I will argue that the participants in this research both subvert and, occasionally, (re)produce heteronormative discourses in complex ways. Rather than 'slightly askew' realisations and articulations of gender, instances of reinventions of gender dynamics are noted, in ways that could be either transformative or heteronormative, or both, but where gender relations are always contested.

The division of labour in lesbian households

The idea that same-gender couples are more likely to share housework equally has been around for some time. Research on lesbian couples has shown that they tend to divide household labour on an equal basis (e.g. Blumstein & Schwartz, 1983; Peplau & Cochran, 1990; Kurdek, 1993). Most of these studies have focused on lesbian couples without children. Studies of heterosexual couples with children have often found that the transition to parenthood is typically associated with a movement towards increasing specialisation of roles (e.g. Gregson & Lowe, 1994; Sullivan, 2000; Sundström & Duvander, 2002). In a study of 26 lesbian couples' division of labour, Patterson (1995a) found that although couples shared housework and decision-making tasks equally, some biological mothers reported greater involvement in childcare and correspondingly co-parents reported spending longer hours in paid employment. The families where couples participated equally in childcare and paid labour reported greater levels of satisfaction with the division of labour. The author concluded that even under the pressure of child-rearing responsibilities, lesbian couples seemed to maintain relatively egalitarian division of household responsibilities in a number of areas. In this way, lesbian couples with children resembled lesbian couples without children.

Several studies have found that both biological and nonbiological lesbian mothers were more involved in childcare than heterosexual fathers (e.g. Chan *et al.*, 1998). Tasker and Golombok (1998), studied the role of co-parents in children's lives by comparing the role of co-mothers in 15 British lesbian mother families with the role of resident father in two different groups of heterosexual families (43 families where the study-child was conceived through donor insemination, and 41 families where the child had been conceived 'naturally'). Their results indicated that co-parents played a more active role in daily caretaking than did most fathers.

Most Swedish and Irish participants described an equal division of labour in their relationships. It is interesting to note that an egalitarian division of labour did not necessarily imply that both partners performed the same tasks equally. While participants referred to equal divisions of labour, they often expressed a preference for particular tasks. However, these preferences did not usually fall along traditional gendered lines (as in many heterosexual relationships or perhaps butch/ femme dichotomies). For example, one partner might prefer ironing, while the other enjoyed cooking. Both are stereotypically 'women's labour' with the same (lack of) value attributed to them in society. But rather than share household tasks along a rigid distribution of equal participation in all work, participants were capable in all areas and chose their preferences in ways that were not based on gender dichotomies. Sullivan (1996) found a similar pattern of flexible division of labour based on preference among 34 lesbian couples, where equitable practices among couples was the norm. However, there were a minority of couples in her study (n = 5) who divided labour along a primary breadwinner/primary caregiver model. She concluded that the experience of this minority of couples highlighted the powerful negative effect of economic dependency on women who are full-time caregivers. The division of labour among these couples was linked to the relative earning power of the women and complex factors such as one woman in the couple being more highly motivated to become a parent than her partner.

Most Swedish and Irish participants in this research described their division of labour in egalitarian terms. Katarina, a Swedish participant, stated: 'We share the housework very equally...we try to do as little as possible, both of us!' She later qualified this statement by explaining that both she and her partner had an aversion to work that was stereotypically female and resisted expectations that they should conform to social expectations regarding housework. She attributed this in part to her experience of living in a lesbian lifestyle, which she felt had made her aware of traditional gender roles in relationships:

> I think both of us have a kind of problem with ordinary housework, like we both feel uncomfortable to do this ordinary female work, neither feels comfortable to be the housekeeper. [...] I don't have to play this female role [with partner]. But sometimes I miss it too [...] it's a role that you are growing up with, that you know that you are nice, cute, that people like when you play the role so you get attention when you play it. I think I have found it very positive about being aware of those different roles and that I have learned a lot that other people don't seem to think about.
>
> – Katarina, Swedish participant

Although the majority of Swedish and Irish participants followed an egalitarian pattern of preference-based division of labour, there were exceptions (n = 4). An interesting example, are Julie and Deirdre, an Irish couple who had three children, including one foster child. Their current division of labour followed a more traditional full-time breadwinner/part-time caregiver model. This is particularly striking as both women had been involved in radical feminist activism and expressed a strong awareness of gender inequalities. At the time of the interview, Julie performed more of the everyday household work, while Deirdre referred to herself jokingly as more of a *'sugar mommy'*, in that she was the main breadwinner, worked much longer hours in paid employment and performed fewer of the day to day chores. They described their current arrangement as similar to a *'modern-day heterosexual situation'* and Julie said of Deirdre that *'she does more than my father ever did'*.

Their division of labour had changed more than once during the course of their relationship. For example, Deirdre did the majority of carework required for their foster child, Mary, who came to live with them as an adolescent. Mary was extremely disturbed when she moved into their home and required an enormous amount of care and attention. They also had two infant children at the time and decided that Julie (the birth mother) would be their main caregiver, while Deirdre concentrated more on Mary's needs. So for some years, while they focused on different areas, they both made significant contributions to the emotional and practical demands of raising their three children.

However, Mary had moved out as an adult, Julie had begun to work part-time and had more household responsibilities, while Deirdre moved into an area that was very lucrative and required full-time or almost full-time hours. This imbalance was something that they were aware of and actively negotiated. While on the one hand, Julie was sometimes upset because Deirdre did less cooking than she did, she also felt that Deirdre behaved unconventionally in a gendered sense by being less restricted to feminine norms regarding responsibilities for housework and Julie respected this in a woman. This is obviously contradictory, in that Deirdre's ability to avoid cooking and cleaning were premised on relying either on Julie to do it or on eating out, or by hiring a cleaner. They were both adamant that they would not tolerate this behaviour in a man, but that in general they were satisfied with the division of labour in their relationship:

D: We have gone up and down, we have changed around our roles at different times like when Mary was here I did most of the caring for her and Julie didn't but then you did have the other kids certainly [...]. It does feel easy, it does feel like we choose what we do.

J: [who has been murmuring agreement throughout] Definitely. And we talk about it as well I think, I mean that's I suppose like you say because the option's there we've always talked about it. So for example Deirdre O'Connell will not clean, she will not clean, that's it. I was led into this very early on in my life, really.

D: I'll pay cleaners, I don't mind paying cleaners.

J: She'll gladly pay a cleaner which, there have been times in our lives when we've had cleaners. I hate having cleaners. I hate cleaning yeah, but I hate having cleaners more. I would rather do all the cleaning than have to be subjected to a stranger coming into my house and cleaning up my shit

D: Whereas I don't have any problem with this

J: And my having to run round knowing that she's going to come in at ten o'clock tomorrow morning, having to spend the evening before running around and tidying and cleaning the house before she does it.

D: I don't have a problem with that either! [laughs]

J: [...] She [Deirdre] really, she doesn't cook except when she wants to cook, when she feels like cooking, when she fancies cooking, which is usually on a weekend. So often during the weekend, Deirdre will cook up a big slap up meal and it's lovely, but she won't cook when she doesn't want to cook. And I think I respect, I like that, I love that, I think that's powerful in a woman, I think that's absolutely wonderful, great, why not, you know to have that choice and to make the choice, that's wonderful. So I get pissed off with it as well, I get pissed off with always having to be the one who does the cooking, to think, maybe think what are we going to have for dinner kind of thing but because it's Deirdre and because she's a woman I'm quite happy to facilitate it. I would not facilitate that in a man.

D: Oh Jesus neither would I.

J: No way!

D: I'd have the man chained to that sink! [laughter]

J: So yes in that way it is, it's very different, it's very different. I wouldn't support a man in that at all.

– Julie and Deirdre, Irish participants

In one way, Deirdre is privileged by her gender in her relationship because her partner as a feminist views her behaviour as non-conforming to gendered social conventions, while at the same time they both believe that Deirdre does more than most men in terms of domestic labour. This example is interesting in that the division of labour is problematised and discussed in relation to equality, but nonetheless played out in a way that could be interpreted as oppressive. However, it would be a mistake to simplistically construe Julie as a passive victim, or Deirdre as a casual exploiter, although the quote above does perhaps suggest a certain defensiveness on her part: '*you did have the other kids then certainly*'. Their experience is also premised on subtle challenges to gender norms and clearly in terms of Deirdre's work with their foster daughter, not always along traditional demarcations of the gendered division of labour. Julie later referred to her children seeing her '*working under a car*' and engaging in traditionally male jobs around the house and although she did most of the housework at this time and her partner worked longer hours in paid employment, they both participated in activities, such as DIY work for example, that would traditionally be a male-gendered activity. In addition, their division of labour has changed over time, with the current arrangement being a more recent one.

Nonetheless, this couple does not follow the equality model of most other couples in the study.

Another Irish couple – Ciara and Gillian – followed a breadwinner/ caregiver model, but it was Ciara, the co-parent, who cared for their child full-time. So in contrast, to Patterson's (1995a) study where if there was an imbalance in the division of labour, it was the biological mother who participated more in childcare, with the co-parent working longer hours in paid employment, in this case, the co-parent was the primary caregiver. Gillian, the biological mother, found that she did not like staying at home full-time and returned to work a month after their child was born. Ciara was unhappy in her working life and had been considering a change for some time. She also had an independent income, as she owned a rental property. In addition, her family had provided much of the capital for the purchase of the house they lived in. So she continued to have an independent income despite no longer being in paid employment. This was a significant factor for her, as she felt that financial dependency was implicated in power relations. Although her partner was currently the main breadwinner, her own financial contribution remained important. She enjoyed the time spent with their child and also the freedom it gave her to pursue other interests. This example is also illustrative of the fact that not all women have equal access to satisfying paid employment. For this particular participant, her job role required very long hours and an unsatisfactory worklife balance. Crèches in Ireland are very expensive and it was financially practical to stay at home with the child. Her career trajectory had reached a point where caregiving and pursuing other interests felt more personally fulfilling than continuing to work in an area that was no longer pleasurable. She intended to take up part-time employment when her daughter began school, but wanted to 'be there' when she returned home from school, as they had gone to great lengths to have a child and she wanted to enjoy as much time with her daughter as possible. However, she also referred to a model of motherhood whereby the ideal situation for a child is to have a caregiver who is at home at the same time as the child:

C: And then we went to so much trouble to have her, it just seems crazy to boot her off to a crèche and then go back and I think you know [the industry she previously worked in] just isn't the same anymore and I just don't enjoy it as much, so.

R: Are you planning on staying at home with her until she goes to school?

> C: Em yeah I would put her into something social a couple of morn-
> ings a week or something and I'd like to do volunteer work or
> something like that but that would be, yeah, I would be here. Even
> when she goes to school or something, I would only take a job
> where I would be here when she comes home every evening at
> three o'clock. I think I was brought up in that.
>
>   – Ciara, Irish participant, co-parent

In contrast, her partner Gillian felt that full-time caregiving was not for
her and had no desire whatsoever to do so. They did however refer to
discussions they had had regarding retraining for Ciara, which Gillian
encouraged, but which Ciara expressed no interest in. In this case,
their individual career paths and personal preferences around parenting as well as Ciara's financial independence led to the decision to
share childcare in this way.

Ciara's depiction of a parent 'being there' when a child returns from
school, is clearly an Irish discourse, referred to in numerous policy and
media discussions. It may be true of many countries with a male breadwinner norm and contrasts with the Swedish case, where female caregivers of school-age children are regarded as performing an antiquated
mode of femininity (Elvin-Nowak, 1999). But her choice also raises the
issue of state-provided childcare and the degree to which equality of
care is supported or hindered by the state. For some Swedish participants, it was not possible to share parental leave when their children
were born, as at that time it could only be divided between legally
recognised parents. Nonetheless some managed to circumvent these
regulations. For example, one couple owned a business jointly where
they both worked and simply 'swapped places' halfway through parental
leave without alerting the social authorities. Alternative strategies
were also developed by Irish participants to enable equal participation
in carework. For example, one Irish couple both chose to become
full-time caregivers during their child's infancy, articulating their
choice in similar terms to Ciara, above. Others chose to reduce
their working hours, similar to participants in Dunne's (1998a)
work. The parental leave rules in Sweden have since been changed,
enabling registered partners to share it, apart from the compulsory
leave (two months each) that must be taken by the biological mother
and father. But this places pressure on lesbian parent couples to
become registered partners, whereas Swedish heterosexual couples
do not have to marry, or even live together in order to share parental
leave equally.

Some Swedish participants who parented with involved fathers spoke of the benefits of this in terms of sharing childcare as this enabled them to have more time both for their relationship with their partner and for themselves:

> I think it's perfect to have a known man [...] Because like if over the summer, they will go away with the fathers somewhere and you can do things that you cannot do with children. Because I think, I mean if you have a relationship and children, the relationship doesn't live by itself, you have to feed it with different things and if you don't, then it's, you can dump it because it's, it's like a flower, if you don't give it water it's going to die. And you have to have the time to do it
> – Birgitta, Swedish participant

> It's nice to have a third adult around sometimes because then the two of us [Lena and her partner] have time together.
> – Lena, Swedish participant

One lone parent in the study shared custody equally with the father of her child, so their son spent half the week with each of them. This arrangement enabled her to complete a university degree and although she referred to herself as a 'single mother', she differentiated between her situation and that of other solo mothers that she knew. Her own mother was also available to help:

> I could ask him [the father] to take him two more evenings and it wasn't a problem, but they had no father to call, he was living in Stockholm or he didn't exist. They were having a tough time and I told them, they were having really a much tougher time than me. They said oh you're a single mother and no I'm not, not in the same way. Really I was really not spoiled, but it was like being without a child sometimes I could ask him to take him anytime or my mother could take him, if I needed to study more.
> – Stina, Swedish participant

There were two instances of unequal sharing of childcare among the Swedish lesbian couple participants. One Swedish couple – Sofie and Beatrice – followed the breadwinner/caregiver model, in that Sofie the biological parent took all of the parental leave. However, this was because she was unemployed prior to the birth of their children and they felt that it was not economically viable to share parental leave. Beatrice had managed to create a flexible working pattern, which enabled her to spend more time at home during the day. They said that if they had both been in paid employment prior to the birth of their first child, they would have liked to share parental leave. In this case, Beatrice, who was in paid employment, felt that she had missed out on precious time with their children due to their economic situation. They suggested that their division of care was a result of economic necessity, rather than choice.

Another Swedish couple in the study, Elin and Ylva, had a traditional division of labour in the home, in that one person – the biological parent, Elin – was primarily responsible for day to day domestic chores that are usually gendered as feminine, while her partner did more of the work that routinely involved 'fixing things'. On the one hand, Elin referred to the division of labour as arising from personal preference, but then she also suggested that it follows a pattern which she is less than satisfied with:

E: I mean you do what you are best at, and that means that she never cooks, I do the cooking [laughs]. She is very good to fix things so she I mean, eh I mean I think every family has, in these discussions about who is doing the dishes or whatever it is, em I don't think we ever decide that you are doing that or you are doing that I mean it just, well we do what we are best at.

R: It's not a problem, you are comfortable with that?

E: Comfortable? No, maybe not. I mean I think we have the same problem that many heterosexuals do that if the woman stays at home, it's her to, it's em all the house things, the things that you do in the house, is more on the person that stays at home and then when I started to work, I would like it to be more equal but sometimes you just you know...

R: ....fall into a pattern?

E: Yeah.

R: And has that changed?

E: .....Eh not at first but now I think because now when I'm in school[3] I just have to have time on my own, yeah, it has changed a little bit maybe.

So for Elin and Ylva, the preference approach falls along traditional lines, or perhaps a stereotypical butch/femme model and is not characterised by equality. Yet Elin also suggested that it was important to counter sexist notions of women's capabilities:

> E: It's also important to show that a woman can do everything a man can do [...] and I mean they [children] are very clear about the things that I'm good at and what Ylva is good at. If they wanted to have anything fixed or repaired, they don't [laughs], they don't go to me! [laughs]
>
> – Elin, Swedish participant

These examples indicate the contested, rather than essentialist, nature of gender relations. While not all heterosexual couples have an unequal division of labour, not all lesbian couples follow an egalitarian model. Gendered subjectivities are unstable, rather than following predetermined patterns. However, the fact that most participants in the study did refer to democratic ways of sharing household responsibilities, suggests that the interaction of gender and sexuality in transformative ways is more representative of lesbian households, at least in this study, in the way that Dunne (1998a, 1998b) suggests. Nonetheless, researchers need to acknowledge the diversity of lesbian parenting and address dissonant cases that do not fall into the categories generally assumed to be characteristic of lesbian families. These cases can be interpreted from a queer feminist perspective to produce nuanced debates about the experiences of lesbian parents. Rather than judge these families as deviating from the only politically acceptable form of lesbian parenting, their choices and experiences produce interesting insights about gender and sexuality, which enable theoretical discussion to move beyond simplistic binaries. Both Julie and Deirdre engaged with equality issues in relation to gender. Ciara and Gillian made different career and caregiving choices and appeared happy with their current arrangements. Elin and Ylva had not negotiated the division of labour in ways in which they contributed equally and this was a point of contention. While they felt that they performed tasks according to preference, the fact that in their case these preferences fell along traditional lines contributed to the unequal nature of their contributions. Nonetheless, they felt that their sons were taught that women could do anything a man could. These cases must also be analysed in terms of gendered moral rationalities (Duncan & Edwards, 1999), whereby nonmarket, collective relations and understandings about motherhood and employment inform women's choices around combining paid employment and carework. The role of the state in supporting particular family forms over others – for example, in the rules concerning who is eligible for parental leave or not – clearly impacts on these families in specific ways. Sexual citizenship, particularly in the terrain of 'the family', negotiates understandings of the public and the private. The welfare state, in supporting certain family forms in specific ways impacted on the extent to which the burden of care could be alleviated and participants could share childcare equally. Despite these obstacles, it is notable that the majority of participants shared domestic work and childcare equitably.

In the next section, gender performance and parenting practices will be explored. Participants' discourses regarding the division of labour indicate that particular activities are gendered and the division of labour is often negotiated with reference to other considerations. The significance of gendered meanings attributed to particular practices and the reinvention of gender in these contexts will be addressed.

Gender and parenting practices among lesbian parents

In exploring participants' views on gender and parenting, it became apparent that there are ways in which gender may be taught differently in lesbian families in a positive way. Proponents of non-sexist parenting and education practices have often stressed the importance of exposing children to a range of activities, without attaching a gendered significance to them. For example, boys may be encouraged to play with dolls, or girls may be encouraged to play with trucks and so on. It is often considered important to teach children a variety of skills usually associated with the other gender. So for example, boys may be taught to sew and girls may learn how to construct materials. In this way, it is argued, children are able to develop all their abilities, rather than being forced to concentrate their energies in areas traditionally considered gender appropriate (Browne, 1986; Peets, 2000).

Interestingly, the lesbian parents interviewed often articulated their conviction that their children would be exposed to gender role models who themselves engaged in a wider range of activities. Participants viewed dominant social norms as encouraging a certain gender segregation in household and play activities. Having a partner of the same gender, necessitated the ability to perform a variety of household tasks, rather than only those stereotyped as traditionally 'female'. Furthermore, they were likely to find new models for achieving this, such as both partners choosing to work part-time in order to participate equally in childcare. As indicated in the previous section, participants expressed their domestic work arrangements in terms of equality and preference. Lacking the pressure associated with traditional gender roles in relationships, participants were skilled in housework *and* maintenance. If there were any areas in which they chose to concentrate their energies, it was usually based on personal preference and the other partner would compensate by focusing on another area. So for example, one partner might take care of the laundry, while the other did the ironing. For most participants, being freed from some of the confines of gender roles in relationships enabled them to share housework in a democratic way that was personally satisfying.

This was also perceived to be of benefit to their children, who saw women doing traditional tasks like cooking, but also fixing cars for example. In addition, the men they chose to be in their children's lives were also selected on the basis of the kind of masculinity they embodied. Gay men were often seen as more progressive role models than many heterosexual men.

> But in a way I don't like, I don't want my kids to have a stereotyped male role, I don't like that, or a stereotypical female role model, as it's seen in this society. I really love and like it that our kids are in a gay community as well and I think it's necessary for all kids to see all diversity and for example I really love to see my kids, that they see both their fathers or other gay men who are not these stereotype, not this macho, because they see that both their fathers like to knit and sew and all those things and they can build houses, and take care of the cars and making good food, taking care of their own clothes and clean and all these things, they see that when two men are living together they have to do all these things and they learn that it doesn't depend on if you're a man or a woman, if you want to do something you can do it because and it's okay. And it's the same way they see other men because, for example in the Pride Week and they see men dressed like women and transgender people and they see women running motorbikes and all this, I love it. I would like, that's the kind of role models I want to see because I want my kids to get, to be as free as they can be in this society and see that it doesn't depend if I'm a boy or a girl, whatever I want to do, I can do it and I see all these examples around me that it's possible. And that's the most important thing I think for our kids, not necessarily that they have fathers. Because we live in a gay community, they have all these things.
>
> – Hanna, Swedish participant

The gay community was seen as a positive resource for the production of non-oppressive genders. Gender in lesbian families was described as being transmitted in ways characterised by an emphasis on diversity and flexibility. Although society in general was associated with monolithic gender norms and roles, the lesbian and gay community provided a counterculture which emphasised the multiplicity of genders and provided a basis for a less rigid approach to the acquisition of gender. This is not to say that all participants articulated the belief that gender is entirely socially constructed, but that it was seen as largely socially determined and participants considered it important to enable their children to have a broader gender repertoire than the socially dominant norm. The result of this was that children would develop all sides of themselves, rather than repress some of their interests or aspects of their emotional life. The emphasis was on a more holistic approach to development and awareness of diversity, rather than the acquisition of traditional gender roles.

The potential outcomes of these practices and ideologies may be very similar to those of non-sexist parenting in heterosexual families. It must also be acknowledged that it is perfectly possible for lesbian families to engage in normative discourses and practices. It is not my intention to argue for an essentialist view of lesbian parenting, in which lesbian parents are constructed as the new normative ideal to which others should aspire. Rather, I wish to critically examine the ways in which gender and sexuality dynamics are discursively (re)constituted in the pedagogical practices of gender in lesbian families. Instead of constructing gender as a rigid binary relation, the diversity of gendered practices and support for choosing activities on the basis of enjoyment and ability rather than social norms, was a distinct discourse among lesbian parents interviewed. The ways that lesbian genders were seen to incorporate a broader range of skills was significant in their articulation of themselves as parents. This was irrespective of whether participants viewed gender as entirely socially constructed or expressed a conscious commitment to non-sexist parenting. Their parenting practices resulted from their gendered locations as lesbians, for whom gender was experienced in the context of a lesbian lifestyle. The prevalent social assumption that sex and gender are mutually determined was therefore continually destabilised.

Lesbian parents in Ireland were far less likely to have an involved donor than in Sweden. Nonetheless, while Swedish participants emphasised the importance of male role models, they did not view fathers as the only possible male role model. This was because of different discourses around the importance of having contact with a known biological father. Both groups considered it important for children to spend time with women and men. Men who were involved in the children's lives, whether they were donors, friends, or other kin, were chosen on the basis of the qualities they possessed as individuals, rather than as examples of hegemonic masculinities. Indeed gay men were often viewed as better role models in their subordinate masculinities than many heterosexual men:

> Yeah it's like, I don't know if it's typically for gay men but there are a lot of men who do things that aren't what you consider in today's society to be typically male and at the same time if you have a son and he sees this, my daddy does this as well and it's okay then you change an attitude in somebody and hopefully that, I would hope it makes the world a little better.
>
> – Lena, Swedish participant

In families where donors did not play an active role, participants pointed out that children were taught traditionally male activities as well. One parent of two sons expressed this in the following way:

> Yeah, they're lucky in a way, I mean they are lucky in a way because em as well as those things, em we've always done [...] a lot of DIY and so they've always had tools around and learned how to use tools so you know it's not, not as though it's only been the more 'female' in quotation marks, activities that they've been offered, they've also been offered the more traditionally male things as well and they've seen me under a car you know.
>
> – Julie, Irish participant

This participant considered her sons lucky because they were exposed to a variety of activities and free to choose to concentrate their energies in areas that were personally appealing, rather than being socialised to follow gender traditional norms. The fact that her sons learned these traditionally male activities from women, rather than from a man, could be seen as a new form of pedagogy, where the dominant essentialist association between gender and certain activities is constantly undermined. Indeed, some lesbians expressed positive feelings about having sons, whom they hoped would share their enjoyment in certain traditionally male domains such as football. However, they acknowledged that daughters could be equally enthusiastic about this sport. In this way, lesbian parents were open to a multiplicity of gendered behaviours in their children, which were not necessarily dependent on biological sex. They also saw themselves as providing support and encouragement in different areas, not just traditionally female ones. Interviewees negotiated their practices in relation to a dominant social order by gendering certain activities. The necessary connection between gender and various activities was then destabilised through the pedagogical practices of parenting.

Participants pointed out that they themselves engaged in traditionally male-dominated activities, for example in their professional lives, as well as in domestic tasks around the house. This was considered to challenge sexist ideologies about gender appropriate behaviour. One participant, who worked in a male-dominated profession, talked about her son's possible view of women and work in the following way:

> I certainly don't think he'd see it as odd [having a mother who works in a male-dominated profession], you know I mean there's no way he could because I am a [occupation] and I prove a point just with what I do you know and em you know his friends going to be the ones who might say god you know [...] I don't think he'd bat an eye at what a woman can do at all. But I think it won't be through me saying it to him, it will just be through my actions of what I do you know.
>
> – Clodagh, Irish participant

An interesting aspect of this example is her suggestion that her son will learn that women are not restricted by their gender as a result of her actions, the way she lives her life, rather than through equality rhetoric.

Participants appropriated dominant narratives of gender, but reinscribed them with their own meanings in the context of their families. While gendering certain activities, they subvert this gendered significance by emphasising their abilities in both traditionally male and female areas, as a result of being in relationships with other women. By acting as a role model for their children in both traditionally male and female activities, the children are provided with a greater degree of choice and encouraged to develop their skills in all areas, not just those stereotyped as gender appropriate.

In both contexts, participants considered wider society to promote a view of gender as a binary divide with clearly segregated activities. This is perhaps to be expected, given the nature of gender politics in Ireland, but it seems surprising that participants did not relate to Swedish society as particularly deconstructive of gender norms. This may be associated with age – most participants in the study were in their late thirties and early forties. However it could also be argued that the experience of being lesbian or gay requires a significant re-evaluation of gender identity, as so much of what constitutes appropriate gender behaviour is intricately bound up with heterosexuality. All participants expressed awareness that gender roles are reinforced by social norms and expectations.

Participants expressed the view that their children were far more likely to be conventionally gendered than not, regardless of their home environment, as they will inevitably be raised in a predominantly heteronormative society. However, lesbian parents are under particular pressure to perform well as parents, as they experience extra surveillance by a society which challenges their very existence. Some participants referred to feelings of constraint as a result. One parent, who was often perceived as butch, felt particularly vulnerable. She described these feelings in relation to raising her daughter:

It would have been a lot easier for me to have a boy because I could never have come under the kind of finger pointing thing or accusation thing that goes along with like do you have to dress her so butchly? I make a big effort to not dress Danae [daughter] in anything boyish you know. And went through a big long stage, in the very early part of her life where everybody was saying how old is he, how old is he and I was feeling so paranoid about the fact that like everybody is thinking this butch dyke is dressing her beautiful baby [as a] boy and trying to turn her into a dyke as well or trying to corrupt her into this, so all that stuff.

– Sorcha, Irish participant

A Swedish couple, who had bought dolls and cars for both their son and daughter, found that their children nonetheless followed gender conventional behaviour in their interests. Despite having exposed them to a range of activities, Sofia expressed some relief at the fact that her son was quite masculine in his behaviour. However, she felt that this was a shortcoming on her part:

But in one way I'm pleased that he is so much a boy and that's a bit em, that's my problem, not his problem. Because if he was a girlish boy, I would think that everyone else would think that it's because we're lesbian, because he didn't have a father, it's our fault and so on. So in one way I'm a little bit pleased that he's not too girlish or so. But that's my problem.

                                                    – Sofia, Swedish participant

Heaphy *et al.* (1999) point out that power dynamics are inevitably present in lesbian and gay and indeed all relationships. However, they suggest that sexual identity may mediate awareness of power dynamics in complex ways. In their research, lesbian and gay participant couples identified an egalitarian relationship model that they strove for in the context of other forms of difference within their relationships – across 'race'/ethnicity, income and educational level for example. The authors suggest that it is the reflexive nature of participants' concerns with equality that enabled them to creatively negotiate more egalitarian relations. They identify this equality model ideal as an emerging ethic within same sex relationships. Similarly, this process is apparent in the two quotes by Sorcha and Sofia, above. Both participants problematise their concern with normative readings of their children's behaviour. This awareness of their own conventional expectations is apparent because it is contrary to their own preferences and represents in their view a conformist compromise.

These two examples show how the interpretation of lesbian parenting practices can be linked to homophobic myths and that these assumptions must be challenged on a multilevel basis. Returning to the debates about assimilative versus transformative approaches to parenting that I began the chapter with, these examples illustrate that it is important to address the complexity of people's experiences and acknowledge how powerful gender binary norms can make it difficult for those who transgress them, particularly in parenting. While participants seemed to welcome the prospect of unconventionally gendered children, they were realistic about the possibilities of this occurring. Further, they were aware of the difficulties they would face as parents of children who engaged in transgressive gender behaviour. In the case of Sorcha, her awareness was also based on her own history as a butch lesbian and the particular prejudice she had encountered throughout her adult life as a result. This further indicates the importance of discursive interventions that challenge gender norms. Lesbian parents may find themselves in a difficult position of trying to pass on particular values to their children, while negotiating parenting in a homophobic and sexist world.

Conclusion

There is a large body of research that refutes the homophobic assumption that children thrive only in heterosexual families. The notion that queer families are a 'deviant Other' whose parenting must be constantly subjected to scrutiny on the basis of their sexuality, has been challenged on numerous grounds. More recently researchers have turned their attention to more productive aspects of lesbian parenting experience. In this chapter, discourses of gender and equality among lesbian parents in Sweden and Ireland were explored. Relatively little attention has been paid to the role of social policy in mediating lesbian parents' choices regarding the equitable distribution of domestic labour and caregiving. This research indicates that policies pertaining to the combining of paid employment with obligations of care can affect the ways lesbian parents share caring responsibilities. Nonetheless, despite different constraints the care and household practices of most participants were characterised by equality.

Participants emphasised the flexibility of gender and undermined hegemonic discourses about sex roles through the pedagogical practices of gender in their families. In this way, heteronormative ideologies and codes were continually challenged and critiqued. However, there were also instances in which lesbian parenting could be normative. These cases provide interesting critical insights when contextualised in relation to the particular social pressures faced by lesbian parents. While much previous research on LGBT-headed families has implicitly assumed that these families may be marked differently in a negative way – often a homophobic assumption – lesbian parent families may also exhibit positive traits, as the work on the gendered division of labour in these households suggests. However, it is possibly the case that there are more overall similarities than differences between lesbian parent and heterosexual families, given the mundane practices of care common to all families and the role of wider society in shaping children's identities and behaviours.

Although research about gendered practices in lesbian parent families suggests a move away from the emphasis on normative performance in previous research, nonetheless both areas remain imbued with similar theoretical concerns about sameness and difference. What does the teleological nature of discourses of sameness/difference and assimilation/transgression with regard to academic work on lesbian parent family practices reveal about the ways in which these families are theorised? I would argue that it is indicative of the socio-political context in which lesbian parenting occurs. Further, it is illustrative of the emphasis on subversion and transgression within much queer theory. In this chapter, I have attempted to unravel these dichotomies and reconceptualise notions of resistance in view of the contexts within which lesbian parenting is enacted. The emphasis on sameness/difference in debates about lesbian parenting also highlights the particular norms that are central to all forms of parenting. The actual diversity of family forms in contemporary society is not always evident within theoretical debates and empirical trends pertaining to lesbian parenting, which often assume a particular heteronormative standard to be representative of all non-lesbian/gay families, irrespective of whether a particular author is sympathetic to lesbian parenting or not. This obscures the plurality of heterosexual family forms.

Munt (1998: 9) argues that 'the profound jubilation/melancholia that attends lesbian identity evolves from the pride/shame dichotomy which is implicit within models of outside and inside'. This perhaps provides another perspective on the centrality of sameness/difference to theoretical discussions of lesbian parenting. If Otherness is characterised through an implicit lens of relative difference, then the Other may utilise the discursive resources of sameness/difference in efforts to assert subjectivity. In this chapter I have attempted to disrupt this dichotomy by contextualising lesbian parenting experiences and examining the significance of inside/outside binaries to ontological understandings of gender, sexuality and parenting. Thus, the heterocentric polarity at the heart of this binary is also displaced, challenging the centrality of the heteronormative model or 'inside', which often functions as the inherent comparative standard for all families.

7
Conclusions: Beyond Assimilation and Transgression

This book began with an acknowledgment of the growing phenomenon of a new generation of lesbians embarking on parenthood in the context of an openly lesbian lifestyle. The preceding chapters have attempted to contextualise lesbian parents' experiences and unravel some of the implications of this relatively new family form for theoretical and empirical work in relation to gender, sexuality and kinship. While much previous research has been centrally concerned with the effects of lesbian and gay parental sexuality on children, this study has integrated lesbian parents' narratives into contemporary theoretical analysis and debate. The relational choices and perspectives of lesbian parents in Sweden and Ireland have been explored and their experiences have been addressed with reference to the importance of socio-political context and place. In addition, the teleological nature of the discussions concerning the relative similarity or difference of lesbian parent families to their heterosexual counterparts, or to a heteronormative standard, has been challenged through a deconstruction of the heterocentric polarity at the heart of these debates. This concluding discussion consists of five sections, in which the implications of the research findings and theoretical concerns of this work are explored: a brief overview of the key findings; suggestions for further research; lesbian parenthood in a comparative perspective; a reconceptualisation of lesbian Otherness; implications for theoretical work on family practices; and finally a reconsideration of the question 'Is kinship always already heterosexual?' (Butler, 2002).

Overview of key findings: moving beyond binaries

The comparative dimension of this research project has explored patterns of similarity and difference between the two samples, thus highlighting the significance of culture and legislative frameworks to lesbian women's reproductive decision-making and experiences of parenting. A consideration of lesbian parents' narratives in two different national contexts has not, however, been solely concerned with comparing their relative similarity or difference. The comparative nature of this research enabled lesbian parent narratives to be at the forefront of analysis. Previous research has largely compared lesbian parents' experiences to an implicit heterosexual norm. By examining participants' narratives relationally according to country of residence, this heteronormative focus was displaced.

The implications of (in)visibility were highlighted in a spatial analysis with regard to the everyday contexts of lesbian parenting. The narratives of lesbian parents in this research suggests that the emphasis on visibility in previous work is insufficient for analysis of the spaces of lesbian parenting. Their parenting practices are not for the most part enacted in spaces either exclusive to lesbian parents, or where they constitute a visible group or presence. This does not, however, render these spaces any less significant in the shaping of their identities as *lesbian* parents. In addition, a spatial analysis of lesbian parent experience provided new understandings of the rural, challenging the metrocentrism in much previous work on sexuality and space.

New research questions have also been posed with regard to kinship formation among lesbian parents. Previous authors have raised the possibility of new forms of relatedness in lesbian and gay families. This research project has enabled a sustained critical interrogation of the symbolic function of biology, gender and kinship among lesbian parents. Perhaps the most striking finding of this study with regard to the comparative component of the research is the contrasting nature of discourses of fatherhood among Swedish and Irish lesbian parents. Clearly, the emphasis on involved donors among the majority of Swedish participants reflects the nature of fatherhood debates in Sweden generally and the evolution of a model of participatory fatherhood which has achieved particular hegemony in contemporary Swedish society. In contrast, Irish women expressed considerable self-confidence in their ability to provide sufficient security for their children independently of male involvement. However, in both contexts a preference for knowledge of paternity was largely retained, irrespective of whether the donor participated in parenting or not. This highlights the continued importance of biological origins to notions of self and identity in lesbian parents' narratives in relation to considerations informing their concerns for children's well being.

Traditional conceptualisations of biology were also continually undermined and reinvented within these families. In particular, the relative lack of importance attached to biological motherhood compared to social parenting, was a recurring feature of participant narratives. This is not to suggest that there was no distinction made between biological mothers and co-parents, rather that this distinction related to an associated difference with regard to legal recognition and wider validation that was socially constructed, in addition to biological relatedness. Within couple relationships, this difference was openly acknowledged and negotiated, rather than constituting a sensitive issue that could only be tacitly recognised. This contributes to understandings of motherhood as a fluid concept. For many participants, a mother was not simply a female parent. Participants articulated a plurality of identifications that were often ostensibly contradictory. The multiple applications of terms were however internally coherent and congruent to participants, highlighting the complex and contextualised meanings of kinship terminology.

In this book, 'motherhood/mothers' and 'parenthood/parents' have been used at times interchangeably but also to refer to specific relationships. When used in the latter way, this has been explicitly demarcated – for example in the discussion of the meanings of motherhood in Chapter 5. However, an interesting finding of this research relates to the preference among many co-parents for the term 'parent' to refer to their personal identity, rather than 'mother', particularly among Swedish participants. As discussed, this was to acknowledge a particular biological relatedness, but the meanings attributed to this biological 'difference' varied. This did not appear to delineate a difference in either carework or emotional relationship, but represented an attempt to negotiate hegemonic concepts and understandings. The utilisation of the terms 'lesbian mothers' and 'lesbian parents' therefore acknowledges those co-parents and biological mothers who claim 'mother' as a personal identity, but also illustrates some of the complexities of these discussions and attempts to incorporate all participants, irrespective of biological relationship to children, within an inclusive terminology. The analytic tensions arising from this endeavour highlight the unstable and constructed nature of kinship appellations.

As a pioneering generation of lesbian women embarking on parenthood, these women are developing new understandings and conceptualisations of kinship, which are continually evolving. Many of these families did appear to create new 'cultures of relatedness', where biology and kinship were reconfigured along axes of identity, parenting practices and affective bonds or relationships. However, irrespective of whether lesbian parents did challenge the hegemony of biology to kinship in Western society or not, the discourses of relational possibilities among participants highlight the ways in which the legal regulation of kinship and biology relatedness are mutually implicated, rather than exclusive entities. It also illustrates the elasticity of biology as a concept within lesbian parent families, where it may be deployed in variable and fluid ways, rather than as a singular entity.

An interesting aspect of this research is the way similar debates regarding sameness/difference recur in different guises across disciplines and thematic explorations. The binary opposition underlying debates centred around lesbian parents' relationship to practices of assimilation or transformation was further deconstructed in Chapter 6. An examination of the division of labour among lesbian couples and the pedagogical practices of gender in lesbian parent families, highlighted the ways in which hegemonic narratives of gender were destabilised in these families. However, the implicit comparison with heterosexual families underlying considerations of sameness and difference with regard to lesbian parent families is illustrative of the heterocentric polarity at the heart of much research on lesbian parents and their children. It also reveals the particular heteronormative standards by which all families are judged in hegemonic normative discourse. It must be noted however that the heteronormativities implicitly related to in participants' discourses throughout the research are also a reflection of their own situatedness as ethnic (primarily white) actors and as geographical citizens. A research sample of lesbian parents belonging to ethnic minorities for example might yield different understandings of, or variations on, hegemonic normative discourses of gender and kinship.

Future directions in research

The 'Other' is usually invoked epistemologically as the marker of boundaries, the relational opposite who makes hegemonic categories meaningful. On an empirical level the Other is often understood as a non-normative lifestyle or marginalised identity. Previous research on lesbian parenting that operates within these frameworks often neglects the significance of context. Although partnership recognition, adoption and access to NRTs for LGBT people are increasingly part of the legislative agenda in European countries, there has been less debate about diversity among LGBT parent families. How is for example kinship reimagined by the Other and how is the Other embedded within local contexts? In other words, how are lesbian parents' subjectivities shaped by cultural underpinnings and how do they as agentic subjects negotiate social policy frameworks in formulating their own visions of kinship?

Relatively little is known about the perspectives, choices and relational frameworks of lesbian parents, as previous research (including that used to inform political debate and social policy) has largely focused on the impact of lesbian and gay parents' sexuality on their children's development. While children's well-being should be central to any consideration of intergenerational family change, the overwhelming emphasis on the implications for children has obscured the experiences of lesbian parents. Furthermore, arguments ostensibly advocating 'the best interests of the child' have often served as a screen for homophobic rhetoric that is premised on the belief that a heteronormative family form constitutes the only acceptable one.

This book has explored a wide range of areas pertaining to lesbian parent kinship, practices and experiences. Numerous areas for further research remain, particularly in relation to diversity in lesbian parent families. This book has contributed to knowledge of diversity among lesbian parents by challenging the US/UK hegemony in research. However, notable gaps in the overall literature remain, including the lack of attention to 'race', ethnicity and other axes of difference within research on lesbian parenting. Another area of lesbian parent experience that could be examined further in theoretical analysis is that of lesbians who conceive in the context of a heterosexual relationship. Although there are numerous anthologies containing experiential accounts by these women, rather less attention has been paid to the theoretical implications of their life experiences. In this research, several participants had children from previous heterosexual relationships. Their narratives were fascinating in their own right and I have often reflected that it is a pity that more work has not been done to explore their experiences from a feminist perspective. In addition, much research on lesbian parenting has focused primarily on couple relationships, another imbalance which could be redressed.

Other areas for further research include gay fatherhood, another relatively neglected topic, despite important exceptions (e.g. Dunne, 2001a, 2001b). Given the need for appropriate policy provision, separation and break-ups among lesbian parent couples also constitutes an important area of research.[1] Comparative work is not appropriate for every research topic, but has provided a useful means for centring lesbian parents' narratives in this research study. However, nation-state analysis necessarily has limitations given the increasing proliferation of globalising processes.

An interesting area arising from this study and worthy of further exploration via transnational analysis is that of lesbian women's access to new reproductive technologies beyond national borders and the implications of this for international legislation and regulation.

Lesbian parenthood in a comparative perspective

Choosing to do comparative work on lesbian parenthood in Sweden and Ireland has proved fruitful for several reasons. Firstly, comparative work highlights how lesbian motherhood must be situated within specific cultural and social policy contexts. In order to examine the situation for lesbian women contemplating parenthood, we must be sensitive to the wider context in terms of sexual citizenship, family policies, kinship norms, and gender and sexual politics. Sweden and Ireland clearly present varied contexts for sexual citizenship, family politics and gender relations. While Sweden has been very innovative and progressive in these fields, there remain ways in which sexual citizenship is conceptualised and established along heteronormative lines. For example, it is only possible to have two legally recognised parents in Sweden, despite the fact that many Swedish lesbian parent families are created with more than two parents, as the discussion of reproductive decision-making among Swedish lesbian parents in Chapter 3 demonstrates. Theories of sexual citizenship attempt to take account of the specific needs of lesbian and gay citizens. Further empirical work is required in order to ascertain those needs.

A comparative perspective highlights the particular issues faced by lesbian and gay citizens in different contexts. It also presents specific challenges for researchers. Fieldwork may be easier or more difficult to carry out in different places. The wider political context may make lesbian and gay participants – always a challenging group to recruit in any study – more or less willing to participate in research. Questions of ethics and representation may be a thorny issue for any researcher working with a minority group.[2] The high profile nature of lesbian and gay family politics in Sweden made it easier to recruit participants for my study than in Ireland, where lesbian parenthood has a low profile. Swedish participants seemed particularly eager for further research about their families, seeing it as necessary for social and political change.

Swedish policy has clearly regulated lesbian and gay families. The introduction of registered partnerships expressly curtailed all parenting possibilities for lesbian and gay citizens. Interestingly, this moment of legal regulation also brought lesbian and gay parenthood into the spotlight. It had the effect of sparking a social movement that addressed lesbian and gay parenthood and pressed for social change. The effects of this visibility could be explored in more depth. In what ways has such explicit legal regulation and the resulting visibility been both productive and problematic for LGBT citizens? It also raises questions regarding invisibility. Discussions of lesbian and gay politics often address questions of voice and representation. What are the implications for researchers of studying a socially excluded group that is in some ways able to navigate the social context rather more easily by virtue of its very invisibility? Ireland follows a more conventional model of family politics in many ways, with a more entrenched tradition of male breadwinner and female caregiver family norms. Lesbian and gay parenthood has not been a high profile issue. As a result, assisted reproduction has been less explicitly exclusionary towards lesbian women in Ireland, compared to the situation in Sweden prior to recent legislative changes.

The ways in which gendered discourses of the family in both countries have developed present interesting conditions for lesbians contemplating parenthood. The emphasis on participatory fatherhood has been both integrated into and reconstructed within lesbian parent families, as was illustrated in Chapter 3. Lesbians in Sweden incorporated notions of participatory fatherhood into their family forms, but also utilised shared parenthood in ways that were advantageous. Irish women emphasised choice, independence and self-confidence in raising children on their own in their discourses around reproductive decision-making. Exploring how sexual citizenship can be made more equitable requires addressing how heteronormativity is constructed cross-culturally. Similarly, it requires consideration of the ways in which lesbians are situated within specific cultural, social and political contexts.

Reconceptualising Otherness

The distinctive ways in which Irish and Swedish participants negotiate local contexts have important implications for the theorising of gender relations and queer theory. As noted in Chapter 3, a construction of heteronormativity as a monolithic concept is an inadequate theoretical tool. The form of heteronormativity that participants resisted and subverted varied cross-culturally. Thus, *multiple heteronormativities* is a more appropriate conceptualisation. This enables an incorporation of varied contexts into queer analyses, acknowledging the different concerns of queer actors situated across a diversity of places and identities.

This further suggests a reconsideration of lesbian Otherness. In situating lesbian parents within the contexts of state policy and cultural frameworks, the multifaceted nature of identity becomes apparent. Thus, Swedish lesbian parents who reinvent discourses of fatherhood while simultaneously supporting participatory fatherhood, are clearly engaging in notions of kinship that are grounded in broader understandings within Swedish society. Similarly, Irish women's self-confidence in their ability to provide for their children without the involvement of active fathers, reflects the genealogy of motherhood in Ireland. Lesbians are often assumed, as the Other, to be entirely outside social norms and conventions. Hegemonic discourses may construct them as the relational Other who renders the hegemonic ideal normative. For example, in the discussions about lesbian and gay adoption in Sweden, a discourse regarding the needs of adopted children was endlessly invoked, in which 'lesbian' and 'adopted child/person' were posited as oppositional categories. Yet the possibility of a lesbian or lesbian parent who had herself been adopted never figured conceptually in these debates. Lesbians, as the Other, were outside such a realm of possibility in the popular imagination. This research, in illustrating that lesbians engage with dominant kinship formulations, illustrates the extent to which sexuality is negotiated by context and identity. Thus, lesbian parents are not simply the Other, they are also individuals grounded in particular cultural norms and ideologies.

A construction of lesbians as exclusively Other ignores the multifaceted intersectional nature of identity and their simultaneous sites of privilege and marginalisation. It further denies the possibility of lesbian subjectivities that are not solely characterised by a marginalised status. Heteronormative ontological frameworks in which lesbian is synonymous with Otherness, are dependent upon a mutually exclusive polarity between 'lesbian' and 'heterosexual', in which these categories are understood as monolithic entities, rather than diverse identifications. Thus, a failure to critically interrogate diversity among lesbian parents contributes to this understanding of lesbian as Other. Increased consideration of lesbian parents' axes of belonging is therefore necessary, in terms of both sites of privilege and diverse marginalised identifications.

Implications for social policy

These research findings and theoretical concerns have numerous implications for understandings of family practices and the social construction of family forms. Clearly, an equality perspective requires all parenting possibilities, including adoption, fostering and access to NRTs to be equally available to citizens irrespective of their sexuality. The restriction of these domains to heterosexuals therefore constitutes homophobic discrimination. This research has explored some of the implications of these restrictions for lesbian women. Some participants were denied the medical assistance they required to conceive and were unable or unwilling to travel abroad for. Those participants who had the resources to access services such as IVF or DI abroad, found their emotional plight compounded by the financial and practical strain this involved. Restricting these services to heterosexuals will only prevent some of the most vulnerable lesbian women – those with the least financial resources – from obtaining this service and exacerbates an already difficult situation for those who can afford to travel for these services. The policy of compulsory donor identity disclosure in Sweden indicates a clear policy preference for known donors. Interestingly, by restricting these services to heterosexuals, the possibility of lesbian women choosing insemination by an unknown donor increased, as the only other way of getting a known donor through DI is by importing from the Sperm Bank of California, an expensive addition to an already costly process.

While Sweden has made significant progress with the extension of adoption to lesbian and gay people, problems with the way this has been formulated remain. Although the Swedish debates focused primarily on international adoption, clearly second parent or 'närstående' adoption, is the most immediately relevant form of adoption for lesbian parents. However, while the introduction of this latter type of adoption safeguards the rights of co-parents, it is only applicable to cases where the father rescinds his parental rights and obligations and is therefore premised on the nuclear family two-parent model. Yet as this research suggests, many lesbian parents in Sweden appear to have a preference for a known and involved donor. Current legislative formulations therefore remain inadequate, despite important recent reforms. A more inclusive proposal would be to enable recognition of more than two parents. Some families in this research had two mothers and two fathers involved in raising a child collectively from birth, but only two parents can be recognised by law.

As the experiences of lesbian couples in this research whose partner relationship has ended illustrates, the lack of legal recognition of co-parents renders them particularly vulnerable. They are dependent on their former partner's goodwill in terms of visitation and should the biological mother die, their situation becomes even more assailable.

The complex nature of power dynamics in this situation can also cause biological mothers to be dependent on their former partners' willingness to meet their financial and care responsibilities, in the absence of a formal framework for their obligations to children post-separation. Second parent adoption should therefore be made available retrospectively. This would enable couples who have already broken up but wish to avail of it to do so and would alleviate some of the vulnerabilities and inequalities of parties concerned.

Ireland's policy framework of relegating decisions regarding access to new reproductive technologies to the medical profession has enabled some lesbian women to procure these services. However, a situation where adequate information and services are difficult to obtain is unacceptable. All such services should be openly available to women regardless of their sexuality. The current adoption laws also reflect a heteronormative discriminatory bias. The issue of second parent adoption is a particularly pressing one in an Irish context. Participants were keenly aware of their legal vulnerability. Unlike in Sweden, unmarried biological fathers have few formal rights before the law. Yet this did not appear to afford participants much sense of security should their guardianship or custody be challenged by a known donor. This highlights the necessity of a legislative framework that is clearly committed to equality and inclusiveness. Even when a lack of comprehensive guidelines – for example regarding NRTs – can accrue advantages to a limited number of individuals, the importance of more rigorous and non-discriminatory legislation remains.

Swedish participants experienced relative advantages in relation to labour market participation compared to their Irish counterparts, due to the widespread availability of affordable good quality childcare and generous parental leave provisions. However, the fact that a Swedish lesbian parent can only share parental leave with her partner if they are in a registered partnership is a heterosexist requirement, enforcing a particular normative ideology of kinship on parents that unfairly imposes a differential expectation of them as parents compared to heterosexual couples. The strictures of a normative ideology are also evident in the case of adoption in Sweden, where only lesbian (and gay) couples who are registered partners can avail of adoption.

Participants in both countries experienced homophobia and prejudice in a wide range of contexts, including during medical care and at their children's schools for example. Clearly, there is a need for more diversity training and awareness among service providers in a variety of areas. Irish participants in particular felt more constrained in their ability to locate sympathetic service providers and this limited the extent to which they could integrate into particular communities and contexts.

Some implications for family studies

The literature on family studies has provided invaluable approaches to the study of new forms of kinship. Previous work has situated kinship within wider social structures and highlighted how particular forms of families are supported over others. Anthropology has played a particularly important role in highlighting the significance of culture to understandings of kinship. The particular convergence of biology and the law in the construction of kinship in Western society is therefore understood as socially and culturally specific. Changes in gender relations, labour markets, and new reproductive technologies have influenced constructions of kinship. Too often, these changes are assumed to be broadly similar throughout the West. This book suggests that context remains significant in the construction of family forms and that there is more variation within the West than might be assumed. As we have seen, in Sweden the mass entry of women into the paid labour market was accompanied by rigorous discussions of the gendered nature of women's and men's participation in family life. Both women and men were seen as entitled to be active in the labour market. Full-time caring is incompatible with modern Swedish femininities. At the same time, fatherhood has become increasingly significant to contemporary Swedish masculinities. Gender equality rhetoric and social change have significantly impacted on the construction of family forms in Sweden. This is most clearly highlighted in Swedish lesbian parents' narratives, which often incorporated active fathers in the creation of their family forms. Irish lesbian parents created families that reflected the importance of legal security and self-confidence in raising children without active fathers.

Nonetheless, a recurring theme cross-nationally was the preference for known donors. This illustrates that knowledge of genetic lineage remains an important part of contemporary identity. While lesbian parents may have differed cross-nationally in the importance placed on familiarity with a donor – whether he should be an active parent or not – they all expressed a preference for knowing who he was. This was invariably articulated as 'in the best interests of the child'. In a society where the social and biological may become conflated in complex ways, where the 'truth' of biological origins is seen as personally revealing, their preference for known donors is understandable. Wider discussions of adoption and the need/right of children to know their biological parents informed these concerns. Reproductive decision-making among lesbian parents highlights how kinship, genetics and identity are potentially both reconfigured and reinforced within non-heteronormative families. These families are being shaped within the context of wider societies that remain unsupportive to varying degrees. Attempts to create families outside of heteronormative parameters require engaging with those parameters. As this book illustrates, this is achieved in complex ways – on the one hand, Swedish lesbian parents may emphasise the need for contact with donors, while also choosing progressive male role models and allowing for greater gender flexibility in family practices. Irish women illustrate considerable independence and concern for legal security in the creation of their family forms. All participants were continually engaged in constructing families that ensured their children's well-being.

A concern for children's well-being also incorporated an awareness of homophobia within society. These families were creating a pioneering family form in the relative absence of state and social approval and support. Their narratives must be interpreted within that context. These families also illustrate the particular freedoms and constraints associated in creating families outside of traditional heteronormative forms, while also negotiating wider heteronormativities. Their choices and imaginaries must be understood as both situated and filled with possibilities. This book has been centrally concerned with locating lesbian parents as social actors, rather than assessing whether or not they disrupt or reinforce heteronormative practices. An approach to family studies that addresses heteronormativity highlights the norms that inform all families. It also allows for an interpretation of lesbian parenthood that goes beyond addressing their potential for subversion of assimilation. In this way, their narratives are revealing of wider kinship practices.

So *is* kinship always already heterosexual?

In the first chapter, Butler's (2002) analysis of the implications of the legal recognition of same sex partnerships was outlined. I will conclude by exploring the implications of her arguments regarding kinship recognition, in light of this research. She suggests that this recent legislative trend has problematic implications for queer kinship imaginaries. I return to these concerns now in order to reconsider the question of whether kinship is 'always already heterosexual'. Previous work on the legal regulation (and legitimation) of queer kinship has been centrally concerned with partnership regulation (e.g. Warner, 1999). This research study has extended this debate further by exploring the implications of legal regulation (and lack thereof) for lesbian *parents* in two different cultural and policy contexts.

Butler's concern with the possible foreclosures in queer kinship imaginaries entailed by legal regulation is a pertinent one. The legislative changes introduced regarding lesbian and gay parenting often reflect heteronormative constraints. Thus for example lesbian and gay couples wishing to avail of second parent adoption in Sweden must be registered partners, rather than a cohabiting couple (although marriage is a requirement that interestingly is also applicable to heterosexuals). Despite such patently problematic potential outcomes, I would argue in favour of a continuing engagement with legal reform. Lesbian and gay parents must in my view continue to attempt to seek redress through the state in order to ensure the security of their families in possible eventualities. Scenarios such as custody disputes between co-parents and biological mothers in the context of relationship breakdown, or between co-parents and either biological fathers or the family of origin of biological mothers should the latter die prematurely, remain a serious concern in the absence of second parent adoption, or multiple adoptive parent possibilities. This is not to deny the constraints of configuring kinship through legal reform, whereby forms of kinship that are not legally recognised are therefore invalidated (or may be forcibly produced through their very marginality). The struggle to maintain identity in the face of legal invalidation constitutes a recurring theme in co-parent narratives. Nonetheless, the awareness of legal vulnerability also shaped their identities in particular ways.

If legislation is utilised as a resource for the protection of lesbian parent families, what are the possible effects of this, other than the obvious impact of legal protection should these efforts be successful? It would appear that more work is needed on queer kinship forms in order to inform social policy. Future research also needs to explore cultural variation and the impact of 'difference' on lesbian parent narratives across a range of locations and identities. As this research study clearly illustrates, the emphasis on participatory fatherhood in Sweden highlights the need for legislative recognition of multiple parents, rather than the two parents ideal intrinsic to the nuclear family model. Irish participants' feelings of vulnerability before the law and judicial system influenced their reproductive decision-making choices. Knowledge of similar complex dynamics informing queer kinship will also enable new forms of relatedness to become visible, challenging the heteronormative hegemony of contemporary kinship discourses. There is a further need to consider a wider range of kinship choices among queer parents, beyond those grounded in sexual partnerships. A critical engagement with legislative recognition requires more knowledge about queer relational possibilities. Critical social theory that incorporates an engagement with anti-heteronormative concerns needs to be informed by the experiences and subjectivities of those constructing kinship in non-normative intimacies who face complex choices in a homophobic world. It is hoped that this book represents one contribution towards this goal.

Notes

Chapter 1

1 See Dunne, G. (1998b), Abstract.
2 Ethical dimensions and epistemological challenges of this research are explored further in Ryan-Flood, R. (2009a, 2009b).

Chapter 2

1 See Stacey (1990, 1996) for a discussion of the development of discourses of the nuclear family.
2 This image is often referred to as 'an Sean Bhean Bhocht' (the Poor Old Woman).
3 This figure is popularly known as Cathleen Ní Houlihan.
4 Divorce is now available and the 'right to travel' abroad for abortion has been established. The traditionally highly contested nature of these issues however is supportive of Meaney's analysis. Indeed, the practice of abortion is still prohibited within the Irish nation state. The complex nature of abortion politics in Ireland has long been acknowledged by Irish feminist writers as a postcolonial signifier, where an anti-abortion stance (originating in Catholic tenets) became conflated with a nationalist stance. Thus Ireland's abortion law can be interpreted as a means of cultural differentiation (Fletcher, 1998; 2001, Smyth, 1998).
5 In Connolly (1995: 14–15).
6 Cited in Connolly (1995: 16).
7 The Oireachtas, or national parliament in the Republic of Ireland, consists of the President and two Houses: Dáil Éireann (the House of Representatives) and Seanad Éireann (the Senate).
8 This information can be downloaded from the central statistics office Ireland website: http://www.cso.ie/index.html
9 Interestingly, according to the 1997 Labour Force Survey, approximately 80 per cent of women who are in paid employment in Ireland are in full-time employment. This figure is slightly higher than the EU average of 73 per cent (O'Connor, 1999).
10 Information about the P2000 Expert Working Group on Childcare in Ireland can be downloaded from the European Industrial Relations Observatory website: http://www.eiro.eurofound.ie/
11 This involved a billboard campaign with a picture of a mother and daughter accompanied by the slogan 'How should you feel if your daughter's a lesbian? The same way you'd feel if she wasn't.' The campaign was launched in Dublin with the aid of Deputy Jan O'Sullivan, Mary Coughlan (an Irish folk singer), MEP Patricia McKenna, Deputy John Gormley and the director of Women's Studies at University College Dublin, Ailbhe Smyth.

12 Group 222 initiated many of the political debates with respect to gender equality. They were also instrumental in the formulation of related social policy. The number 222 was the address of one of its members, Annika Baude, a prominent social democrat (Baude, 1992).

13 The Swedish women's movement has been criticised for a heterosexist bias. Rosenberg (2002) suggests that the Swedish women's movement has a history of neglecting lesbian-specific issues.

14 Statistics Sweden (2003) *Women and Men in Sweden: Facts and Figures 2002.* Sweden: Statisiska Centralbyrån.

15 Cited in Murphy-Lawless, J. & McCarthy, J. (1999: 89).

16 However, although most women work full-time, they are over-represented in the part-time sector. Part-time employment represented nearly 15 per cent of total employment in Sweden in 1998. The average female share of part-time employment from 1995–1998 was 76.4 per cent (International Labour Organisation website) [http://www.ilo.org].

17 These initiatives were largely inspired by Alva and Gunnar Myrdal's famous book *Kris i Befolkningsfrågan* [Crisis in the Population Question] (1934). Hirdman (1989) in her discussion of the Swedish welfare state model emphasises the socialist sympathies of the Myrdals. She suggests that Alva Myrdal in particular believed that institutions such as childcare centres were the best way to raise children, rather than children being cared for by their mothers, who had not received special education for this role.

18 See Nyberg (2003) for a detailed account of parental leave provisions in Sweden.

19 Statistics indicate that couples who begin cohabiting in their twenties and thirties eventually marry in their forties if the relationship has lasted. Marriage appears to have become a largely pragmatic arrangement, rather than a symbolic one. A brief rise in the number of marriages took place during the 1980s, just prior to the cut off date for access to a widow's pension (Family formation and family dissolution in the 1980s, Official Statistics Sweden, 1990).

20 See for example Dagens Nyheter dagens debattartikel, Ökad tolerans mot homosexuella' [Increased tolerance towards homosexuals], August 28th, 2000. The research was eventually published in an academic journal in 2002.

21 Riksförbundet för sexuellt likaberättigande.

22 Recognition of cohabiting relationships – heterosexual and homosexual – was introduced in 1987. Initially, these were two separate laws. However, the sambo laws were eventually rewritten and combined to cover both heterosexuals and same sex couples under one law in 2003 [Sambolag (2003: 376)].

23 Hans Ytterberg, a former associate judge with substantial experience working for the rights of lesbians, gays and bisexuals. The Ombudsman was interviewed for this research study in February, 2002.

24 The Copenhagen clinic is run by a midwife who was interviewed for this research in February 2002.

25 One Swedish couple who participated in this research did however qualify in 2002 as a 'contact family', or part-time/respite foster carers of a special needs child who was in a long-term foster care placement.

26 For the relevant legislation, see Lagen (1984: 1140) om insemination and Lagen (1988: 711) om befruktning utanför kroppen. Additionally, the National Board of Health and Welfare has issued general guide lines that complement the statutes (SOSFS 2002: 13).

27 Interview, February 2002.
28 In Sweden, very few children are given up for adoption every year and most adoptions involve children born abroad. According to the Adoption Centre, Sweden, the number of Swedes adopted from abroad is in excess of 40,000 and this figure grows by approximately 1,000 every year. Sweden today has more internationally adopted children per capita than any other country in the world. The most common countries of origin for these children are Columbia, South Korea, China, Vietnam, Russia, Belarus, South Africa, India, Bulgaria and Ethiopia. The imperialist dimensions of international adoption have been increasingly debated in recent years (SOU 2001: 10). Nonetheless it remains an accepted practice for (predominantly white) Swedish couples who would otherwise be unable to become parents. (This information is provided on the homepage of the Adoption Centre, Sweden: http://www.adoptions-centrum.se/).

Chapter 3

1 Sourbut (1996) used the term 'gynogenesis' to refer to the process whereby an embryo is created using the genetic material of two women. There is no 'father' in such a situation and all offspring are female, as neither genetic parent carries the Y chromosome, which is required for male offspring. In January 2002 scientists at the Reproductive Genetics Institute in Chicago claimed that they have devised a way to create 'artificial sperm' from any cell in a woman's body, which can be used to fertilise another woman's eggs. The new method was already being tested on human eggs and scientists claimed that it could become available within the next 18 months, although this does not appear to have materialised. This technology was originally created to enable men who do not produce viable sperm to have a biological child with a female partner. In March 2008, the Observer newspaper reported that a change in the law in the UK would allow this type of 'artificial sperm' to be used in IVF treatment, but noted that the science was still in its infancy. The article suggested that such treatment would help those rendered infertile through cancer treatment for example or older women whose eggs were no longer viable.
2 One couple also had a foster child, in addition to two children born to one partner in the context of their relationship. Another couple, who had a son, also fostered part-time.
3 The clinic in question did not allow known donors to be used for its services where the donor is not also the partner of a woman receiving treatment in a heterosexual couple. This decision applies to heterosexual and lesbian couples and to single women as well. The rationale given for this is that complications may arise regarding access and financial provision (personal communication with clinic, September 2003).
4 Also cited in Freeman & Richards (2006).

Chapter 4

1 Sinfield (2000: 21) clarifies the scope of the term 'metropolitan' for Queer Studies. Metropolitan refers to 'global centres of capital' but is also used to mean capital cities within nation-states. He notes however that power rela-

tions in a particular metropolis include and exclude residents on the grounds of for example 'race' and ethnicity. Thus, individual experiences are differentially mediated by multiple facets of identity.

2 This image is reproduced at the beginning of this book.

3 Thus, NRTs are often presented as a means to enable a heterosexual couple to have a longed-for child, while opponents of NRTs may deride them as unnatural and actively utilise the example of lesbian parents as representative of the dangers of technology (Liljestrand, 1995).

4 This interview has not been included in this book, apart from the reference to it here.

5 The same is also true of heterosexual women who experience infertility but choose not to adopt or undergo medical interventions such as IVF.

6 I have previously omitted this information when publishing or writing up this research, as I did not want to alert authorities to the fact that some lesbians posed as heterosexual to access assisted reproduction services. However, now that the laws in Sweden have changed, I can write about it openly. This dilemma is further elaborated in Ryan-Flood, R. (2009) 'Keeping Mum: Secrecy and Silence in Research on Lesbian Parenthood', in Ryan-Flood, R. & Gill, R. (eds) (2009) *Secrecy and Silence in the Research Process: Feminist Reflections*. London: Routledge.

7 See for example, the third feature in the (2000) HBO film 'If These Walls Could Talk 2'.

8 This relates to earlier discussions about (in)visibility in Chapter 1.

9 The relatively small-scale nature of qualitative research means that it cannot be assumed that this is a representative sample. Nonetheless, the distribution of participants across urban/rural locations remains striking.

10 Her survey of homophobic harassment found that 25 per cent of the 3,000 Swedish lesbians and gay men who participated had experienced hate crime victimisation on the grounds of their sexuality.

Chapter 5

1 Béteille (1991: 25) has commented on the white-centredness of Schneider's (1968) work on kinship. He points out that the dichotomy between substance and code does not acknowledge the complex historical dynamics of race stratification and kinship in the US, whereby for example an African-American may be denied as kin to a white American.

2 This percentage was conveyed by Professor Lewin in a personal communication, June 2003.

3 See Lewin (1993), prologue and pp. 8–9.

4 The Active Management of Labour, while often associated with low caesarean rates, is also frequently criticised as overly interventionist and a compromise to women's integrity and agency in childbirth. For further discussion of these debates, see O'Regan (1998).

5 Adoption is of course a possible alternative for heterosexual women who wish to become mothers without giving birth.

6 See Rival, L. (1998) for a discussion of anthropological debates about the 'couvade', or the participation of fathers in childbirth rites. Examples of the

couvade can be found among the Huaorani Indians of Amazonian Ecuador, where men take the same steps as women, such as fasting or abstaining from particular food during pregnancy, in order to prevent harm coming to the future child. Rival argues that this can be understood, not simply as the assertion of paternity or as a challenge to Western notions of individuation, but rather as a process whereby a 'a new human person is brought to life and new relationships are created' (p. 628).

7 A reference to the political debate regarding second parent adoption, which was taking place in Sweden at that time.
8 'Spit' here is a colloquial expression originating from the term 'spitting image', meaning bears a strong physical resemblance to.
9 *Heather Has Two Mommies* (1990), by Lesléa Newman was one of the first children's books to portray lesbian parent families in a positive way.
10 The appellations 'mamma' and 'mamsan' are similar to 'mom' and 'mommy' respectively.
11 This situation has since been ameliorated with the introduction of second parent adoption in Sweden in 2003. However, this option was not available to participants during my fieldwork.

Chapter 6

1 This is illustrated by the notorious case of Sharon Bottoms in the US. Sharon Bottoms' mother sued for custody of her grandson when her daughter came out as a lesbian. The courts concluded that living in a lesbian household was harmful to the child and awarded full custody to the maternal grandmother with restricted visitation rights by the mother in 1995.
2 Issues of power and difference within lesbian couples regarding biological parenthood, were explored in the previous chapter.
3 Elin had recently embarked on full-time study.

Chapter 7

1 See Ryan-Flood, R. '"It's My Child": Power and vulnerability among separated lesbian parents', *European Societies*, forthcoming.
2 Questions of ethics and representation are discussed further in Ryan-Flood (2009a, 2009b).

Bibliography

Ahmed, S. (2004) *The Cultural Politics of Emotion*. Edinburgh: Edinburgh University Press.

Alexander, M. J. (2005) *Pedagogies of Crossing*. North Carolina: Duke University Press.

Anthias, F. & Yuval-Davis, N. (1993) *Racialised Boundaries: Race, Nation, Gender, Colour and Class*. London: Routledge.

Baude, A. (1992) *Visionen om jämställdhet* [The Vision of Equality Between Women and Men]. Stockholm: SNS.

Bauer, E. & Thompson, P. (2006) *Jamaican Hands across the Atlantic: Families between Jamaica, Britain and North America*. Kingston and London: Ian Randle.

Bell, D. & Binnie J. (2000) *The Sexual Citizen: Queer Politics and Beyond*. Cambridge: Polity Press.

Bell, D. & Binnie, J. (2002) *The Sexual Citizen*. Cambridge: Polity Press.

Bell, D. (2000) 'Eroticizing the Rural', in R. Phillips, Watt, D. & Shuttleton, D. (eds) *De-centring Sexualities: Politics and Representations Beyond the Metropolis*. London: Routledge.

Bell, D. & Valentine, G. (1995b) 'Queer Country: Rural Lesbian and Gay Lives', *Journal of Rural Studies*, 11: 113–22.

Bell, D. & Valentine, G. (1995a) Mapping Desire: geographies of sexualities. London: Routledge.

Benkov, L. (1994) *Reinventing the Family: The Emerging Story of Gay and Lesbian Parents*. New York: Crown.

Beresford, S. (1998) 'The Lesbian Mother: Questions of Gender and Sexual Identity', in L. J. Moran, D. Monk & S. Beresford (eds) *Legal Queries: Lesbian, Gay, and Transgender Legal Studies*. London: Cassell.

Berggren, C. (1997) 'Sweden', in Griffin, K. & Mulholland, L. A. (eds) *Lesbian Motherhood in Europe*. London: Cassell.

Bergman, H. & Hobson, B. (2002) 'Compulsory Fatherhood: The Coding of Fatherhood in the Swedish Welfare State', in B. Hobson (ed.) *Making Men into Fathers: Masculinities, Gender Logics, and Social Politics*. Cambridge: Cambridge University Press.

Bergqvist, C., Borchest, A., Christensen, A. D., Ramstedt-Silén, V., Raaum, N. C. & Styrkársdóttir, A. (1999) *Equal Democracies? Gender and Politics in the Nordic Countries*. Oslo: Scandinavian University Press.

Bergqvist, C. (1999) 'Childcare and Parental Leave Models', in Bergqvist, C., Borchest, A., Christensen, A. D., Ramstedt-Silén, V. Raaum, N. C. & Styrkársdóttir, A. (eds) *Equal Democracies? Gender and Politics in the Nordic Countries*. Oslo: Scandinavian University Press.

Bernstein, M. & Reimann, R. (2001) *Queer Families, Queer Politics: Challenging Culture and the State*. New York: Columbia University Press.

Béteille, A. (1991) *Society and Politics in India: Essays in a Comparative Perspective*. London: Athlone Press.

Binnie, J. (2004) *The Globalization of Sexuality*. London: Sage.

Birenbaum-Carmeli, D. & Carmeli, Y. (2002) Physiognomy, Familism and Consumerism: Preferences among Jewish Israeli Recipients of Donor Insemination', *Social Science and Medicine*, 54(3): 363–76.

Björnberg, U. (1998) 'Family Orientation Among Men: A Process of Change in Sweden', in E. Drew, R. Emerek & E. Mahon (eds) *Women, Work and the Family in Europe*. London: Routledge.

Blumstein, P. & Schwartz, P. (1983) *American Couples*. New York: Morrow.

Bowyer, S. (2001) Coming Out to the Neighbourhood/Coming On to the Neighbours: Same Sex Desire, Speaking it and Being it in Dublin 2001, *International Association for the Study of Sex, Culture and Society*. Melbourne, Australia.

Brewaeys, A., Ponjaert-Kristoffersen, I., Van Steirteghem, A. C. & Devroey, P. (1993) 'Children from Anonymous Donors: An Inquiry into Homosexual and Heterosexual Parents' Attitudes', *Journal of Psychosomatic Gynaecology and Sexology*, 14: 23–35.

Butler, J. (2002) 'Is Kinship Always Already Heterosexual?', *Differences: A Journal of Feminist Cultural Studies*, 13: 14–44.

Byrne, A. & Leonard, M. (1997) *Women and Irish Society: A Sociological Reader*. Belfast: Beyond the Pale Publications.

Carsten, J. (2000) *Cultures of Relatedness: New Approaches to the Study of Kinship*. Cambridge: Cambridge University Press.

Chan, R. W., Brooks, R. C., Raboy, B. & Patterson, C. J. (1998) 'Division of Labor Among Lesbian and Heterosexual Parents: Associations with Children's Adjustment', *Journal of Family Psychology*, 12: 402–19.

Chesnais, J. C. (1996) 'Fertility, Family and Social Policy in Contemporary Western Europe', *Population and Development Review*, 22: 729–39.

Clarke, V. (2002) 'Sameness and Difference in Research on Lesbian Parenting', *Journal of Community & Applied Social Psychology*, 12: 210–22.

Collins, A. (2006) (ed.) *Cities of Pleasure*. London: Routledge.

Connolly, A. (1995) 'The Constitution', in A. Connolly (ed.) *Gender and the Law in Ireland*. Dublin: Oak Tree Press.

Cook, G. & McCashin, A. (1997) 'Male Breadwinner: A Case Study of Gender and Social Security in the Republic of Ireland', in Byrne, A. & Leonard, M. (eds) *Women and Irish Society: A Sociological Reader*. Belfast: Beyond the Pale Publications.

Corber, R. J. & Valocchi, S. (2003) *Queer Studies: An Interdisciplinary Reader*. Oxford: Blackwell.

Dahlström, E. (1962) *Kvinnors liv och arbete* [Women's Life and Work]. Sweden: Publica.

Davidoff, L. (2006) 'Close Marriage in the Nineteenth and Twentieth Century Middle Strata', in M. Richards and F. Ebtehaj (eds) *Kinship Matters*. Cambridge: Hart Publishers.

De Lauretis, T. (1994) 'Habit Changes', *Differences: A Journal of Feminist Cultural Studies*, 6(2): 296–313.

Donovan, C. (2000) 'Who Needs a Father? Negotiating Biological Fatherhood in British Lesbian Families Using Self-Insemination', *Sexualities*, 3: 149–64.

Duncan, S. & Edwards, R. (1999) *Lone Mothers, Paid Work and Gendered Moral Rationalities*. Houndmills [England]: Macmillan Press.

Duncan, N. (1996) *Bodyspace: Destabilising Geographies of Gender and Sexuality*. New York: Routledge.

Dunne, G. (1998a) '"Pioneers Behind Our Own Front Doors": New Models for the Organization of Work in Partnerships', *The Journal of Work Employment and Society*, 12: 273–97.

—— (1998b) Opting into Motherhood: Blurring the Boundaries and Redefining the Meaning of Parenthood, *LSE Gender Institute discussion paper series*. London: London School of Economics and Political Science; Gender Institute.

—— (2001a) The Different Dimensions of Gay Fatherhood: Exploding the Myths, LSE Gender Institute discussion paper, January 2001. http://www.lse.ac.uk/collections/genderInstitute/pdf/gayfatherhood.pdf

—— (2001b) 'The Lady Vanishes? Reflections on the Experiences of Married and Divorced Gay Fathers', *Sociological Research Online*. Volume 6, Number 3 (November) http://www.socresonline.org.uk/6/3/dunne.html. pp. 1–17.

Edwards, J. & Strathern, M. (2000) 'Including Our Own', in J. Carsten (ed.), *Cultures of Relatedness: New Approaches to the Study of Kinship*. Cambridge: Cambridge University Press.

Elman, A. (1996) *Sexual Subordination and State Intervention: Comparing Sweden and the United States*. Oxford: Bergahn Books.

Elvin-Nowak, Y. (1999) *Accompanied by Guilt: Modern Motherhood the Swedish Way*. Stockholm: Stockholm University Press.

Fincher, R. & Jacobs, J. (eds) (1998) *Cities of Difference*. London: Guilford Press.

Finkler, K. (2001) 'The Kin in the Gene: The Medicalization of Family and Kinship in American Society', *Current Anthropology*, 42(2): 235–63.

Fletcher, R. (1998) '"Pro-Life" Absolutes; Feminist Challenges: The Fundamentalist Narrative of Irish Abortion Law 1986–92', *Osgoode Hall Law Journal*, 36: 1–62.

—— (2001) 'Post-colonial Fragments: Representations of Abortion in Irish Law and Politics', *Journal of Law and Society*, 28: 568–89.

Franklin, S. & McKinnon, S. (eds) (2001) *Relative Values: Reconfiguring Kinship Studies*. North Caroline: Duke University Press.

Freeman, M. (1996) 'The New Birth Right? Identity and the Child of the Reproduction Revolution', *The International Journal of Children's Rights*, 4: 273–97.

Freeman, T. & Richards, M. (2006) 'DNA Testing and Kinship: Paternity, Genealogy, and the Search for the "Truth" of Genetic Origins', in M. Richards & F. Ebtehaj (eds) *Kinship Matters*. Cambridge: Hart Publishers.

Gabb, J. (2002) '(In)Essential Ingredients? Selectivity and Silences in Lesbian Parent Families' Research', conference paper, paper presented at *Parenting Under the Rainbow conference*. University of Sunderland.

Gabb, J. (2005) 'Locating Lesbian Parent Families', *Gender, Place, Culture*. Vol. 12(4): 419–32.

Galligan, Y. (1998) *Women and Politics in Contemporary Ireland*. London: Pinter.

Giddens, A. (1992) *The Transformation of Intimacy: Sexuality, Love and Eroticism in Modern Societies*. Oxford: Polity Press.

Golombok, S. & Tasker, F. (1997) *Growing Up in a Lesbian Family: Effects on Child Development*. New York: Guilford Press.

Golombok, S., Spencer, A. & Rutter, M. (1983) 'Children in Lesbian and Single-Parent Households: Psychosexual and Psychiatric Appraisal', *Journal of Child Psychology and Psychiatry*, 24: 551–72.

Gray, B. & Ryan, L. (1997) '(Dis)locating "Woman" and Women in Representations of Irish National Identity', in Byrne, A. & Leonard, M. (eds) *Women and Irish Society: A Sociological Reader*. Belfast: Beyond the Pale Publications.

Green, S. (1997) *Urban Amazons: Lesbian Feminism and Beyond in the Gender, Sexuality, and Identity Battles of London*. Basingstoke: Macmillan Press.

Gregson, N. & Lowe, M. (1994) 'Waged Domestic Labour and the Renegotiation of the Domestic Divisions of Labour within Dual Career Households', *Sociology*, 28: 55–78.

Griffin, K. & Mulholland, L. A. (1997) *Lesbian Motherhood in Europe*. London: Cassell.

Guitiérrez, R. A. (1997) 'Response to Schneider's "The Power of Culture"', *Cultural Anthropology*, 12: 278–81.

Gustafsson, S. (1994) 'Childcare and Types of Welfare States', in D. Sainsbury (ed.) *Gendering Welfare States*. London: Sage.

Haavind, H. (1998) 'Understanding Women in the Psychological Mode: the Challenge from the Experiences of Nordic Women', in D. von der Fehr, A. Jónasdóttir & B. Rosenbeck (eds) *Is There a Nordic Feminism?: Nordic Feminist Thought on Culture and Society*. London: UCL Press.

Halberstam, J. (2003) 'The Brandon Teena Archive', in R. J. Corber & S. Valocchi (eds) *Queer Studies: An Interdisciplinary Reader*. Oxford: Blackwell Publishing.

Haltvorsen, L. (1998) 'The Ambiguity of Lesbian and Gay Marriages. Change and Continuity in the Symbolic Order', in J. Löfström (ed.) *Scandinavian Homosexualities: Essays on Gay and Lesbian Studies*. New York: Haworth Press.

Hanscombe, G. E. & Forster, J. (1982) *Rocking the Cradle. Lesbian Mothers: A Challenge in Family Living*. London: Peter Owens.

Hayden, C. (1995) 'Gender, Genetics, and Generation: Reformulating Biology in Lesbian Kinship', *Cultural Anthropology*, 10: 41–63.

Heaphy, B., Donovan, C. & Weekes, J. (1999) 'Sex, Money and the Kitchen Sink: Power in Same-Sex Couple Relationships', in J. Seymour (ed.) *Relating Intimacies: Power and Resistance*. London: Macmillan.

Herdt, Gilbert H. (ed.) (1984) *Ritualized Homosexuality in Melanesia*. Berkeley: University of California Press.

Herek, G. M. (1998) *Stigma and Sexual Orientation: Understanding Prejudice Against Lesbians, Gay Men, and Bisexuals*. Thousand Oaks, CA: Sage Publications.

Hicks, S. & McDermott, J. (1999) *Lesbian and Gay Fostering and Adoption: Extraordinary Yet Ordinary*. London: Jessica Kingsley Publishers.

Hicks, S. (2002) 'I Was Shamed on "Richard and Judy": Responding to Claims that Same-Sex Parenting is Bad for You', paper presented at *Parenting Under the Rainbow conference*. University of Sunderland.

Hicks, S. (2005) 'Is Gay Parenting Bad for Kids?, Responding to the "Very Idea of Difference" in Research on Lesbian and Gay Parents', *Sexualities*, 8: 153–68.

Hill-Collins, P. (1990) *Black Feminist Thought*. New York: Routledge.

—— (1994) 'Shifting the Center: Race, Class and Feminist Theorizing about Motherhood', in D. Bassin, M. Honey & M. M. Kaplan (eds) *Representations of Motherhood*. London: Yale University Press.

Hirdman, Y. (1989) *Att lägga livet tillrätta: Studier i svensk folkhemspolitik* [To put life in order: Studies in Swedish social democratic policies]. Stockholm: Carlssons.

—— (1998) 'State Policy and Gender Contracts: the Swedish Experience', in E. Drew, R. Emerek & E. Mahon (eds), *Women, Work and the Family in Europe*. London: Routledge.

Hobson, B. (1993) 'Gendered Discourses and Feminist Strategies in Welfare States: The Debates over Married Women's Right to Work in Sweden and the United States', in S. Koven & S. Michel (eds) *Mothers of a New World: Gender and Origins of Welfare States in Western Europe and North America*. London: Routledge.

Hobson, B. & Takahashi, M. (1997) 'The Parent-Worker Model: Lone Mothers in Sweden', in J. Lewis (ed.) *Lone Mothers in European Welfare Regimes: Shifting Policy Logics*. England: Jessica Kingsley Publishers.

Hobson, B. (2003) 'Frames and Claims: The Interplay Between Recognition and Redistribution in Sweden and Ireland', in B. Hobson (ed.) *Recognition Struggles and Social Movements: Contested Identities, Agency and Power*. Cambridge: Cambridge University Press.

Hobson, B. & Bergman, H. (2002) 'Compulsory Fatherhood: The Coding of Fatherhood in the Swedish Welfare State', in B. Hobson (ed.) *Making Men into Fathers: Men, Masculinities and the Social Politics of Fatherhood*. England: Cambridge University Press.

Hoem, J. M. (1990) 'Social Policy and Recent Fertility Change in Europe', *Population and Development Review*, 16: 735–48.

Inglis, T. (1998) *Lessons in Irish Sexuality*. Dublin: University College Dublin Press.

Ingram, G., Bouthilette, A. and Retter, Y. (eds) (1997) *Queers in Space*. Seattle, WA: Bay Press.

Irigaray, L. (1985) *This Sex Which Is Not One*. New York: Cornell University Press.

Johnson, S. M. & O'Connor, E. (2002) *The Gay Baby Boom: The Psychology of Gay Parenthood*. London: New York University Press.

Johnston, L. (2005) *Queering Tourism: Paradoxical Performances of Gay Pride Parades*. London and New York: Routledge.

Kearney, Jeremy, Sven-Axel Mansson, Lars Plantin, Keith Pringle & Sheila Quaid (2000) *Fatherhood and Masculinities*. Sunderland: University of Sunderland.

Kenney, J. & Tash, D. T. (1992) 'Lesbian Childbearing Couples' Dilemmas and Decisions', *Health Care for Women International*, 13: 209–19.

Kitzinger, C. & Coyle, A. (1995) 'Lesbian and Gay Couples: Speaking of Difference', *The Psychologist*, 8: 64–9.

Kitzinger, S. (1992) *Ourselves as Mothers: The Universal Experience of Motherhood*. London: Doubleday.

Knopp, L. (1995) 'Sexuality and Urban Space: A Framework for Analysis', in D. Bell & G. Valentine (eds) *Mapping Desire: Geographies of Sexualities*. London: Routledge.

—— (1998) 'Sexuality and Urban Space: Gay Male Identity Politics in the United States, the United Kingdom and Australia', in R. Fincher & J. Jacobs (eds) *Cities of Difference*. London: Guilford Press.

Kurdek, L. (1993) 'The Allocation of Household Labour in Homosexual and Heterosexual Cohabiting Couples', *Journal of Social Issues*, 49: 127–39.

Laird, J. (1999) *Lesbians and Lesbian Families: Reflections on Theory and Practice*. New York: Columbia University Press.

Landén, M., & Innala, S. (2002) 'The Effect of a Biological Explanation on Attitudes towards Homosexual Persons: a Swedish National Sample Study', *Nordic Journal of Psychiatry*, 56.

Lehr, V. (1999) *Queer Family Values: Debunking the Myth of the Nuclear Family*. Philadelphia: Temple University Press.

Leira, A. (1993) 'The "Woman-Friendly" Welfare State? The Case of Norway and Sweden', in J. Lewis (ed.) *Women and Social Policies in Europe*. London: Edward Elgar.

Lentin, R. (1998) '"Irishness", the 1937 Constitution and Citizenship: A Gender and Ethnicity View', *Irish Journal of Sociology*, 8: 5–24.

Lentin, R. & McVeigh, R. (2002) *Racism and Anti-racism in Ireland*. Belfast: Beyond the Pale.

Lewin, E. (1993) *Lesbian Mothers: Accounts of Gender in American Culture*. New York: Cornell University Press.

—— (2001) 'It's All in the Family', *GLQ: A Journal of Lesbian and Gay Studies*, 7: 655–62.

—— (1993) *Women and Social Policies in Europe*. London: Edward Elgar.

Lewis, J. & Ostner, I. (1995) 'Gender and the Evolution of European Social Policies', in S. Liebfried & P. Pierson (eds) *European Social Policy*. Washington: Brookings Institution.

Liljestrand, P. (1995) 'Legitimate State and Illegitimate Parents: Donor Insemination Politics in Sweden', *Social Politics: International Studies in Gender, State and Society*, 2: 270–304.

Lister, R. (1997) *Citizenship: Feminist Perspectives*. Macmillan: Basingstoke.

Lott-Whitehead, L. & Tully, C. T. (1999) 'The Family Lives of Lesbian Mothers', in J. Laird (ed) *Lesbians and Lesbian Families: Reflections on Theory and Practice*. New York: Columbia University Press.

Mahon, E. (1998) 'Changing Gender Roles, State, Work and Family Lives', in E. Drew, R. Emerek & E. Mahon (eds) *Women, Work and the Family in Europe*. London: Routledge.

Malone, K. & Cleary, R. (2002) '(De)Sexing the Family: Theorising the social Science of Lesbian Families', *Feminist Theory*, 3: 271–93.

McCarthy, J. & Murphy-Lawless, J. (1999) 'Recent Fertility Change in Ireland', *Population Bulletin of the United Nations*, (40–1): 235–46.

McDonnell, O. (1999) 'Shifting Debates on New Reproductive Technology: Implications for Public Discourse in Ireland', in P. O'Mahony (ed.) *Nature, Risk and Responsibility: Discourses of Biotechnology*. Basingstoke: Macmillan.

McDowell, L. (1999) *Gender, Identity and Place: Understanding Feminist Geographies*. Oxford: Polity Press.

McLaughlin, E. & Yeates, N. (1999) 'The Biopolitics of Welfare in Ireland', *Irish Journal of Feminist Studies*, 2: 49–69.

Meaney, G. (1991) 'Sex and Nation: Women in Irish Culture and Politics', in E. Boland (ed.) *A Dozen Lips*. Dublin: Attic Press.

Moane, G. (1997) 'Lesbian Politics and Community', in Byrne, A. & Leonard, M. (eds) *Women and Irish Society: A Sociological Reader*. Dublin: Beyond the Pale Publications.

Mohler, M. & Frazer, L. (2002) *A Donor Insemination Guide Written By and For Lesbian Women*. New York: Haworth Press.

Moraga, C. (1997) *Waiting in the Wings: Portrait of a Queer Motherhood*. New York: Firebrand Books.

Morgan, D. (1996) *Family Connections: An Introduction to Family Studies*. Cambridge: Polity Press.

Morgan, P. (2002) *Children as Trophies? Examining the Evidence on Same-Sex Parenting*. Newcastle-upon-Tyne, England: The Christian Institute.

Morningstar, B. (1999) 'Lesbian Parents: Understanding Developmental Pathways', in J. Laird (ed.) *Lesbians and Lesbian Families: Reflections on Theory and Practice*. New York: Columbia University Press.

Munt, S. (1998) *Butch/femme: Inside Lesbian Gender*. London: Cassell.

Muzio, C. (1999) 'Lesbian Co-Parenting: On Being/Being with the Invisible (M)Other', in Laird, J. (ed.) *Lesbians and Lesbian Families: Reflections on Theory and Practice*. New York: Columbia University Press.

Myrdal, A. & Myrdal, G. (1934) *Kris i Befolkningsfrågan* [Crisis in the Population Question]. Stockholm: Bonnier.

Nandy, A. (1983) *The Intimate Enemy: Loss and Recovery of Self under Colonialism*. Oxford: Oxford University Press.

Nash, C. (1993) 'Re-mapping and Re-naming: new cartographies of identity, gender and landscape in Ireland', *Feminist Review*, 44: 39–57.

Nelson, F. (1996) *Lesbian Motherhood: An Exploration of Canadian Lesbian Families*. Toronto: University of Toronto Press.

Nestle, J. (1992) *The Persistent Desire: A Femme-Butch Reader*. Boston: Alyson Publications.

Newman, L. (1990) *Heather Has Two Mommies*. California: Heretic Books.

Nyberg, A. (2002) 'Gender, (de)Commodification, Economic (In)dependence and Autonomous Households: The Case of Sweden', *Critical Social Policy*, 22: 72–95.

—— (2003) 'Economic Crisis and the Sustainability of the Dual Earner, Dual Carer Model: Working Paper, *ESRC seminar series 'Work, Life and Time in the New Economy'*. University of Manchester.

O'Connor, P. (1998) *Emerging Voices: Women in Contemporary Irish Society*. Dublin: Institute of Public Administration.

O'Connor, P. (1999) *Emerging Voices: Women in Contemporary Irish Society*. Ireland: IPA Press.

O'Donnell, K. (1999) 'Lesbian and Gay Families: Legal Perspectives', in G. Jagger & C. Wright (eds) *Difference, Diversity and the Decline of Male Order*. London: Routledge.

Oerton, S. (1998) 'Reclaiming the "Housewife"? Lesbians and Household Work', *The Journal of Lesbian Studies*, 2: 69–84.

O'Regan, M. (1998) 'Active Management of Labour – The Irish Way of Birth', *AIMS Journal*. Summer.

Oyen, E. (1990) *Comparative Methodology, Theory and Practice in International Social Research*. London: Sage.

Patterson, C. (1994) 'Children of the Lesbian Baby Boom: Behavioral Adjustment, Self-Concepts, and Sex-Role Identity', in B. Greene & G. M. Herek (eds) *Contemporary Perspectives on Lesbian and Gay Psychology: Theory, Research and Applications*. California: Sage.

—— (1992) 'Children of Lesbian and Gay Parents', *Child Development*, 63: 1025–42.

Patterson, C. (1995a) 'Families of the Lesbian Baby Boom: Parents' Division of Labor and Children's Adjustment', *Developmental Psychology*, 13: 115–23.

—— (1995b) 'Lesbian Mothers, Gay Fathers, and Their Children', in A. D'Augelli & C. Patterson (eds) *Lesbian, Gay and Bisexual Identities over the Lifespan: Psychological Perspectives*. England: Oxford University Press.

Peets, C. (2000) 'Feminist Mothers and Sons: Making a Difference', *Journal of the Association for Research on Mothering: Mothers and Sons*, 2: 98–103.

Peplau, L. A. & Cochran, S. D. (1990) 'A Relational Perspective on Homosexuality', in D. P. McWhirter, A. Sanders & J. M. Reinisch (eds) *Homosexuality/Heterosexuality: Concepts of Sexual Orientation*. New York: Oxford University Press.

Pepper, R. (1999) *The Ultimate Guide to Pregnancy for Lesbians*. London: Cleis Press.

Petersen, A. & Bunton, R. (2002) *The New Genetics and the Public's Health*. London: Routledge.

Phillips, R. & Watt, D. (2000) 'Introduction', in R. Phillips, D. Watt & D. Shuttleton (eds) *In De-centring Sexualities: Politics and Representations Beyond the Metropolis*. London: Routledge.

Phillips, R., Watt, D. & Shuttleton, D. (eds) (2000) *De-Centering Sexualities: Politics and Representations Beyond the Metropolis*. London: Routledge.

Pies, C. (1988) *Considering Parenthood*. London: Spinsters Book Company.

Plantin, L. (2001) *Mäns föräldraskap. Om mäns upplevelser och erfarenheter av faderskapet* [Men's Parenting. On Men's Perceptions and Experiences of Fatherhood]. Gothenburg: Gothenburg University Press.

Pollack, S. & Vaughn, J. (1987) *Politics of the Heart: A Lesbian Parenting Anthology*. New York: Firebrand Books.

Popenoe, D. (1988) *Disturbing the Nest: Family Change and Decline in Modern Societies*. New York: A. de Gruyter.

Prendiville, P. (1997) 'Ireland', in Griffin, K. & Mulholland, L. A. (eds) *Lesbian Motherhood in Europe*. London: Cassell.

Reinharz, S. (1992) *Feminist Methods in Social Research*. Oxford: Oxford University Press.

RFSL (1997) *Fakta från RFSL: Homosexuella och barn* [Facts from RFSL: Homosexuals and children]. Stockholm: RFSL.

Rival, L. (1998) 'Androgynous Parents and Guest Children: The Huaorani Couvade', *Journal of the Royal Anthropological Institute*, 4: 619–42.

Rohrbaugh, J. (1989) 'Choosing Children: Psychosocial Issues in Lesbian Parenting', in E. D. Rosenblum & E. Cole (eds) *Lesbianism: Affirming Nontraditional Roles*. New York: Haworth.

Romlid, C. (1998) *Makt, motstånd och förändring. Vårdens historia speglad genom det svenska barnmorskeväsendet 1663–1908* [Power, resistance and change: the history of Swedish health care reflected through the official midwife system 1663–1908]. Stockholm: Vårdförbundet.

Rose, K. (1994) *Diverse Communities: The Evolution of Lesbian and Gay Politics in Ireland*. Cork: Cork University Press.

Rosenberg, T. (2002) *Queerfeministisk agenda*. Stockholm: Atlas.

Ryan-Flood, R. (2009a) 'Keeping Mum: Secrecy and Silence in Research on Lesbian Parenthood', in Ryan-Flood, R. & Gill, R. (eds) (2009) *Secrecy and Silence in the Research Process: Feminist Reflections*. London: Routledge.

Ryan-Flood, R. (2009b) 'Queering Representation: Ethics and Visibility in Research', *Journal of Lesbian Studies*, 13(2): 216–28.

Ryan-Flood, R. & Gill, R. (eds) (2009) *Secrecy and Silence in the Research Process: Feminist Reflections*. London: Routledge.

Saffron, L. (2001) *It's a Family Affair: The Complete Lesbian Parenting Book*. London: Diva.

Sainsbury, D. (1994) Gendering Welfare States. London: Sage.

—— (1996) *Gender, Equality and Welfare States*. Cambridge: Cambridge University Press.

—— (1999) *Gender and Welfare State Regimes*. Oxford: Oxford University Press.

Scheib, J. E., Riordan, M. & Shaver, P. R. (2000) 'Choosing Between Anonymous and Identity Release Sperm Donors: Recipient and Donor Characteristics. *Reproductive Technologies*, 10: 50–8.

Scheib, J. E., Riordan, M. & Rubin, S. (2003) 'Choosing Identity-Release Sperm Donors: The Parents' Perspective 13–18 Years Later', *Human Reproduction*, 18: 1115–27.

Schneider, D. (1984) *A Critique of the Study of Kinship*. Michigan: University of Michigan Press.

Schneider, D. (1968) *American Kinship: A Cultural Account*. New Jersey: Prentice-Hall.

—— (1997) 'The Power of Culture: Notes on Some Aspects of Gay and Lesbian Kinship in America Today', *Cultural Anthropology*, 12: 270–4.

Schwartz, A. E. (1998) *Sexual Subjects: Lesbians, Gender and Psychoanalysis*. London: Routledge.

Sedgewick, E. (1994) 'How to Bring Your Kids Up Gay', in M. Warner (ed) *Fear of a Queer Planet: Queer Politics and Social Theory*. Minneapolis: University of Minnesota Press.

Sinfield, A. (2000) 'The Production of Gay and the Return of Power', in Phillips, R., Watt, D. & Shuttleton, D. (eds) (2000) *De-Centering Sexualities: Politics and Representations Beyond the Metropolis*. London: Routledge.

Slater, S. (1995) *The Lesbian Family Life Cycle*. New York: The Free Tree Press.

Smyth, A. (1988) 'The Contemporary Women's Movement in the Republic of Ireland', *Women's Studies International Forum*, 11: 331–41.

Smyth, A. (1991) 'The Floozie in the Jacuzzi', *Feminist Studies*, 17(1): 7–28.

Smyth, E. (1997) 'Labour Market Structures and Women's Employment in the Republic of Ireland', in A. Byrne & M. Leonard (eds) *Women and Irish Society: A Sociological Reader*. Belfast: Beyond the Pale Publications.

Søland, B. (1998) 'A Queer Nation? The Passage of the Gay and Lesbian Partnership Legislation in Denmark, 1989', *Social Politics: International Studies in Gender, State and Society*, 5: 48–69.

SOU (2001) *Barn i homosexuella familjer: betänkande av Kommittén om barn i homosexuella familjer* [Children in homosexual families: Report from the Commission on children in homosexual families].

—— (1984) *Homosexuella och samhället – betänkande av utredningen om homosexuellas situation i samhället* [Homosexuals and the society – Report from the parliamentary inquiry on homosexuals' situation in the society].

Sourbut, E. (1996) 'Gynogenesis: A Lesbian Appropriation of Reproductive Technologies', in N. Lykke & R. Braidotti (eds) *Between Monsters, Goddesses and Cyborgs: Feminist Confrontations with Science, Medicine and Cyberspace*. London: Zed Books.

Spillane, F. (2001) *Lesbian Non-Mothers Reproductive Decisions*. Unpublished BA dissertation, Trinity College.

Stacey, J. (1990) *Brave New Families: Stories of Domestic Upheaval in Late Twentieth-Century America*. Basic Books.

Stacey, J. (1996) *In the Name of the Family: Rethinking Family Values in the Postmodern Age*. Boston: Beacon Press.

—— (1991) 'Can There Be a Feminist Ethnography?', in S. B. Gluck & D. Patai (eds) *Women's Words: The Feminist Practice of Oral History*. London: Routledge.

Stacey, J. & Biblarz, T. J. (2001) '(How) Does the Sexual Orientation of Parents Matter?', *American Sociological Review*, 66: 159–83.

Strathern, M. (1993) 'Families We Choose: Lesbians, Gays, Kinship (Review)', *Man*, 28: 195–6.

Sullivan, M. (1996) 'Rozzie and Harriet? Gender and Family Patterns of Lesbian Coparents', *Gender and Society*, 10: 747–67.

Sullivan, O. (2000) 'The Division of Domestic Labour: Twenty Years of Change?', *Sociology*, 34: 437–56.

Sullivan, M. (2001) 'Alma Mater: Family "Outings" and the Making of the Modern Other Mother (MOM)', in Bernstein, M. & Reimann, R. (eds) *Queer Families, Queer Politics: Challenging Culture and the State*. New York: Columbia University Press.

Sullivan, M. (2004) *The Family of Woman: Lesbian Mothers, Their Children, and the Undoing of Gender*. California: University of California Press.

Sundström, M. & Duvander, A. E. (2002) 'Gender Division of Childcare and the Sharing of Parental Leave among New Parents in Sweden', *European Sociological Review*, 18: 433–47.

Tasker, F. & Golombok, S. (1997) *Growing Up in a Lesbian Family: Effects on Child Development*. New York: The Guilford Press.

Tasker, F. & Golombok, S. (1998) 'The Role of Co-Mothers in Planned Lesbian-Led Families', *The Journal of Lesbian Studies*, 2: 49–68.

Thompson, J. M. (2002) *Mommy Queerest: Contemporary Rhetorics of Lesbian Maternal Identity*. Boston: University of Massachusetts Press.

Tiby, E. (1999) *Hatbrott? Homosexuella kvinnors och mäns berättelser om utsatthet för brott* [Hate Crime? Homosexual women's and men's stories about exposure to crime]. Stockholm: Stockholm University Press.

Valentine, G. (2001) *Social Geographies: Space and Society*. London: Prentice-Hall.

—— (2002) 'People Like Us: Negotiating Sameness and Difference in the Research Process', in P. J. Moss (ed.) *Feminist Geography in Practice: Research and Methods*. Oxford: Blackwell.

Vanfraussen, K., Ponjaert-Kristoffersen, I. & Brewaeys, A. (2001) 'An Attempt to reconstruct Children's Donor Concept: A Comparison between Children's and Lesbian Parents' Attitudes towards Donor Anonymity', *Human Reproduction*, 16: 2019–25.

Walshe, E. (2000) 'Ireland', in G. E. Haggerty (ed.) *Gay Histories and Cultures: An Encyclopedia*. New York: Garland.

Warner, M. (1994) *Fear of a Queer Planet: Queer Politics and Social Theory*. Minneapolis: University of Minnesota Press.

—— (1999) *The Trouble With Normal: Sex, Politics, and The Ethics of Queer Life*. New York: Free Press.

Weeks, J., Heaphy, B. & Donovan, C. (2001) *Same Sex Intimacies: Families of Choice and Other Life Experiments*. London: Routledge.

Wells, J. (2000) *Homefronts: Controversies in Nontraditional Parenting*. New York: Alyson Publications.

Weston, G. (1993) *Families We Choose: Lesbians, Gays, Kinship*. New York: Columbia University Press.

Weston, K. (1992) *Families We Choose: Lesbians, Gays, Kinship*. New York: Columbia University Press.

Weston, K. (1998) 'Get Thee to a Big City: Sexual Imaginary and the Great Gay Migration', in K. Weston (ed.) *Long Slow Burn: Sexuality and Social Science*. New York: Routledge.

Weston, K. (1991) *Families We Choose: Lesbians, Gays, Kinship*. New York: Columbia University Press.
Widegren, B. & Ytterberg, H. (1995) *Homosexuellas Rättigheter [Homosexuals' Rights]*. Stockholm: Folkhälsoinstitutet.

Index

22222222

performance, of identities, 80–1
  gay and lesbian, 80
  heterosexual, 80
Phillips, R., 81
political debates
  lesbian and gay parenting, 6, 14, 83, 183
  lesbian and gay rights, 6, 13
  new reproductive technologies (NRTs), 28–9
  same sex marriage, 28
positivist tradition, 149, 151
postcolonialism, 20, 108
postnatal depression, 93–4
power
  and biological ties, 115, 122, 131, 139, 143, 145, 146, 147–8, 154
  and fertility, 122
  and co-parenting, 131, 137, 146, 147, 154
prenatal care, 73, 88–9, 116, 128
preschool, 25, 157
press, *see* media
Pride Week, 83–4, 171
psychological development of children, 2, 5–6, 150–1, 183

queer activism, 14, 37, 42, 90
  see also LGBT movement
queer metropolis, 81–2, 102–3
queer theory, 2–3, 105, 109, 178, 185

race, 80, 176, 183
  of donors, 65–9
  of mothers, 14
  of children, 67, 68
racism, 66–7 *see also* discrimination
Reinharz, S., 41
relatedness
  cultures of, 111–15, 127, 133, 148, 181–2
  epistemology of, 111
  see also biology
  see also kinship
relationship break-ups, 8, 111, 121, 142–7, 183, 188
  see also divorce
reproductive rights, 3, 20, 21

resistance, 11, 15, 17, 80, 86, 94, 154, 178
resistance/accommodation dichotomy, 11
RFSL (The Swedish Federation for Gays and Lesbians), 37, 84, 90
Richards, M., 22, 76
rights
  adoption, 8, 13, 39–41, 112
  children's, 9, 32–3, 39, 45, 46, 76, 101, 190
  guardianship, 23, 27, 75
  lesbian and gay, 13, 26, 27, 37, 40, 42
  parental, 5, 6, 7, 13, 27–8, 33, 36, 38, 40, 110, 112, 114, 139, 187
  fathers', 23, 27, 33, 38, 47, 51, 188
  mothers', 27–8, 38, 47, 51, 52
Rohrbaugh, J., 110
Ryan, L., 20, 21

Sainsbury, D., 31
sambo law, 38, 40, 95
same sex marriage, 11, 13, 27, 37, 38, 78, 83, 112, 154, 191
same sex partnerships, 8, 27, 28, 191
  see also same-sex marriage
sameness, 17, 127, 149, 156, 177, 182
sameness/difference, 2, 148, 150, 177–8, 182
Scandinavia, *see* Denmark, Finland, Norway, Sweden
Scheib, J. E., 9, 10
Schneider, D., 18, 111–12
schools, 3, 16, 78, 79, 84, 97–100, 102, 133, 188
  in Ireland, 26, 97
  multi-denominational schools, 97
  secular schools, 97
  in Sweden, 97
  state-run schools, 97
second-parent adoption, 16, 38, 40–1, 148, 187, 188, 191
  see also närstående adoption
Sedgewick, E., 154–5
separation, *see* relationship break-ups

LaVergne, TN USA
28 April 2010
180844LV00003B/33/P